Software Engineering for Internet Applications

Eve Andersson, Philip Greenspun, and Andrew Grumet

Software Engineering for Internet Applications

The MIT Press
Cambridge, Massachusetts
London, England

MIT Press books may be purchased at special quantity discounts for business or sales promotional use. For information, please email special_sales@mitpress.mit.edu or write to Special Sales Department, The MIT Press, 55 Hayward Street, Cambridge, MA 02142.

This book was set in Times New Roman on 3B2 by Asco Typesetters, Hong Kong, and printed and bound in the United States of America.

Library of Congress Cataloging-in-Publication Data

Andersson, Eve Astrid.
Software engineering for Internet applications / Eve Andersson, Philip Greenspun, and Andrew Grumet.
    p.   cm.
Includes bibliographical references and index.
ISBN 978-0-262-51191-9 (pb. : alk. paper)
1. Internet programming. 2. Application software. 3. Software engineering. I. Greenspun, Philip. II. Grumet, Andrew. III. Title.

QA76.625.A55   2006   005.2′76—dc22   2005049144

10 9 8 7 6 5 4

Contents

Preface

This is the textbook for the MIT course "Software Engineering for Internet Applications." The course is intended for juniors and seniors in computer science. We assume that they know how to write a computer program and debug it. We do not assume knowledge of any particular programming languages, standards, or protocols. The most concise statement of the course goal is that "The student finishes knowing how to build amazon.com by him or herself."

Other people who might find this book useful include the following:

- professional software developers building online communities or other multi-user Internet applications
- managers who are evaluating packaged software aimed at supporting online communities—various chapters contain criteria for judging the features of products such as Microsoft Sharepoint or Microsoft Content Management Server
- university students and faculty looking to add some structure to a "capstone" project at the end of a computer science degree

If you're confused by the "student knows how to build amazon.com" statement, we can break it down in terms of principles and skills. The fundamental difference between server-based Internet applications and the desktop applications that students have already learned to build is that server-based applications have multiple simultaneous users. Coupled with the unreliability of networks, this gives rise to the problems of concurrency and transactions. Stateless communications protocols such as HTTP mean that the student must learn how to build a stateful user experience on top of stateless protocols. For persistence between clicks and management of concurrency and transactions, the student needs to learn how to use the relational database management system. Finally, though this goes beyond the simple stand-alone amazon.com-style service, students ought to learn about object-oriented distributed computing where each object is a Web service.

In addition to learning these principles, we'd like the student to learn some skills. This is a laboratory course, and we want students who graduate to be competent software engineers. We'd like our students to be able to take vague and ambitious specifications and turn them into a system design that can be built and launched within a few months, with the features most important to users and easiest to develop built first and the difficult bells and whistles deferred to a second version. We'd like our students to know how to test prototypes with end-users and refine their application design once or twice within even a three-month project. When business requirements are extreme, for example, "build me amazon.com by yourself in three months," we want our students to understand how to cope with the challenge via automatic code generation and use of open-source toolkits where appropriate.

We can recast the "student knows how to build amazon.com" statement in terms of technologies used. By the time someone has finished reading and doing the exercises in this book, he or she will understand HTTP, HTML, SQL, mobile browsers on telephones, VoiceXML, data modeling, page flow and interaction design, server-side scripting, and usability analysis.

Eve Andersson, Philip Greenspun, Andrew Grumet
Cambridge, Massachusetts
December 2005

Acknowledgments

The book is an outgrowth of six semesters of teaching experience at MIT and other universities. So our first thanks must go to our students, who taught us what worked and what didn't work. It is a privilege to teach at MIT, and every instructor should have the opportunity once in a lifetime.

We did not teach alone. Hal Abelson and the late Michael Dertouzos were our partners on the lecture podium. Hal was Mr. Pedagogy and also pushed the distributed computing ideas to the fore. Michael gave us an early push into voice applications. Lydia Sandon was our first teaching assistant. Ben Adida was our teaching assistant at MIT in the fall of 2003 when this book took its final pre-print shakedown cruise.

In semesters where we did not have a full-time teaching assistant, the students' most valuable partners were their industry mentors, most of whom were MIT alumni volunteering their time: David Abercrombie, Tracy Adams, Ben Adida, Mike Bonnet, Christian Brechbuhler, James Buszard-Welcher, Bryan Che, Bruce Keilin, Chris McEniry, Henry Minsky, Neil Mayle, Dan Parker, Richard Perng, Lydia Sandon, Mike Shurpik, Steve Strassman, Jessica Wong, and certainly a few more whose names have slipped from our memory.

We've gotten valuable feedback from instructors at other universities using these materials, notably Aurelius Prochazka at Caltech and Oscar Bonilla at Universidad Galileo.

1   **Introduction**

The concern for man and his destiny must always be the chief interest of all technical effort. Never forget it between your diagrams and equations.
—Albert Einstein

A twelve-year-old can build a nice Web application using the tools that came standard with any Linux or Windows machine. Thus it is worth asking ourselves, "What is challenging, interesting, and inspiring about Internet-based applications?"

There are some easy-to-identify technology-related challenges. For example, in many situations it would be more convenient to interact with an information system by talking and listening. You're in the bathtub reading *New Yorker*. You want to know whether there are any early morning appointments on your calendar that would prevent you from staying in the tub and finishing an interesting article. You've bought a new DVD player. You could read the manual and master the remote control. But in a dark room, wouldn't it be easier if you could simply ask the house or the machine to "back up thirty seconds"? You're driving in your car and curious to know the population of Thailand and the country's size relative to the state of California; voice is your only option.

There are some easy-to-identify missing features in typical Web-based applications. For example, shareable and portable sessions. You can use the Internet to share your photos. You can use the Internet to share your music. You can use the Internet to share your documents. The one thing that you can't typically share on the Internet is your experience of using the Internet. Suppose that you're surfing a travel site, planning a trip for yourself and three friends. Wouldn't it be nice if your companions could see what you're looking at, page-by-page, and speak comments into a shared voice-session? If everyone has the same brand of computer and special software, this is easy enough. But shareable sessions ought to be a built-in feature of sites that are usable from any browser. The same infrastructure could be used to make sessions portable. You could start browsing on a desktop computer with a big screen and finish your session in a taxi on a mobile phone.

Speaking of mobile browsers, their small screens raise the issues of multi-modal user interfaces and personalization. With the General Packet Radio Service or "GPRS," rolled out across the world in late 2001, it became possible for a mobile user to simultaneously speak and listen in a voice connection while using text screens delivered via a Web connection. As an engineer, you'll have to decide when it makes sense to talk to the user, listen to the user, print out a screen of options to the user, and ask the user to highlight and click to choose from that screen of options. For example, when booking an airline flight it is much more convenient to speak the departure and arrival cities than to choose from a menu of thousands of airports worldwide. But if there are ten options for making the connection you don't want to wait for the computer to read out those ten and you don't want to have to hold all the facts about those ten options in your mind. It would be more convenient for the travel service to send you a Web page with the ten options printed and scrollable.

On the personalization front, consider the corporate "knowledge sharing" or "knowledge management" system. Initially, workers are happy simply to have this kind of system in place. But after a few years, the system becomes so filled with stuff that it is difficult to find anything relevant. Given an organization in which 1,000 documents are generated every day, wouldn't it be nice to have a computer system smart enough to figure out which three are likely to be most interesting to you? And display the titles on the three lines of your phone's display?

A more interesting challenge is presented by asking the question, "Can a computer help me be all that I can be?" Engineers often build things that are easy to engineer. Fifty years after the development of television, we started building high-definition television (HDTV). Could engineers build a higher resolution standard? Absolutely. Did consumers care? So far it seems that not too many do care.

Let's put it this way: Given a choice between watching *Laverne and Shirley* in HDTV and being twenty pounds thinner, which would you prefer?

Thought so.

If you take a tape measure down to the self-help section of your local bookstore you'll discover a world of unmet human goals. A lot of these goals are tough to reach because we lack willpower. Olympic athletes also lack willpower at times. But they get to the Olympics, and we're still fat. Why? Maybe because they have a coach and we don't. Where are the engineering challenges in building a network-based diet coach? First look at a proposed interaction with the computer system that we'll call "Dr. Rachel":

0900:   you're walking to work; you call Dr. Rachel from your mobile:

- Dr. Rachel: "What did you have for breakfast this morning?" (She knows that it is morning in your typical time zone; she knows that you've not called in so far today.)
- You: "Glass of orange juice. Two eggs. Two slices of bread. Coffee with milk and sugar."
- Dr. Rachel: "Was the orange juice glass small, medium, or large?"
- You: "Medium."
- Dr. Rachel: "Anything else?"
- You: hang up.

1045:   your programmer officemate brings in a box of donuts; you eat one. Since you're at your computer anyway, you pull down the Dr. Rachel bookmark from the Web browser's "favorites" menu. You quickly inform Dr. Rachel of your consumption. She confirms the donut and shows you a summary page with your current estimated weight, what you've reported eating so far today, the total calories consumed so far today, and how many are left in your budget. The page shows a warning red "Don't eat more than one small sandwich for lunch" hint.

1330:   you're at the cafe down the street, having a small sandwich and a Diet Coke. It is noisy and you don't want to disturb people at the neighboring tables. You use your mobile phone's browser to connect to Dr. Rachel. She knows that it is lunchtime and that you've not told her about lunch so the lunch menus come up first. You report your consumption.

1600:   your desktop machine has crashed (again). Fortunately the software company where you work provides free snacks and soda. You go into the kitchen and power down on a bag of potato chips and some Mountain Dew. When you get back to your desk, your computer is still dead. You call Dr. Rachel from your wired phone and tell her about the snack and soda. She cautions you that you'll have to go to the gym tonight.

1900:   driving back from the gym, you call Dr. Rachel from your car and tell her that you worked out for 45 minutes.

2030:   you're finished with dinner and weigh yourself. You use the Web browser on your home computer to report the food consumption and weight as measured by the scale. Dr. Rachel responds with a Web page informing you that the measured weight is higher than she would have predicted. She's going to adjust her assumptions about your portion estimates, e.g., in the future when you say "medium" she'll assume "large."

From the sample interaction, you can infer that Dr. Rachel must include the following components: an adaptive model of the user; a database of calorie counts for different foods; some knowledge about effective dieting, for example, how many calories can be consumed per day if one intends to reach Weight X by Date Y; a Web browser interface; a mobile browser interface; a conversational voice interface (though perhaps one could get by with a simple VoiceXML interface).

What if, after two months, you're still fat? Should Dr. Rachel call you up in the middle of meals to suggest that you don't need to clean your plate? Where's the line between being effective and annoying? Can the computer system read your facial expression to figure out when to back off?

What are the enduring unmet human goals? To connect with other people and to learn. Email and "reference library" were the two universally appealing applications of the Internet, according to a December 1999 survey conducted by Norman Nie and Lutz Erbring and reported in "Internet and Society," a January 2000 report of the Stanford Institute for the Quantitative Study of Society (http://www.stanford.edu/group/siqss/Press_Release/Preliminary_Report.pdf). Entertainment and business-to-consumer e-commerce were far down the list.

Let's consider the "connecting with other people" goal. Suppose the people already know each other. They may be able to meet face-to-face. They can almost surely pick up the telephone and call each other using a system that dates from the nineteenth century. They may choose to exchange email, a system that dates from the 1960s. It doesn't look as though there is any challenge for twenty-first century engineers here.

Suppose the people don't already know each other. Can technology help? First we might ask "Should technology help?" Why would you want to talk to a bunch of strangers rather than your close friends and family? The problem with your friends and family is that by and large they (a) know the same things that you know, and (b) know the same people that you know. Mark Granovetter's classic 1973 study "The Strength of Weak Ties" (*American Journal of Sociology* 78: 1360–80) showed that most people got their jobs from people whom they did not know very well. Friends of friends of friends, perhaps. There are aggregate social and economic advantages to networks of people with a lot of weak ties. These networks have much faster information flow than networks in which people stick to their families and their villages. If you're exploring a new career or area of interest, you want to reach out beyond the people whom you know very well. If you're starting a new enterprise, you'll need to hire people with very different skills from your own. Where better to meet those new people than on the Internet? You probably won't become as strongly tied to them as you are to your best friends. But they'll give you the help that you need.

How will you find the people who can help you, though? Should you send a broadcast email to all one billion Internet users? That seems to be a popular strategy but it isn't clear how effective it is at generating the good will that you'll need. Perhaps we need an information system where individuals interested in a particular subject can communicate with each other, that is, an *online community*. This is precisely the kind of information system on which the chapters that follow will dwell.

What about the second big goal (learning)? Heavy technological artillery has been applied to education starting in the 1960s. The basic idea has always been to amplify the efforts of our greatest current teachers, usually by canning and shipping them to new students. The canning mechanism is almost always a video camera. In the 1960s we shipped the resulting cans via closed-circuit television. In the 1970s the Chinese planned to ship their best educational cans all over their nine-million-square-kilometer land via satellite television. In the 1980s we shipped the cans on VHS video tapes. In the 1990s we shipped the cans via streaming Internet media. We've been pursuing essentially the same approach for forty years. If it worked you'd expect to have seen dramatic results.

What if, instead of increasing the number of learners per teacher, we increased the number of teachers? There are already plenty of opportunities to learn at your convenience. If it is 3:00 A.M. and you want to learn about quantum mechanics, you need only pull a book from your shelf and turn on the reading light. But what if you want to teach at 3:00 A.M.? Your friends may not appreciate being called up at 0300 and told "Hey, I just learned that the Franck-Hertz Experiment in 1914 confirmed the theory that electrons occupy only discrete, quantized energy states." What if you could go to a server-based information system and say "show me a listing of all the unanswered questions posted by other users"? You might be willing to answer a few, simply for the satisfaction of helping another person and feeling like an expert. When you got tired, you'd go to bed. Teaching is fun if you don't have to do it forty hours per week for thirty years.

Imagine if every learning photographer had a group of experienced photographers answering his or her questions? That's the online community photo.net, started by one of the authors as a collection of tutorial articles and a question-and-answer forum in 1993 and, as of August 2005, home to 426,000 registered users engaged in answering each other's questions and critiquing each other's photographs. Imagine if every current MIT student had an alumnus mentor? That's what some folks at MIT have been working on. It seems like a much more effective strategy to get some volunteer labor out of the 90,000 alumni than to try to squeeze more from the 930 faculty members. Most of MIT's alumni don't live in the Boston area. Students can benefit from the volunteerism of distant alumni only if (1) student-faculty interaction is done in a computer-mediated fashion so that it becomes visible to authorized mentors, and (2) mentors can use the same information system as the students and faculty to get access to handouts, assignments, and lecture notes. We're coordinating people separated in space and time who share a common purpose. Again, that's an online community.

Online communities are challenging because learning is difficult and people are idiosyncratic. Online communities are challenging because the software that works for a community of 200 won't work for a community of 2,000 or 20,000. Online communities are inspiring engineering projects because they deliver to users two of the things that they want most out of life: connections to other people and education.

If your interest in this book stems from the desire to build a straightforward e-commerce site, don't despair. It turns out that the most successful e-commerce and collaborative commerce sites are, at their core, actually online communities. Amazon is the best known example. In 1995 there were dozens of online bookstores with comprehensive catalogs. Amazon had a catalog but, with its reader review facility, Amazon also had a mechanism for users to communicate with each other. Thus did the programmers at Amazon crush their competition.

As you work through this book, you're going to build an online learning community. Along the way, you'll pick up all the important principles, skills, and technologies for building desktop Web, mobile Web, and voice applications of all types.

More

- on GPRS: "Emerging Technology: Clear Signals for General Packet Radio Service" by Peter Rysavy in the December 2000 issue of *Network Magazine*, available at http://www.rysavy.com/Articles/GPRS2/gprs2.html
- on the state-of-the-art in easy-to-build voice applications: Chapter 10 on VoiceXML (stands by itself reasonably well)

2   Basics

In this chapter you'll learn how to evaluate Internet application development environments. Then you'll pick one. Then you'll learn how to use it.

You're also going to learn about the stateless and anonymous protocol that makes Web development different from classical inter-computer application development. You'll learn why the relational database management system is key to controlling the concurrency problem that arises from multiple simultaneous users. You'll develop software to read and write Extensible Markup Language (XML).

Old-Style Communications Protocols

In a traditional communications protocol, Computer Program A opens a connection to Computer Program B. Both programs run continuously for the duration of the communication. This makes it easy for Program B to remember what Program A has said already. Program B can build up *state* in its memory. The memory can in fact contain a complete log of everything that has come over the wire from Program A. See figure 2.1.

HTTP: Stateless and Anonymous

HyperText Transfer Protocol (HTTP) is the fundamental means of exchanging information and requesting services on the Web. HTTP is also used when developing text services for mobile phone users and, with VoiceXML, also used to implement voice-controlled applications.

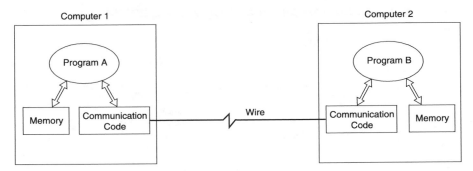

Figure 2.1   In a traditional stateful communications protocol, two programs running on two separate computers establish a connection and proceed to use that connection for as long as necessary, typically until one of the programs terminates.

The most important thing to know about HTTP is that it is *stateless*. If you view ten Web pages, your browser makes ten independent HTTP requests of the publisher's Web server. At any time in between those requests, you are free to restart your browser program. At any time in between those requests, the publisher is free to restart its server program.

Here's the anatomy of a typical HTTP session:

- user types "www.yahoo.com" into a browser

- browser translates www.yahoo.com into an IP address and tries to open a TCP connection with port 80 of that address (TCP is "Transmission Control Protocol" and is the fundamental system via which two computers on the Internet send streams of bytes to each other.)

- once a connection is established, the browser sends the following byte stream: "GET / HTTP/1.0" (plus two carriage-return line-feeds). The "GET" means that the browser is requesting a file. The "/" is the name of the file, in this case simply the root index page. The "HTTP/1.0" says that this browser would prefer to get a result back adhering to the HTTP 1.0 protocol.

- Yahoo responds with a set of headers indicating which protocol is actually being used, whether or not the file requested was found, how many bytes are contained in that file, and what kind of information is contained in the file (the Multipurpose Internet Mail Extensions or "MIME" type)

- Yahoo's server sends a blank line to indicate the end of the headers

- Yahoo sends the contents of its index page
- The TCP connection is closed when the file has been received by the browser.

You can try it yourself from an operating system shell:

```
bash-2.03$ telnet www.yahoo.com 80
Trying 216.32.74.53...
Connected to www.yahoo.akadns.net.
Escape character is '^]'.
GET / HTTP/1.0

HTTP/1.0 200 OK
Content-Length: 18385
Content-Type: text/html

<html><head><title>Yahoo!</title><base
href=http://www.yahoo.com/>...
```

In this case we've used the Unix `telnet` command with an optional argument specifying the port number for the target host—everything typed by the programmer is here indicated in bold. We typed the "GET ..." line ourselves and then hit Enter twice on the keyboard. Yahoo's first header back is "HTTP/1.0 200 OK." The HTTP status code of 200 means that the file was found ("OK").

Don't get too lost in the details of the HTTP example. The point is that when the connection is over, it is over. If the user follows a hyperlink from the Yahoo front page to "Photography," for example, that's a brand new HTTP request. If Yahoo is using multiple servers to operate its site, the second request might go to an entirely different machine. This sounds fine for browsing Yahoo. But suppose you're shopping at an e-commerce site such as Amazon. If you put something in your shopping cart on one HTTP request, you still want it to be there ten clicks later. Or suppose you've logged into photo.net on Click 23 and on Click 45 are responding to a discussion forum posting. You don't want the photo.net server to have forgotten your identity and demand your username and password again.

This presents you, the engineer, with a challenge: creating a stateful user experience on top of a fundamentally stateless protocol.

See the HTTP standard at http://www.w3.org/Protocols/ for more information on HTTP.

Where can you store state from request to request? Perhaps in a log file on the Web server. The server would write down "Joe Smith wants three copies of *Bus Nine to Paradise* by Leo Buscaglia." On any subsequent request by Joe Smith, the server-side script can simply check the log and display the contents of the shopping cart. A problem with this idea, however, is that HTTP is *anonymous*. A Web server doesn't know that it is Joe Smith connecting. The server only knows the IP address of the computer making the request. Sometimes this translates into a host name. If it is joe-smiths-desktop.stanford.edu, perhaps you can identify subsequent requests from this IP address as coming from the same person. But what if it is cache-rr02.proxy.aol.com, one of the HTTP proxy servers connecting America Online's 20 million users to the public Internet? The same user's next request will very likely come from a different IP address, that is, another physical computer within AOL's racks and racks of proxy machines. The next request from cache-rr02.proxy.aol.com will very likely come from a different person, that is, another physical human being among AOL's 20 million subscribers who share a common pool of proxy machines.

Somehow you need to write some information out to an individual user that will be returned on that user's next request.

If all of your pages are generated by computer programs as opposed to being static HTML, one idea would be to rewrite all the hyperlinks on the pages served. Instead of sending the same files to everyone, with the same embedded URLs, customize the output so that a user who follows a link is sending extra information back to the server. Here is an example of how amazon.com embeds a session key in URLs:

1. Suppose that a shopper follows a link to a page that displays a single book for sale, e.g., http://www.amazon.com/exec/obidos/ASIN/1588750019/. Note that 1588750019 is an International Standard Book Number (ISBN) and completely identifies the product to be presented.

2. The amazon.com server redirects the request to a URL that includes a session ID after the last slash, e.g., "http://www.amazon.com/exec/obidos/ASIN/1588750019/103-9609966-7089404"

3. If the shopper rolls a mouse over the hyperlinks on the page served, he or she will notice that all the hyperlinks contain, at the end, this same session ID.

Note that this session ID does not change in length no matter how long a shopper's session or how many items are placed in the shopping cart. The session ID is being used as a key to look up the shopping basket contents in a database within amazon.com. An alternative implementation would be to encode the complete contents of the shopping cart in the URLs instead of the session ID. Suppose, for example, that Joe Shopper puts three books in his shopping cart. Amazon's server could simply add three ISBNs to all the hyperlink URLs that he might follow, separated by slashes. The URLs will be getting a bit long but Amazon's programmers can take encouragement from this quote from the HTTP spec:

The HTTP protocol does not place any a priori limit on the length of a URI. Servers MUST be able to handle the URI of any resource they serve, and SHOULD be able to handle URIs of unbounded length if they provide GET-based forms that could generate such URIs. A server SHOULD return 414 (Request-URI Too Long) status if a URI is longer than the server can handle (see section 10.4.15).

There is no need to worry about turning away Amazon's best customers, the ones with really big shopping carts, with a return status of "414 Request-URI Too Long." Or is there? Here is a comment from the HTTP spec:

Note: Servers ought to be cautious about depending on URI lengths above 255 bytes, because some older client or proxy implementations might not properly support these lengths.

Perhaps this is why the real live amazon.com stores only session ID in the URLs.

Cookies

Instead of playing games with rewriting hyperlinks in HTML pages we can take advantage of an extension to HTTP known as *cookies*. We said that we needed a way to write some information out to an individual user that will be returned on that user's next request. The first paragraph of Netscape's "Persistent Client State HTTP Cookies—Preliminary Specification" (http://wp.netscape.com/newsref/std/cookie_spec.html) reads:

Cookies are a general mechanism which server side connections (such as CGI scripts) can use to both store and retrieve information on the client side of the connection. The addition of a simple, persistent, client-side state significantly extends the capabilities of Web-based client/server applications.

How does it work? After Joe Smith adds a book to his shopping cart, the server writes

```
Set-Cookie: cart_contents=1588750019; path=/
```

As long as Joe does not quit his browser, on every subsequent request to your server, the browser adds a header:

```
Cookie: cart_contents=1588750019
```

Your server-side scripts can read this header and extract the current contents of the shopping cart.

Sound like the perfect solution? In some ways it is. If you're a computer science egghead you can take pride in the fact that this is a distributed database management system. Instead of keeping a big log file on your server, you're keeping bits of information on thousands of users' machines worldwide. But one problem with cookies is that the spec limits you to asking each browser to store no more than 20 cookies on behalf of your server and each of those cookies must be no more than 4 kilobytes in size. A minor problem is that cookie information will be passed back up to your server on every page load. If you have indeed indulged yourself by parking 80 kilobytes of information in 20 cookies and your user is on a modem, this is going to slow down Web interaction.

A deeper problem with cookies is that they aren't portable for the user. If Joe Smith starts shopping from his desktop computer at work and wants to continue from a mobile phone in a taxi or from a Web browser at home, he can't retrieve the contents of his cart so far. The shopping cart resides in the memory of his computer at work.

A final problem with cookies is that a small percentage of users have disabled them due to the privacy problems illustrated in figure 2.2.

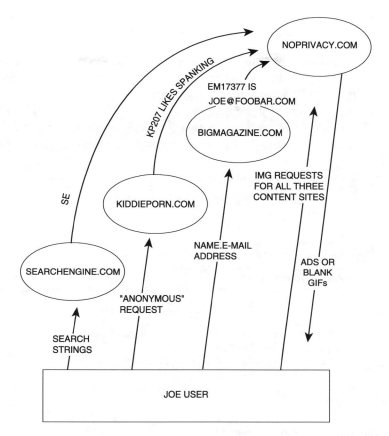

Figure 2.2 Cookies coupled with the open-hearted behavior of 1990s browsers meant the end of privacy on the Internet. Suppose that three publishers cooperate and agree to serve all of their banner ads from http://noprivacy.com. When Joe User visits search-engine.com and types in "acne cream," the page comes back with an IMG referencing noprivacy.com. Joe's browser will automatically visit noprivacy.com and ask for "the GIF for SE9734." If this is Joe's first time using any of these three cooperating services, noprivacy.com will issue a Set-Cookie header to Joe's browser. Meanwhile, search-engine.com sends a message to noprivacy.com saying "SE9734 was a request for acne cream pages." The "acne cream" string gets stored in noprivacy.com's database along with "browser_id 7586." When Joe visits bigmagazine.com, he is forced to register and give his name, email address, snail mail address, and credit card number. There are no ads in bigmagazine.com. They have too much integrity for that. So they include in their pages an IMG referencing a blank GIF at noprivacy.com. Joe's browser requests "the blank GIF for BM17377" and, because it is talking to noprivacy.com, the site that issued the Set-Cookie header, the browser includes a cookie header saying "I'm browser_id 7586." When all is said and done, the noprivacy.com folks know Joe User's name, his interests, and the fact that he has downloaded six spanking JPEGs from kiddieporn.com.

A reasonable engineering approach to using cookies is to send a unique identifier for the data rather than the data, just as in the amazon.com "session ID in the URL" example previously described. Information about the contents of the shopping cart will be kept in some sort of log on the server. This means that it can be picked up from another location. To see how this works in practice, go to an operating system shell and request the home page of eveandersson.com:

```
bash-2.03$ telnet www.eveandersson.com 80
Trying 64.94.245.206...
Connected to www.eveandersson.com.
Escape character is '^]'.
GET / HTTP/1.0

HTTP/1.0 200 OK
Set-Cookie: ad_browser_id=3291092; Path=/; Expires=Fri, 01-
Jan-2010 01:00:00 GMT
Set-Cookie:
ad_session_id=3291093%2c0%2c6634C478EF46FC%2c10622158;
Path=/; Max-Age=86400
Set-Cookie: last_visit=1071622158; path=/; expires=Fri, 01-
Jan-2010 01:00:00 GMT
Content-Type: text/html; charset=iso-8859-1
MIME-Version: 1.0
Date: Thu, 03 Feb 2005 00:49:18 GMT
Server: AOLserver/3.3.1+ad13
Content-Length: 8289
Connection: close

<html>
  <head>
...
```

Note that two cookies are set. The first one, `ad_browser_id` is given an explicit expiration date in January 2010. This instructs the browser to record the cookie value, in this case "3291092," on the hard drive. The cookie's value will continue to be sent back up to the server for the next four years, even if the user quits and restarts the browser. What's the point of having a browser cookie? If the user says "I prefer text-only" or "I prefer French language" that's probably worthwhile information to keep with the browser. The text-only preference may be related to a slow Internet connection to that computer. If the computer is in a home full of Francophones, chances are that all the people who share the browser will prefer French.

The second cookie set, `ad_session_id` is set to expire after one hour ("Max-Age = 3600"). If not explicitly set to expire, it would expire when the user quit his or her browser. Things worth associating with a session ID include the contents of a shopping cart on an e-commerce site, though note that if this were a shopping site, it would not be a good idea to expire the session cookie after one hour! It is annoying to build up a cart, be called away from your computer for a few hours, and then have to start over when you return to what you thought was a working Web page.

If we were logged into the site, there would be a third cookie, one that identifies the user. Languages and presentation preferences stored on the server on behalf of the user would then override preferences kept with the browser ID.

Server-Side Storage

You've got ID information going out to and coming back from browsers, via either the cookie extension to HTTP or URL rewriting. Now you have to figure out a way to keep associated information on the Web server.

For flexibility in how you present and analyze user-contributed data, you'll probably want to keep the information in a structured form. For example, it would be nice to have a table of all the items put into shopping carts by various users. And another table of orders. And another table of reader-contributed product reviews. And another table of questions and answers.

What's a good tool for storing tables of information? Consider first a spreadsheet program. These are inexpensive and easy to use. One should never apply more complex technology than necessary for solving a problem. Something like Visicalc, Lotus 1-2-3, Microsoft Excel, or StarOffice Calc would seem to serve nicely.

The problem with a spreadsheet program is that it is designed for one user. The program listens for user input from two sources: mouse and keyboard. The program reports its results to one place: the screen. Any source of persistence for a Web server has to contend with potentially thousands of simultaneous users both reading and writing to the database. This is the problem that *database management systems (DBMS)* were intended to solve.

A good way to think about a relational database management system (RDBMS, the most popular type of DBMS) is as a spreadsheet program that sits inside a dark closet. If you need to create a new table you slip a little strip of paper under the door with "CREATE TABLE ..." written on it. To add a row of data to that table, you slip another little strip under the door saying "INSERT ..." To change some data within the table, you write "UPDATE ..." on a paper strip. To remove a row, you send in a strip starting with "DELETE."

Notice that we've solved the *concurrency* problem here. Suppose that you have only one copy of *Bus Nine to Paradise* left in inventory and 1000 users at the same instant request Dr. Buscaglia's work. By arranging the strips of paper in a row, the program in the closet can decide to process one INSERT into the orders table and reject the 999 others. This is better than 1000 people fighting over a single keyboard and mouse.

Once we've sent information into the closet, how do we get it back out? We can write down a request for a report on a strip of paper starting with "SELECT" and slide it under the door. The DBMS in the dark closet will prepare a report for us and slide that back to us under the same door.

How do we evaluate whether or not a DBMS is powerful enough for our application? Starting in the 1960s IBM proposed the "ACID test":

Atomicity   Results of a transaction's execution are either all committed or all rolled back. All changes take effect, or none do. Suppose that a user is registering by uploading name, address, and JPEG portrait into three separate tables. A Web script tells the database to perform three inserts as part of a transaction. If the hard drive fills up after the name and address have been inserted but before the portrait can be stored, the changes to the name and address tables will be rolled back.

Consistency   The database is transformed from one valid state to another valid state. A transaction is legal only if it obeys user-defined integrity constraints. Illegal transactions aren't allowed and, if an integrity constraint can't be satisfied, the transaction is rolled back. For example, suppose that you define a rule that postings in a discussion forum table must be attributed to a valid user ID. Then you hire Joe Novice to write some admin pages. Joe writes a delete-user page that doesn't bother to check whether or not the deletion will result in an orphaned discussion forum posting. An ACID-compliant DBMS will check, though, and abort any transaction that would result in you having a discussion forum posting by a deleted user.

Isolation   The results of a transaction are invisible to other transactions until the transaction is complete. For example, suppose you have a page to show new users and their photographs. This page is coded in reliance on the publisher's directive that there will be a portrait for every user and will present a broken image if there is not. Jane Newuser is registering at your site at the same time that Bill Olduser is viewing the new user page. The script processing Jane's registration has completed inserting her name and address into their respective tables. But it is not done storing her JPEG portrait. If Bill's query starts before Jane's transaction commits, Bill won't see Jane at all on his new-users page, even though Jane's insertion into some of the tables is complete.

Durability   Once committed (completed), the results of a transaction are permanent and survive future system and media failures. Suppose your e-commerce system inserts an order from a customer into a database table and then instructs CyberSource to bill the customer $500. A millisecond later, before your server has heard back from CyberSource, someone trips over the machine's power cord. An ACID-compliant DBMS will not have forgotten about the new order. Furthermore, if a programmer spills coffee into a disk drive, it will be possible to install a new disk and recover the transactions up to the coffee spill, showing that you tried to bill someone for $500 and still aren't sure what happened over at CyberSource. Notice that to achieve the D part of ACID requires that your computer have more than one hard disk.

Why the Relational Database Management System?

Why is the relational database management system (RDBMS) the dominant technology for persistence behind a Web server? There are three main factors.

The first pillar of RDBMS popularity is a declarative query language called "SQL." The most common style of programming is not declarative; it is called "imperative" or "procedural." You tell the computer what to do, step by step:

- do this
- do this
- do this
- if it is after March 17, 2023, do this, this, and then this; otherwise do this
- do this

  ...

Programs written in this style have two drawbacks. First, they quickly become complex and then can be developed and maintained only by professional programmers. Second, they contain a lot of errors. For example, the program sketched above may have quite a few bugs. It is not after March 17, 2023. So we can't be sure that the steps specified in the THEN clause of the IF statement are error-free.

An alternative style of programming is "declarative." We tell the computer what we want, for example, a report of users who've been registered for more than one year but who haven't answered any questions in the discussion forum. We don't tell the RDBMS whether to scan the users table first and then check the discussion forum table or vice versa. We just specify the desired characteristics of the report and it is the job of the RDBMS to prepare it.

Stop someone in the street. Pick someone with fashionable clothing so you can be sure he or she is not a professional programmer. Ask this person, "Have you ever programmed in a declarative computer language?" Follow that up with "Have you ever used a spreadsheet program?" Chances are that you can find quite a few people who will tell you that they've never written any kind of computer program but yet they've developed fairly sophisticated spreadsheet models. Why? The spreadsheet language is declarative: "Make this cell be the sum of these three other cells." The user doesn't tell the spreadsheet program in what order to perform the computation, merely the desired result.

The declarative language of the spreadsheet created an explosion in the number of people who were able to develop working computer programs. Through the mid-1970s, organizations that worked with data kept a staff of programmers. If you wanted some analysis performed you'd call one into your office, explain the assumptions and formulae to be used, then wait a few days for a report. In 1979 Dan Bricklin (MIT EECS '73) and Bob Frankston (MIT EECS '70) developed Visicalc and suddenly most of the people who'd been hollering for programming services were able to build their own models.

With an RDBMS the metaphoric little strips of paper pushed under the door are declarative programs in the SQL language. (See *SQL for Web Nerds* at http://philip.greenspun.com/sql/ for a SQL language tutorial.)

The second pillar of RDBMS popularity is isolation of important data from programmers' mistakes. With other kinds of database management systems, it is possible for a computer program to make arbitrary changes to the data set. This can be convenient for applications such as computer-aided design systems with very complex data structures. However, if your goal is to preserve a data set over a twenty-five-year period, letting arbitrarily buggy imperative programs make arbitrary changes isn't a good idea. The RDBMS limits programmers to uttering very simple statements of the form INSERT, DELETE, and UPDATE. Furthermore, if you're unhappy with the contents of your database you can simply review all the strips of paper that were pushed under the door. Each strip will contain an SQL statement and the name of the program or programmer that authored the strip. This makes it easy to correct mistakes and reform offenders.

The third and final pillar of RDBMS popularity is good performance with many thousands of simultaneous users. This is more a reflection on the refined state of commercial development of systems such as IBM DB2, Oracle, Microsoft SQL Server, and the open-source PostgreSQL than an inherent feature of the RDBMS itself.

The Steps

When building any Internet application you're going to go through the following steps:

1. Develop a data model. What information are you going to store and how will you represent it?

2. Develop a collection of legal transactions on that model, e.g., inserts and updates.

3. Design the page flow. How will the user interact with the system? What steps will lead up to one of those legal transactions? (Note that "page flow" embraces interaction design on Web and mobile browsers, and also via hierarchical voice menus in VoiceXML, but *not* conversational speech systems.)

4. Implement the individual pages. You'll be writing scripts that query information from the data model, wrap that information in a template (in HTML for a Web application), and return the combined result to the user.

It is very unlikely that you'll have a choice of tools for persistent storage. You will be using an RDBMS and won't be making any fundamental technology decisions at Steps 1 or 2. Designing the page flow is a purely abstract exercise. There are some technology-imposed limits on the interface, but those are generally derived from public standards such as HTML, XHTML Mobile Profile, and VoiceXML. So you need not make any technology choices for Step 3.

Step 4 is intellectually uninteresting and also uninteresting from an engineering point of view. An Internet service lives or dies by Steps 1 through 3. What can the service do for the user? Is the page flow comprehensible and usable? The answers to these questions are determined at Steps 1 through 3. However, Step 4 is where you have a huge range of technology choices and therefore it seems to generate a lot of discussion. This course and this book are neutral on the subject of how you go about Step 4, but we provide some guidance on how to make choices.

First, though, let's step back and make sure that everyone knows HTML.

HTML

Here is some legal HTML:

```
My Samoyed is really hairy.
```

That is a perfectly acceptable HTML document. Type it up in a text editor, save it as index.html, and put it on your Web server. A Web server can serve it. A user with Netscape Navigator can view it. A search engine can index it.

Suppose you want something more expressive. You want the word *really* to be in italic type:

```
My Samoyed is <I>really</I> hairy.
```

HTML stands for Hypertext Markup Language. The <I> is markup. It tells the browser to start rendering words in italics. The </I> closes the <I> element and stops the italics. If you want to be more tasteful, you can tell the browser to emphasize the word *really*:

```
My Samoyed is <EM>really</EM> hairy.
```

Most browsers use italics to emphasize, but some use boldface and browsers for ancient ASCII terminals (e.g., Lynx) have to ignore this tag or come up with a clever rendering method. A picky user with the right browser program can even customize the rendering of particular tags.

There are a few dozen more tags in HTML. You can learn them by choosing View Source from your Web browser when visiting sites whose formatting you admire. You can look at the HTML reference chapter of this book. You can learn them by starting at Yahoo's directory of HTML guides and tutorials,

http://dir.yahoo.com/Computers_and_Internet/Data_Formats/HTML/Guides
_and_Tutorials/. Or you can buy *HTML & XHTML: The Definitive Guide*
(Chuck Musciano and Bill Kennedy [O'Reilly, 2002]).

Document Structure

Armed with a big pile of tags, you can start strewing them among your words
more or less at random. Though browsers are extremely forgiving of technically
illegal markup, it is useful to know that an HTML document officially consists
of two pieces: the *head* and the *body*. The head contains information about the
document as a whole, such as the title. The body contains information to be
displayed by the user's browser.

Another structure issue is that you should try to make sure that you close
every element that you open. If your document has a <BODY> it should have
a </BODY> at the end. If you start an HTML table with a <TABLE> and
don't have a </TABLE>, a browser may display nothing. Tags can overlap,
but you should close the most recently opened before the rest, for example, for
something both boldface and italic:

```
My Samoyed is <B><I>really</I></B> hairy.
```

Something that confuses a lot of new users is that the <P> element used to
surround a paragraph has an optional closing tag </P>. Browsers by convention assume that an open <P> element is implicitly closed by the next <P> element. This leads a lot of publishers (including lazy old us) to use <P> elements
as paragraph separators.

Here's the source HTML from a simply formatted Web document:

```
<html>
 <head>
  <title>Nikon D1 Digital Camera Review</title>
 </head>
 <body bgcolor=white text=black>
  <h2>Nikon D1</h2>
  by <a href="http://philip.greenspun.com/">Philip Greenspun</a>
  <hr>
  Little black spots are appearing at the top of every ...
  <h3>Basics</h3>
  The Nikon D1 is a good digital camera for ...
  <p>
  The camera's 15.6x23.7mm CCD image sensor ...
```

```
<h3>User Interface</h3>
If you wanted a camera with lots of buttons, switches, and dials ...
<hr>
<address>
  <a href="mailto:philg@mit.edu">philg@mit.edu</a>
</address>
</body>
</html>
```

Let's go through this document piece by piece (see http://philip.greenspun .com/seia/examples-basics/simple-page.html for how it looks rendered by a browser).

The <HTML> tag at the top says "I'm an HTML document." Note that this tag is closed at the end of the document. It turns out that this tag is unnecessary. We've saved the document in the file "simple-page.html." When a user requests this document, the Web server looks at the ".html" extension and adds a MIME header to tell the user's browser that this document is of type "text/ html."

The HEAD element here is useful mostly so that the TITLE element can be used to give this document a name. Whatever text you place between <TITLE> and </TITLE> will appear at the top of the user's browser window, on the Go (Netscape) or Back (MSIE) menu, and in the bookmarks menu should the user bookmark this page. After closing the head with a </HEAD>, we open the body of the document with a <BODY> tag, to which are added some parameters that set the background to white and the text to black. Some Web browsers default to a gray background, and the resulting lack of contrast between background and text is so tough on users that it may be worth changing the colors manually. This is a violation of interface design principles since it potentially introduces an inconsistency in the user's experience of the Web. However, we do it at photo.net without feeling too guilty about it because (1) a lot of browsers use a white background by default, (2) enough other publishers set a white background that our pages won't seem inconsistent, and (3) it doesn't affect the core user interface the way that setting custom link colors would.

Just below the body, we have a headline, size 2, wrapped in an <H2> tag. This will be displayed to the user at the top of the page. We probably should use <H1> but browsers typically render that in a frighteningly huge font. Underneath the headline, the phrase "Philip Greenspun" is a hypertext *anchor* which is why it is wrapped in an A element. The <A HREF= says "this is a

hyperlink." If the reader clicks anywhere from here up to the </A> the browser should fetch http://philip.greenspun.com/.

After the headline, author, and optional navigation, we put in a horizontal rule tag: <HR>. One of the good things that we learned from designer Dave Siegel (see http://philip.greenspun.com/wtr/getting-dates) is not to overuse horizontal rules: Real graphic designers use whitespace for separation. We use <H3> headlines in the text to separate sections and only put an <HR> at the very bottom of the document.

Underneath the last <HR>, we sign our documents with the email address of the author. This way a reader can scroll to the bottom of a browser window and find out who is responsible for what they've just read and where to send corrections. The <ADDRESS> tag usually results in an italics rendering by browser programs. Note that this one is wrapped in an anchor tag with a target of "mailto:" rather than "http:." If the user clicks on the anchor text (Philip's email address), the browser will pop up a "send mail to philg@mit.edu" window.

Picking a Programming Environment

Now you get to pick a programming environment for the rest of the semester. If you've been building RDBMS-backed Internet applications for some time, you can just use whatever you've been using. Switching tools is seldom a path to glory. If you haven't built this kind of software before, read on.

Choosing an RDBMS

There are probably three reasonable choices for an RDBMS this semester: (1) Microsoft SQL Server, (2) Oracle, and (3) PostgreSQL.

For experienced Windows programmers, Microsoft SQL Server is easy to install and administer. And if you expect to spend the rest of your professional life in a Microsoft environment, you might as well learn it.

Concurrency is Oracle's strongest suit relative to its commercial competitors. In Oracle, readers never wait for writers, and writers never wait for readers. Suppose the publisher at a large site starts a query at 12:00 P.M. summarizing usage by user. Oracle might have to spend an hour sifting through 200 GB of tracking data. The disk drives grind and one CPU is completely used up until 1:30 P.M. Further, suppose that User 356712 comes in at 12:30 P.M. and changes his email address, thus updating a row in the users table. If the usage tracking query arrives at this row at 12:45 P.M., Oracle will notice that the row was last modified after the query started. Under the "I" in ACID, Oracle is required to isolate the publisher from the user's update. Oracle does this by reaching into the rollback segment and producing data from user row 356712 as it was at 12:00 P.M. when the query started. Here's the scenario in a table:

Time	Publisher	Public Web Application
12:00 P.M.	Starts a ninety-minute query summarizing usage for preceding year	—
12:30 P.M.	usage summary continues to chug away	User 356712 updates email address from "joe@foobar.com" to "joe@yahoo.com"
12:45 P.M.	usage summary arrives at User 356712; Oracle reaches into rollback segment and pulls out "joe@foobar.com" for the report, since that's what the value was at 12:30 P.M.	—
1:30 P.M.	usage summary report completes	—

How would this play out in Microsoft SQL Server? When you're reading, you take read locks on the information that you're about to read. Nobody can write until you release them. When you're writing, you take write locks on the information that you're about to update. Nobody can read or write until you release the locks. In the preceding example, User 356712 would submit his request for the address change at 12:30 P.M. The thread on the Web server would be blocked waiting for the read locks to clear. How long would it wait? A full hour with a spinning/waving "browser still receiving information" icon in the upper right corner of the browser window. If you're thoughtful, you can program around this locking architecture in SQL Server, but most Internet service operators would rather just install Oracle than train their programmers to think more carefully about concurrency.

The open-source purist's only realistic choice for an RDBMS is PostgreSQL, available from www.postgresql.org/. In some ways, PostgreSQL has more advanced features than any commercial RDBMS, and it has an Oracle-style multi-version concurrency system. PostgreSQL is easy to install and administer, but is not used by operators of large services because there is no way to build a truly massive PostgreSQL installation or one that can tolerate hardware failures.

Most of the SQL examples in this book will use Oracle syntax. This is partly because Oracle is the world's most popular RDBMS, but mostly because Oracle is what we had running at MIT when we started working in this area back in 1994 and therefore we have whole file systems full of Oracle code. Problem set supplements (see end of chapter) may contain translations for ANSI SQL databases such as Microsoft SQL Server and PostgreSQL.

Choosing a Procedural Language

As mentioned above, most of the time your procedural code, a.k.a. "Web scripts," will be doing little more than querying the RDBMS and merging the results with an HTML, XHTML Mobile Profile, or VoiceXML template. So your productivity and code maintainability won't be affected much by your choice of procedural language.

That said, let us put in a kind word for scripting languages. If you need to write some heavy-duty abstractions, you can always do those in Java running inside Oracle or C# running within Microsoft .NET. But for your presentation layer, that is, individual pages, don't overlook the advantages of using simpler and terser languages such as Perl, Tcl, and Visual Basic.

Choosing an Execution Environment

Below are some things to look for when choosing Web servers and Web/application servers.

One URL = one file   The first thing you should look for in an execution environment is the property that one user-visible URL corresponds to one file in the file system. It is much faster to debug a system if, given a complaint about http://photo.net/foobar, you can know that you'll find the responsible computer program in the file system at /web/photonet/www/foobar.something. Programming environments where this is true:

- Perl CGI
- Microsoft Active Server Pages
- Java Server Pages
- AOLserver ADP templates and .tcl scripts

A notable exception to this property is Java servlets. One servlet typically processes several URLs. This proves cumbersome in practice because it slows you down when trying to fix a bug in someone else's code. The ideas of modularity and code reuse are nice, but try to think about how many files a programmer must wade through in order to fix a bug. One is great. Two is probably okay. N where N is uncertain is not okay.

Filters   We said that modularity and code reuse could be tossed in favor of preserving the sacred principle of "one URL = one file." The way that you get modularity and code reuse back is via *filters*, the ability to instruct the Web server to "run this fragment of code before serving any URL that starts with /yow/." This is particularly useful for access control code. Suppose that you have fifteen scripts that constitute the administration experience for a contest system. You want to make sure that only authorized administrators can use the pages. Checking for administrative access requires an SQL query. You could write a procedure called `CheckForContestAdminAuthority` and instruct your script authors to include a call to this procedure in each of the fifteen admin scripts. You've still got fifteen copies of some code: one IF statement, one procedure call, and a call to an error message procedure if `CheckForContestAdminAuthority` returns "unauthorized." But the SQL query occurs only in one place and can be updated centrally.

The main problem with this approach is not the fifteen copies of the IF statement and its consequents. The problem is that inevitably one of the script authors will forget to include the check. So your site has a security hole. You close the hole and eliminate fourteen copies of the IF statement by installing the code as a server filter. Note that for this to work the filter mechanism must include an API for aborting service of the requested page. Your filter needs to be able to tell the Web server "Don't proceed with serving the user with the script or document requested."

Abstract URLs   As an engineer your primary contributions to an Internet service will be data model and interaction design (Steps 1 through 3). When you're sketching the page flow for a discussion forum on a whiteboard you give the pages names such as "all-topics," "one-topic," "one-thread," "post-reply," "post-reply-confirm," and so on. Let's call these *abstract URLs*. Suppose that you elect to implement your service in Java Server Pages. Does it make sense to have the URLs be "all-topics.jsp," "one-topic.jsp," "one-thread.jsp," and so forth? Why should the users see that you've used JSP? Should they care? And if you change your mind and switch to Perl, will you change the user-visible URLs to "all-topics.pl," "one-topic.pl," "one-thread.pl," and so on? This will break everyone's bookmarks. More importantly, this change will break all of the links from other sites to yours. That's a high price to pay for an implementation change that should have been invisible to end-users.

You need a Web programming environment powerful enough that you can build something that we'll call a *request processor*. This program looks at an incoming abstract URL, for example, "one-topic," and follows the following logic:

- is there a .jsp file in the file system; if so, execute it
- look for headers requesting XHTML Mobile Profile for a cell phone browser; if so and there is a .mobile file in the file system, serve it, if not, continue
- look for a .html file
- look for a .jpg
- look for a .gif

(You'll want to customize the preference order for your server.)

Centralized logging of RDBMS queries   The main job of your Web scripts will be to formulate SQL queries and transactions. If things go wrong, the most valuable information that you can get is "what did my Web scripts tell the RDBMS to do and in what order." The best Web/application server programs have a single error log file into which they will optionally write all the queries that are sent to the RDBMS.

Exercises

After solving these problems you will know

- How to log into your development server
- Rudiments of whatever programming language you've chosen

- How to create, execute, test, and debug a dynamic Web page
- How to write a Web page that queries a foreign server
- Rudiments of SQL
- How to query an RDBMS from the shell
- How to write a Web page that queries an RDBMS
- How to personalize Web applications by issuing and reading cookies
- How to read and write data in XML
- How to load a flat-file of data into an RDBMS table

If you're using Microsoft .NET, you'll find the examples helpful in http://philip.greenspun.com/seia/examples-basics/dot-net-examples/.

Exercise 1: Finding Your Place in the World

Find your Web server's page root, the directory where the Web server begins looking for files. Put a file there named "index.html" and fill it with text identifying this as your server. Include your hyperlinked email address at the bottom of the page.

Connect to your server from a Web browser, using only the host name. For the rest of this problem set, we're going to assume that your hostname is "yourhostname.com." Verify that when you request http://yourhostname .com your customized page is presented. (If you get a directory listing instead, your Web server is probably not configured to look for index files named "index.html"; you'll have to reconfigure your server.) Now use an HTML validator to make sure that your HTML is legal. (See Yahoo's directory of HTML validators at http://dir.yahoo.com/Computers_and_Internet/ Data_Formats/ HTML/Validation_and_Checkers/ for a list of programs and services.)

You've made at least two requests from your Web server now. These will have been logged in the server access log. Find it in the file system and verify that the times and files requested shown make sense to you.

Exercise 2: Your First Program

Create a subdirectory called "basics" at the same level in the file system as the index.html file that you just created, that is, basics should be one level below the Web server root. This directory should be accessible at http://yourhostname .com/basics/.

Put a file in the directory so that it is accessible at http://yourhostname.com/ basics/my-first-program. If you haven't yet figured out how to implement abstract URLs, this may be "my-first-program.pl" or "my-first-program.asp" or similar.

When we visit http://yourhostname.com/basics/my-first-program, we should see the current time wrapped in a legal HTML page of some sort, signed with your email address.

Add some code that will generate a divide-by-zero error to your program. Find and visit the server error log to see how this error is communicated to you. With some execution environments, it may be possible to have the error message and stack backtrace presented to you in the browser window when the error occurs. If you can configure your server thusly, you'll find that debugging goes much faster this semester. If not, make sure that you know how to quickly display the latest errors. (On a Unix machine you'd use the command "tail -f error.log" in a shell or "M-x revert-buffer" in an Emacs editor visiting the error log.)

Just before the code that generates the divide-by-zero error, add a line of code to write the following message into the error log: "About to divide by zero." Request http://yourhostname.com/basics/my-first-program from a browser again and then visit the error log to verify that your "About to divide by zero" statement precedes the actual error.

Exercise 3: Processing Forms

Visit http://philip.greenspun.com/seia/examples-basics/lens and look at the focal length calculator under "Exactly how long a lens do you need?"

Make this service work on your server. Note that this will involve (1) learning a bit about HTML forms, (2) following the "view the source code" link on the results page at photo.net and pulling the mathematical formula out of the program there, (3) parking a static .html file containing the form on your server at /basics/lens-calculator, and (4) parking a program to process the form at /basics/lens-calculator-2.

(Note the naming convention above. When possible, this semester we'd like you to adhere to the idea that a script that processes a form at "foobar" is found at "foobar-2." If there is a pipeline of steps that a user must follow, we like to see them at "foobar," "foobar-2," "foobar-3," etc.)

Exercise 3a: Add a View Source Link

A big part of our work this semester is looking at other folks' source code. We do this so that we can examine alternative approaches to the same problem. You can facilitate this by adding a "view source" link to the bottom of the page that you just made. A user who clicks on this link ought to be served a file showing all of the source code behind the page in question, but not including procedures shared with other pages on the site.

Hints: you'll want to deliver your script and any template file, if applicable, with a MIME type of "text/plain." This way the receiving browser won't try to render the HTML source. Some Web browsers are super aggressive and try to render anything that looks like HTML, even if it comes through without the text/html MIME type. An alternative approach that works with such browsers is to quote all of your HTML by replacing < with <, > with >, and & with &, then wrap source code in a <PRE> tag.

Servers That Query Foreign Servers

Some of the highest achievement-to-effort ratios can be achieved by aggregating information from multiple existing data sources. Consider, for example, the Bill Gates Personal Wealth Clock, at http://philip.greenspun.com/WealthClock (figure 2.3). This program queries a public stock quote server (the first "foreign server") to find the current price of Microsoft Corporation stock. The second foreign server queried is a U.S. Census Bureau "population clock" for an estimate of the current U.S. population.

There are several interesting things about this program, which was built by one of the authors in 1995. One is that it was enabled by the existence of a procedure built into AOLserver that went out and grabbed a page from the wider Internet, ns_httpget. This enabled the entire project to be completed in one hour. Engineering is all about cost. If building this little application would have required several days of work it probably would not have been done. A second item worth noting is that the program has required substantial maintenance over the years, far exceeding its initial development cost. The program relies on using regular expressions to pull data out of HTML pages that are designed for human eyes. As the publishers of the underlying data sources have changed their HTML formatting over the years, these regular expressions have had to be updated.

Thu Mar 24 02:31:15 EST 2005

Microsoft Stock Price:	$24.18
Bill Gates's Wealth:	$57.901977 billion
U.S. Population:	295,723,917
Your Personal Contribution:	**$195.80**

"If you want to know what God thinks about money, just look at the people He gives it to."
-- Old Irish Saying

Figure 2.3   The Bill Gates Personal Wealth Clock. This program queries a public stock quote server to find the price of Microsoft stock and the U.S. Census Bureau's server for the current U.S. population, then combines the numbers on one page.
Sources: Population: U.S. Census Bureau, http://www.census.gov/cgi-bin/popclock. N shares of Microsoft owned by Bill Gates: 1995 Microsoft Proxy Statement (141,159,990 shares adjusted for splits in December 1996, February 1998, March 1999, and February 2003). Microsoft Stock Price: Yahoo! Finance, http://yahoo.finance.com.

The final point worth mentioning about this program is that part of the hour of coding went into building a general-purpose caching or *memoization* system to record the results of evaluating any Tcl expression in a global variable. Why? It seemed like bad netiquette to write a program that had the potential to impose an unreasonable load on the Census Bureau and stock quote servers. Also, in the event that the Wealth Clock became popular, it would be asking the underlying servers several times a second for the same data. Lastly it seemed that users shouldn't have to wait for the two subsidiary pages to be fetched if they didn't need up-to-the-minute data. With the complete HTML page stored in a global variable, it is available from AOLserver's virtual memory space and can be accessed much faster than even a static file. Users who want a real-time answer can demand one with an extra mouse click. The calculation performed for them then updates the cache for casual users.

The caching mechanism might sound like overengineering, but from time to time the Wealth Clock would be linked to from extremely popular news sites and receive several requests per second. The ability to handle a reasonably high load like that, back in the mid-1990s, without an enormous server farm was rather rare. Had those requests been passed directly through to the Census Bureau, for example, the entire service would have slowed to a crawl.

The source code for this program is available at http://philip.greenspun.com/examples-basics/wealth-clock.tcl.txt and may prove helpful in doing the next exercise.

Exercise 4: Comparative Book Shopping

Drawing upon the Bill Gates Personal Wealth Clock and its source code as a model, build a new Web application that takes the ISBN of a book from a form and queries several online bookstores to find price and stock information. The results should be displayed in an HTML table (price and in stock/out of stock at each store). Make your service available at /basics/books (the entry form) and /basics/books-2 (the results page).

We suggest querying barnesandnoble.com and www.powells.com. Your program should be robust to timeouts, errors at the foreign sites, and network problems. In other words, in no situation should your user ever get a "Server Error 500" page. To ensure this, you'll have to learn about exception handling in your chosen language. In Java, for example, you'll want to use `try` and `catch`. Test your program with the following ISBNs: 0590353403, 0140260404, 0679762906, 1588750019.

Try adding more bookstores, but you may have trouble getting them to work. For example, amazon.com and wordsworth.com tend to respond with a 302 redirect if the client doesn't give them a session ID in the query.

Extra credit: Which of the preceding books states that "The obvious mathematical breakthrough would be development of an easy way to factor large prime numbers"?

Remember that it is a mistake to compare Harry Potter to Shakespeare.... That's because Harry Potter is a fictional character whereas Shakespeare was an author. What you really ought to be doing is comparing J. K. Rowling to Shakespeare.

—Jin S. Choi

Exercise 5: Talking to the RDBMS

It turns out that it takes less time to learn the basics of SQL than it does to figure out how to deliver an SQL command to your RDBMS. These instructions are for Oracle. Refer to your supplement if you're using another RDBMS.

On Unix, the most convenient way to drive Oracle is generally from within Emacs, assuming you're already an Emacs user. Type "M-x shell" to get a Unix shell. Type "M-x rename-buffer" to rename the shell to "sql-shell" so that you can always type "M-x shell" again and get an operating system shell. In the sql-shell buffer, type "sqlplus" to start SQL*Plus, the Oracle shell client. If you're using Windows, look for the program "SQLPLUS.EXE" or "PLUS80.EXE."

SQL*Plus will prompt you for a username and password. If you're using a school-supplied development server, you may need to get these from your TA. If you set up the RDBMS yourself, you might need to create a new tablespace and user before you can do this exercise.

Type the following at the SQL*Plus prompt to create a table for keeping track of the classes you're taking this semester:

```
create table my_courses (
        course_number  varchar(20)
);
```

Note that you have to end your SQL commands with a semicolon in SQL*Plus. These are not part of the SQL language and you shouldn't use these when writing SQL in your Web scripts.

Insert a few rows, for example,

```
insert into my_courses (course_number) values ('6.171');
```

See what you've got:

```
select * from my_courses;
```

Commit your changes:

```
commit;
```

Note that until you typed this COMMIT, another connected database user wouldn't have been able to see the row that you inserted. "Connected database user" includes the Web server. A common source of student consternation with Oracle is that they've inserted information with SQL*Plus and neglected to COMMIT. The new information does not appear on any of their Web pages, and they tear their hair out debugging. Of course nothing is wrong with their scripts. It is just that the ACID guarantees mean that the Web server sees a different view of the database than the user who is in the middle of a transaction.

Your view of the table shouldn't change after a COMMIT, but maybe check again:

```
select * from my_courses;
```

One of the main benefits of using an RDBMS is *persistence*. Everything that you create stays around even after you log out. Normally, that's a good thing, but in this case you probably want to clean up after your experiment:

```
drop table my_courses;
```

Quit SQL*Plus with the `quit` command.

Reading Interlude

Now would be a good time to take a break and read about SQL. We suggest chapters 1 through 9 of *SQL for Web Nerds* at http://philip.greenspun.com/sql/.

Exercise 6: Web Scripts That Talk to the RDBMS

Look at the file http://philip.greenspun.com/seia/examples-basics/quotations-pseudo-code.txt, which is pseudo-code for a page that displays quotations that have been stored in the Oracle database.

If your instructors are being nice to you, they'll already have translated this pseudo-code into something that works with the infrastructure you're using at your school. If not, you'll have to translate it yourself, along with http://philip.greenspun.com/seia/examples-basics/quotation-add-pseudo-code.txt. Park your finished program at /basics/quotations (plus a file extension if you must). Add a hyperlink from your site index page to this service.

Use the form on the Web page to manually add some quotations. If you don't feel inspired to surf, here are a few to get you going:

- "I feel like those Jewish people in Germany in 1942."—Ted Turner (on being prevented from buying another TV station)
- "If a man speaks in the forest and there is no woman there to hear him, is he still wrong?"—Unknown Heroine
- "Men are like a fine wine. They all start out like grapes, and it's our job to stomp on them and keep them in the dark where they will mature into something you'd want to have dinner with."—Unknown Heroine
- "A woman needs four animals in her life. A mink in the closet. A jaguar in the garage. A tiger in bed. And an ass to pay for it all."—Anne Slater
- "An editor should have a pimp for a brother, so he'd have someone to look up to."—Gene Fowler

- "The newest computer can merely compound, at speed, the oldest problem in the relations between human beings, and in the end the communicator will be confronted with the old problem, of what to say and how to say it."—Edward R. Murrow
- "Egotism is the anesthetic that dulls the pain of stupidity."—Frank Leahy
- "Some for renown, on scraps of learning dote, And think they grow immortal as they quote."—Edward Young

Return to your RDBMS shell client (e.g., SQL*Plus for Oracle) and `select * from` the table to see that your quotation has been inserted into the table.

In your RDBMS shell client, insert a quotation with some hand-coded SQL. To see the form of the SQL INSERT command you should use, examine the code on the page quotation-add. After creating this new table row, do `select * again`, and you should now see two rows.

Hint: Don't forget that SQL quotes strings using single quotes, not double quotes.

Now reload the `quotations` URL from your Web browser. If you don't see your new quotation here, that's because you didn't type "commit;" at SQL*Plus and the Web server is being protected from seeing the unfinished transaction.

Exercise 6a: Eliminating the `lock table` via a Sequence

Read about Oracle's *sequence* database object in the "Data Modeling" and "Transactions" chapters of *SQL for Web Nerds* at http://philip.greenspun .com/sql/data-modeling and http://philip.greenspun.com/sql/transactions. By creating a sequence, you should be able to edit the quotation-add script to

- eliminate the need for `lock table`
- eliminate the transaction machinery (since you're no longer tying multiple SQL statements together)
- generate a unique key for the new quotation within the INSERT statement itself

Exercise 7: Improving the User Interface for Data Entry

Go back to the main quotations page and modify it so that categories entry is done via a select box of existing categories (you will want to use the "SELECT DISTINCT" SQL command). For new categories, provide an alternative text entry box labeled "new category." Make sure to modify quotation-add so that it recognizes when a new category is being defined.

Exercise 8: Searching

Add a small form at the top of /basics/quotations that takes a single query word from the user. Build a target for this form that returns all quotes containing the specified word. Your search should be case-insensitive and also look through the authors column. Hints: `like '%foo%'` and SQL's UPPER and LOWER functions.

Exercise 9: Personalizing Your Service with Cookies

Now implement per-browser personalization of the quotation database. The overall goal should be

- A user can "kill" a quotation and have it never show up again either from the top-level page or the search page.
- Killing a quotation is persistent and survives the quitting and restarting of a browser.
- Quotations killed by one user have no effect on what is seen by other users.
- Users can erase their personalizations and see the complete quotation database again by clicking on an "erase my personalization" link on the main page. This link should appear only if the user has personalized the quotation database.

You'll implement this using cookies. From your technology supplement you'll need to learn how to read the incoming HTTP request headers and then parse out the Cookie header or perhaps you'll have an API that makes it easy to get the value of a particular cookie. Note that you can expire a cookie by reissuing it with an expiration date that has already passed.

Hint 1: It is possible to build this system using an ID cookie for the browser and keeping the set of killed quotations in the RDBMS. However, if you're not going to allow users to log in and claim their profile, there really isn't much point in keeping data on the server.

Hint 2: It isn't strictly copacetic with the cookie spec, but browsers accept cookie values containing spaces. So you can store the killed quotations as a space-separated list if you like.

Hint 3: Don't filter the quotations in your Web script. It is generally a sign of incompetent programming when you query more data from the RDBMS than you're going to display to the end-user. SQL is a very powerful query language. You can use the NOT IN feature to exclude a list of quotations.

Exercise 10: Publishing Data in XML

As you learned above from querying bookstores, data on the Web have not traditionally been formatted for convenient use by computer programs. In theory, people who wish to exchange data over the Web can cooperate using XML, a 1998 standard from the Web Consortium (http://www.w3.org/XML/). In practice, you'll be hard pressed to get any XML-based cooperation from the average Web site right now (2005). Fortunately for your sake in completing this problem set, you can cooperate with your fellow students: the overall goal is to make quotations in your database exportable in a structured format so that other students' applications can read them.

Here's what we need in order to cooperate:

- an agreed-upon URL at everyone's server where the quotations database may be obtained: "/basics/quotations-xml"
- an agreed-upon format for the quotations

(In point of fact, we could avoid the need for prior agreement by setting up infrastructures for *service discovery* and by employing techniques for *self-describing data*—both of which we'll deal with later in the semester—but we'll keep things simple for now.)

We'll format the quotations using XML, a conventional notation for describing structured data. XML structures consist of data strings enclosed in HTML-like tags of the form <foo> and </foo>, describing what kind of thing the data is supposed to be.

Here's an informal example, showing the structure we'll use for our quotations:

```
<quotations>
  <onequote>
    <quotation_id>1</quotation_id>
    <insertion_date>2004-01-26</insertion_date>
    <author_name>Britney Spears</author_name>
    <category>Pop Musician Leisure Activities</category>
    <quote>I shop, go to movies, and go out to eat.</quote>
```

```
    </onequote>
    <onequote>
    .. another row from the quotations table ...
    </onequote>
    ... some more rows
</quotations>
```

Notice that there's a separate tag for each column in our SQL data model:

```
<quotation_id>
<insertion_date>
<author_name>
<category>
<quote>
```

There's also a "wrapper" tag that identifies each row as a `<onequote>` structure, and an outer wrapper that identifies a sequence of `<onequote>` structures as a `<quotations>` document.

Building a DTD

We can give a formal description of our XML structure, rather than an informal example, by means of an XML Document Type Definition (DTD).

Our DTD will start with a definition of the `quotations` tag:

```
<!ELEMENT quotations (onequote)+>
```

This says that the `quotations` element must contain at least one occurrence of `onequote`, but may contain more than one. Now we have to say what constitutes a legal `onequote` element:

```
<!ELEMENT onequote (quotation_id,insertion_date,author_name,category,quote)>
```

This says that the sub-elements, such as `quotation_id` must each appear exactly once and in the specified order. Now we have to define an XML element that actually contains something other than other XML elements:

```
<!ELEMENT quotation_id (#PCDATA)>
```

This says that whatever falls between `<quotation_id>` and `</quotation_id>` is to be interpreted as raw characters rather than as containing further tags ("PCDATA" stands for "parsed character data").

Here's our complete DTD:

```
<!-- quotations.dtd -->
<!ELEMENT quotations (onequote)+>

<!ELEMENT onequote (quotation_id,insertion_date,author_name,category,quote)>

<!ELEMENT quotation_id (#PCDATA)>
<!ELEMENT insertion_date (#PCDATA)>
<!ELEMENT author_name (#PCDATA)>
<!ELEMENT category (#PCDATA)>
<!ELEMENT quote (#PCDATA)>
```

You will find this extremely useful. Hey, actually you won't find this DTD useful at all for completing this part of the problem set. The only situation in which a DTD is useful is when feeding documents to an XML parser because then the parser can automatically tokenize each XML document. For implementing your quotations-xml page, you will only need to look at the informal example.

The meat of this exercise: Write a script that queries the `quotations` table, produces an XML document in the preceding form, and returns it to the client with a MIME type of "application/xml." Place this in the file system at /basics/quotations-xml, so that other users can retrieve the data by visiting that agreed-upon URL.

Exercise 11: Importing XML

Write a program to import the quotations from another student's XML output page. Your program must

- Grab /basics/quotations-xml from another student's server.
- Parse the resulting XML structure into records and then parse the records into fields.
- If a quote from the foreign server has identical author and content as a quote in your own database, ignore it; otherwise, insert it into your database with a new `quotation_id`. (You don't want keys from the foreign server conflicting with what is already in your database.)

Hint: You can set up a temporary table using `create table quotations_temp as select * from quotations` and then drop it after you're done debugging, so that you don't mess up your own quotations database.

You are not expected to write an XML parser as part of this exercise. You will either use a general-purpose XML parser or your TAs will give you a simple program that is capable only of parsing this particular format. If you aren't getting any help from your TAs and you're using Oracle, keep in mind that the Oracle RDBMS has extensive built-in support for processing XML. Read the Oracle documentation, notably the *Oracle XML DB Developer's Guide: Oracle XML DB*. If you're using Java or Perl, there are plenty of free open-source XML parsers available. The Microsoft .NET Framework Class Library contains classes that provide a full set of XML tools.

Exercise 12: Taking Credit

Please go through your source code files. Make sure that there is a header at the top explaining (1) who wrote the code, (2) on what date it was written, and (3) what problem it is trying to solve. Please go through your Web pages. Make sure that at the bottom of each page there is a mailto: link to your permanent email address.

It is your professional obligation to other programmers to take responsibility for your source code. It is your professional obligation to end-users to take responsibility for their experience with your program.

Database Exercises

We're going to shift gears now into a portion of the problem set designed to teach you more about the RDBMS and SQL. See your supplement if you're using an RDBMS other than Oracle.

To facilitate turning in your problem set, keep a text file transcript of relevant parts of your database session at http://yourhostname.com/basics/db-exercises.txt.

DB Exercise 1: SQL*Loader

- Use a standard text editor to create a plain text file containing five lines, each line to contain your favorite stock symbol, an integer number of shares owned, and a date acquired (in the form MM/DD/YYYY). Separate the fields on each line with tabs.

- create an Oracle table to hold these data:

```
create table my_stocks (
        symbol          varchar(20) not null,
        n_shares        integer not null,
        date_acquired   date not null
);
```

- use the `sqlldr` shell command on Unix to invoke SQL*Loader to slurp up your tab-separated file into the `my_stocks` table

Depending on how resourceful you are with skimming documentation, this exercise can take fifteen minutes or a lifetime. The book *Oracle: The Complete Reference*, discussed in the "More" section of this chapter is very helpful. You can also read about SQL*Loader in the official Oracle docs, linked from http://www.oracle.com/, typically in the *Utilities* book. Note that finding Oracle documentation online requires a bit of persistence and oftentimes registration (free). Look for links that say "view library" and tabs that say "books."

DB Exercise 2: Copying Data from One Table to Another

This exercise exists because we found that, when faced with the task of moving data from one table to another, programmers were dragging the data across SQL*Net from Oracle into their Web server, manipulating it in a Web script, then pushing it back into Oracle over SQL*Net. This is not the way! SQL is a very powerful language and there is no need to bring in any other tools if what you want to do is move data around within the RDBMS.

- using only one SQL statement, create a table called `stock_prices` with three columns: `symbol`, `quote_date`, `price`. Within this one statement, fill the table you're creating with one row per symbol in `my_stocks`. The date and price columns should be filled with the current date and a nominal price. Hint: `select symbol, sysdate as quote_date, 31.415 as price from my_stocks;`.

- create a new table:

```
create table newly_acquired_stocks (
        symbol          varchar(20) not null,
        n_shares        integer not null,
        date_acquired   date not null
);
```

- using a single `insert into ... select ...` statement (with a WHERE clause appropriate to your sample data), copy about half the rows from `my_stocks` into `newly_acquired_stocks`

DB Exercise 3: JOIN

With a single SQL statement JOINing `my_stocks` and `stock_prices`, produce a report showing symbol, number of shares, price per share, and current value.

DB Exercise 4: OUTER JOIN

Insert a row into `my_stocks`. Rerun your query from the previous exercise. Notice that your new stock does not appear in the report. This is because you've JOINed them with the constraint that the symbol appear in both tables.

Modify your statement to use an OUTER JOIN instead so that you'll get a complete report of all your stocks, but won't get price information if none is available.

DB Exercise 5: PL/SQL

Inspired by Wall Street's methods for valuing Internet companies, we've developed our own valuation method for this problem set: a stock is valued at the sum of the ASCII characters making up its symbol. (Note that students who've used lowercase letters to represent symbols will have higher-valued portfolios than those who've used all uppercase symbols; "IBM" is worth only $216 whereas "ibm" is worth $312!)

- define a PL/SQL *function* that takes a trading symbol as its argument and returns the stock value. Hint: Oracle's built-in ASCII function will be helpful.
- with a single UPDATE statement, update `stock_prices` to set each stock's value to whatever is returned by this PL/SQL procedure
- define a PL/SQL function that takes no arguments and returns the aggregate value of the portfolio (`n_shares * price` for each stock). You'll want to define your JOIN from DB Exercise 3 (above) as a cursor, and then use the PL/SQL Cursor FOR LOOP facility. Hint: when you're all done, you can run this procedure from SQL*Plus with `select portfolio_value() from dual;`.

SQL*Plus Tip: though it is not part of the SQL language, you will find it very useful to type "/" after your PL/SQL definitions if you're feeding them to Oracle via the SQL*Plus application. Unless you write perfect code, you'll also want to know about the SQL*Plus command "show errors." For exposure to the full range of this kind of obscurantism, see the *SQL*Plus User's Guide and Reference*, one of the books included in Oracle's database documentation.

DB Exercise 6: Buy More of the Winners

Rather than taking your profits on the winners, buy more of them!

- use SELECT AVG( ) to figure out the average price of your holdings
- Using a single INSERT with SELECT statement, double your holdings in all the stocks whose price is higher than average (with `date_acquired` set to `sysdate`)

Rerun your query from DB Exercise 4. Note that in some cases you will have two rows for the same symbol. If what you're really interested in is your current position, you want a report with at most one row per symbol.

- use a `select ... group by ...` query from `my_stocks` to produce a report of symbols and total shares held
- use a `select ... group by ...` query JOINing with `stock_prices` to produce a report of symbols and total value held per symbol
- use a `select ... group by ... having ...` query to produce a report of symbols, total shares held, and total value held per symbol *restricted to symbols in which you have at least two blocks of shares* (i.e., the "winners")

DB Exercise 7: Encapsulate Your Queries with a View

Using the final query above, create a view called `stocks_i_like` that encapsulates the final query.

More

- on HTTP: The Web Consortium's canonical standard at http://www.w3.org/Protocols/

- on HTML: the "HTML" reference chapter of this book
- on ASP.NET: Stephen Walther's *ASP.NET Unleashed* (Sams, 2003)
- on the Oracle RDBMS: a very helpful hardcopy book is Kevin Loney's *Oracle XX: The Complete Reference* from Oracle Press, where "XX" is whatever the latest version of Oracle is. At press time *Oracle 10g: The Complete Reference* (2004) is available. All Oracle documentation is available online at www.oracle.com, but it can be overwhelming for beginners.

Problem Set Supplements

- for people using Microsoft .NET: http://philip.greenspun.com/seia/examples-basics/dot-net-examples/
- for people using Java: http://philip.greenspun.com/seia/examples-basics/java-examples/
- refer to the online version of this chapter periodically to find new supplements: http://philip.greenspun.com/seia/basics

Time and Motion

The luckiest students spend only two hours setting up their RDBMS and development environment. An average student who makes reasonable technology choices can expect to spend a day or two getting things connected properly. Some students who are unlucky with sysadmin, hardware, or who are not resourceful with Internet and face-to-face sources of help can spend many days without building a working environment. At MIT we have the students start on sysadmin/dbadmin at least three weeks before the first class.

Given an established development environment, the exercises in this chapter take between six and twelve hours for MIT students working in a lab where teaching assistants are available and possibly as long as twenty hours for those working by themselves.

3   Planning

If you're reading this chapter, we assume that you've completed the "Basics" problem set and are going to stay with the course for the rest of the semester. Welcome. Now it is time to plan your work during the core of the course.

Everyone in this course will be building an online learning community, a site where users teach each other. The work may be done alone or in groups of two or three students. Ideally, you or your instructors will find a real client for you, someone who wants to publish and administer the community on an ongoing basis. A good client would be a non-profit organization that wants to educate people about the subject surrounding its mission. A good client would be a medium-sized company that wants a knowledge-sharing system for employees. A good client would be a student group at your university. If you can't find a client, pick something that you're passionate about. It could be Islamic architecture. It could be African Cichlids (a family of freshwater fishes, living mostly in the rift lakes of East Africa; see www.cichlid.org). It could be cryptography. Pick something where you think that you can easily get or generate *magnet content*, some tutorial information that will attract users to your service.

You are building the same type of project as everyone else in the class. Thus it will be easy for you to compare approaches to, for example, user registration or content management.

Before you starting writing code, however, we'd like you to do some planning and competitive analysis. Fundamentally you need to answer the questions "Who is going to teach what to whom?" and "What alternatives are currently available for this kind of learning?"

User Classes

Start by dividing your users into classes. Two users should fall into the same class if you expect them to want substantially the same experience with your service. It is almost always useful to think about different levels of administrative privileges as you are dividing the users into classes. It is almost never useful to think about teachers versus learners; the whole point of an online community is that each user is learning some of the time and each user is teaching some of the time.

Example: User Class Decomposition on photo.net

To give you an idea of what a user class decomposition might look like, we'll walk through one for the photo.net service.

First, consider the overall objective of photo.net: A place where a person can go and get the answer to any question about photography.

Second, consider levels of administrative privilege. There are *site-wide administrators*, who are free to edit or delete any content on the site. These administrators also have the power to adjust the authority of other users. We have *moderators* who have authority to approve or delete postings in particular discussion forums. Finally there are *regular users* who can read, post, and edit their own contributions. A less popular service could probably get away with only two levels of admin privilege.

A different way of dividing the users is by purpose in visiting the service:

- wanna-be point-and-shooter—wants quick advice on what point-and-shoot camera to buy and where to buy it; wants to invest minimal time, effort, and money in photography
- novice photographer shopper—wants to begin taking pictures for purposes of artistic expression, but does not have a camera with flexible controls right now
- novice photographer learner—has the right equipment, but wants ideas for where, when, and how to use it; wants critiques of finished work
- expert photographer—wants new ideas, to see what is new in the world of hardware; wants to share expertise; wants community
- wanna-be commercial photographer—might be a high school or college student curious about the future or an older person wanting to change careers;

wants to know whether it is feasible to make a living doing photography and, if so, how to start

- exhibitor—wants to upload photos into the photo-sharing system and develop an audience among the photo.net readership

- traveler—wants to know about locations worldwide for photography incidental to an already planned trip or wants ideas for where to travel for photographic inspiration

- reader—likes the travel stories like *Travels with Samantha* and viewing photographs, but does not want to take photographs him or herself

A final way of dividing users that may be useful is by how they connect. In the case of photo.net, it is easy to envision the *Web-browser user*. This user is uploading and downloading photos, participating in discussions, reading tutorials, shopping for equipment, and so on. The same person may connect via a mobile phone, in which case he or she becomes a *mobile user*. If the mobile user is in the middle of a photographic project, we want to provide information about nearby camera shops, processing labs, repair shops, time of sunset, good locations, and other useful data. If the mobile user is connecting for social purposes, we need to think about what are practical ways for a person on a mobile phone to participate in an online community. Our engineering challenge is similar for the *telephone user*.

Usage Scenarios

For each class of user, you should write down a rough idea of what a person in this class would get from your new service. You may want to hint at page flow.

Example: Novice Photographer Shopper at photo.net

The novice should start by reading a bunch of carefully authored camera-buying advice articles and then reviews of specific cameras. Much of the best shopping advice is contained in question-and-answer exchanges within the discussion forums so editors will need a way to pick out and point to the best threads in the forum archives. After our user has read all of this stuff, it would be ideal if he or she could be directed into a Q&A forum where "here's what I've decided to buy; what do you think?" questions are welcomed. That could be implemented as an explicitly social shopping system with one column for responses from other readers and an adjacent column for bids from camera shops.

Example: Site-Wide Administrator at photo.net

The site-wide administrator should log in and see a page that gives the pulse of the community with statistics on the number of new users registered, the quantity of photos uploaded into the photo-sharing system, the activity in the discussion forums, the relative efforts of the moderators (volunteers from the community). If there are unbanned users who have been responsible for an onerous amount of moderator work in deleting off-topic postings, and so forth, these should be listed with a summary of their problematic activities and an option to ban.

Exercise 1a

Answer the following questions:

- What subject will people be able to learn in the community that you're building?
- What do you want people to say about your service after a visit?
- What are the relevant distinct user classes?
- What should a user on a mobile phone be able to do? Is it productive to mix voice and text interaction? (See "Multimodal Requirements for Voice Markup Languages" from the Web Consortium at http://www.w3.org/TR/multimodal-reqs for some hints as to what will be possible.)

Make sure that your answers to this and all subsequent exercises are Web accessible. It is a good idea to get into the discipline of ensuring that all documents relevant to your project are available on the project server itself, perhaps in the /doc/ directory.

Exercise 1b: Build User Profile Pages

When building an application it would be ideal to have the potential users in the room with you at all times. Their needs would then be concrete and manifest. This isn't very practical, however, and therefore as an aid to making the people for whom you're building the application concrete, you should build two or three profile pages. A profile page contains the following information: (a) a picture of the user, (b) the user's name, age, occupation, marital status, housing situation, and income, (c) the user's short-term and long-term goals relevant to the online community that you're building, (d) the immediate questions that this user will bring to the site, (e) the kind of computer equipment and connection in this person's house, and (f) any other information that will help to humanize this fictitious person.

To assist you in this task we've created a couple of examples for an online learning community in the area of general aviation:

- Rachel Lipschitz (http://philip.greenspun.com/seia/examples-planning/user-profile-1)
- Melvin Cohen (http://philip.greenspun.com/seia/examples-planning/user-profile-2)
- Mindy Silverblatt (http://philip.greenspun.com/seia/examples-planning/user-profile-3)

If you don't have a good photo library of your own, lift photos (with credit) from photo.net and other online sources.

Don't spend more than one hour on this exercise; plenty of truly awful software has been written with fancy user profiles on the programmers' desks. There is no substitute for launching a service to real users and then watching their behavior attentively.

Exercise 1c

For each class of user identified in Exercise 1a, produce a textual or graphical usage scenario for how that user will experience your service.

Evaluating Alternatives: Offline

Whenever Nick Gittes (1902–2000; grandfather of one of the authors) would see a computer advertised on television, he'd say "A home computer. Why would anyone want a thing like that?"

Figure 3.1   Nick Gittes and Alex, 1998. Photo copyright Philip Greenspun.

The dotcom boom is over. You ought to have a good reason for building an information system. If a curmudgeon wants to know why you need all these fancy computers instead of a book, some chalk, and pencil and paper, it would be nice to have a convincing answer.

There are good reasons to look at the best elements of offline resources and systems. After several millenia, many of these systems are exquisitely refined and extremely effective. Your online community and technology-aided learning environment can be much improved by careful study of the best offline alternatives.

Example: *Popular Photography* Magazine

The largest circulation offline publication in the U.S. world of photography is the sixty-five-year-old magazine *Popular Photography*. It is extremely effective at answering the following questions: What is the price of a Nikon 50/1.4 lens? What are the latest cameras available? How does the new Canon Elan 7 body perform on a test bench?

The magazine is ineffective for start-to-finish learning. It is impossible for *Popular Photography* to sell enough ads to run a twenty-page tutorial article much less a complete beginner's textbook on photography. The magazine is ineffective for finding the average price for a used or obscure item. (*Shutterbug* is the place for used and classic camera dealer ads.)

The magazine is ineffective as a means of getting answers to arbitrary questions. There is a "Too Hot to Handle" section in every issue that promises "Honest, forthright answers to your most probing questions." Unfortunately, only four questions are answered per issue. Presumably these were submitted at least a couple of months previously. And the answers come only from the editors of the magazine; they don't tap the reserves of knowledge that may reside among the hundreds of thousands of subscribers.

The magazine is ineffective as a means of exhibiting reader work. The "Your Best Shot" column displays five or six reader-contributed photos in every issue, but being selected is a slow and uncertain process.

Example: Face-to-Face Course

The main strength of a face-to-face course in photography is guaranteed mentoring. The instructor keeps track of each student's progress and questions. Another strength of a face-to-face course is the availability of critiques from other students and the instructor.

Face-to-face courses require more travel, time, effort, and commitment than many people are able to give. Once the course is over, the student is unable to avail him or herself of mentoring and critiques from the instructor and other students.

Exercise 2

Write down the best features of offline alternatives for learning the subject matter of the service that you're building. Indicate those features that you think can be translated into an online community and, if so, how. Write a three-sentence justification for why your online learning community will be an improvement over offline alternatives for at least some group of people.

Evaluating Alternatives: Online

In performing your analysis of online competitors you should look at any service or resources for learning in your subject area. But pay special attention to online learning communities. Before setting off to surf, you might find it useful to think about the following elements of sustainable online community:

1. magnet content authored by experts

2. means of collaboration

3. powerful facilities for browsing and searching both magnet content and contributed content

4. means of delegation of moderation

5. means of identifying members who are imposing an undue burden on the community and ways of changing their behavior and/or excluding them from the community without them realizing it

6. means of software extension by community members themselves

When you visit a site ask yourself "Did they author or license a substantial body of tutorial content?" Look at the ratio between publisher-authored and user-authored content. If more than half of the content is authored by users, the site is heading away from *publishing* and toward *community*. Note the number of different ways in which a user can post some information that then becomes available to other users ("means of collaboration"). See whether the default search utility on the site returns results from things like discussion forum postings. As an unprivileged user, it will be hard for you to determine whether or not the site has provisions for distributing the content moderation burden or excluding difficult users. However, you can sometimes make inferences about Element 6, whether or not the software can be extended by people who are regular users and administrators of the community, but aren't expert programmers. If the site is commercial, check the job listings to see what skills are required. If the site hasn't adopted the abstract URL religion (see "Basics" chapter) the file extensions may give you a clue as to implementation technology. A ".pl," ".asp," ".php," ".adp," or ".tcl" indicates the use of a scripting language amenable to program extensions by novices. A ".jsp" or the term "servlet" in the URL indicates the use of Java, a language that is intended only for professional programmers.

Exercise 3

Find the best existing online communities in your subject area. Note how closely they conform to the six elements of sustainability listed above. Also write down anything strikingly good or bad about the registration process and the mechanisms of collaboration, for example, in discussion forums, comments on articles, and chat rooms. Look for voice and mobile interfaces. If present, try them out. (The "Adding Mobile Users To Your Community" chapter provides a list of desktop browser-based phone emulators so that you won't have to use your mobile phone; alternatively type "WAP emulator" or "Mobile browser emulator" into a public search engine.) Look for evidence of personalization and direct controls over preferences.

Does the World Need More Than One Online Community?

Suppose that in Exercise 3 you found 100 online communities in your subject area. Should you be discouraged? A search at amazon.com for "aquarium" yields 679 books on the subject of keeping fish at home. The National Center for Educational Statistics (nces.ed.gov) found that there were 3,913 colleges and universities in the United States in 1998. The computing world historically has tended toward concentration. There is only room for one or two desktop user interfaces, one or two word processors, one or two spreadsheets, a handful of enterprise accounting systems, and so forth. Two factors prevent similar concentration in the world of online learning communities. One is the idiosyncracy of authorship. A person may believe that *Anna Karenina* is the best novel ever written and simultaneously be interested in reading C. D. Payne's *Youth in Revolt*. A moviegoer may believe that *Gone with the Wind* will never be excelled and yet still invest two hours in *Charade*. The range of idiosyncracy is narrower in explicitly tutorial works. Nonetheless one can admit the towering accomplishment of Leslie Stroebel et al.'s *Basic Photographic Materials and Processes* (Focal Press, 2000) and still profit from working through *Mastering Black-And-White Photography* (Bernhard Seuss, [Allworth Press, 1995]).

The second force that prevents concentration in the world of online learning communities is the nature of community itself. Christopher Alexander, Sara Ishikawa, and Murray Silverstein argue in *A Pattern Language* (Oxford University Press, 1977) against countries of more than a few million people:

It is not hard to see why the government of a region becomes less and less manageable with size. In a population of N persons, there are of the order of N^2 person-to-person links needed to keep channels of communication open. Naturally, when N goes beyond a certain limit, the channels of communication needed for democracy and justice and information are simply too clogged, and too complex; bureaucracy overwhelms human process. . . .

We believe the limits are reached when the population of a region reaches some 2 to 10 million. Beyond this size, people become remote from the large-scale processes of government. Our estimate may seem extraordinary in the light of modern history: the nation-states have grown mightily and their governments hold power over tens of millions, sometimes hundreds of millions, of people. But these huge powers cannot claim to have a natural size. They cannot claim to have struck the balance between the needs of towns and communities, and the needs of the world community as a whole. Indeed, their tendency has been to override local needs and repress local culture, and at the same time aggrandize themselves to the point where they are out of reach, their power barely conceivable to the average citizen.

If it were possible for everyone to pile into a single community and have a great learning experience, America Online would long ago have subsumed all the smaller communities on the Internet. One of the later chapters of this book is devoted to the topic of growing an online community gracefully to a large size. But, for now, rest assured that it is a hard problem that nobody has solved. Given sufficiently high quality magnet content and an initial group of people dedicated to teaching, there will always be room for a new learning community.

Exercise 4

Identify sources of magnet content for your community this semester. If some of this content is going to come from other people, write to them and ask for permission. Even if you're only using their work experimentally, one concern that an author or publisher might have is that your site will get indexed by search engines and readers will be misdirected to your site instead of theirs. In practice, this is not a problem if your server isn't accessible from the public Internet or if you include a `robots.txt` file that will instruct search engines to exclude certain content. You may get a friendlier response from copyright holders if you agree to provide a hyperlinked credit and to ensure that their content does not become multiply indexed.

If you have a client who is supplying all the magnet content, write down a summary of what is going to be available and when. Next to each class of documents note the person responsible for assembling and delivering them. As an engineer, it isn't your job to assemble and develop content, but it is your job to identify risks to a project, such as "not enough magnet content" or "nobody has thought about magnet content."

Domain Name System

The Domain Name System (DNS) translates human-readable hostnames, for example, `www.google.com`, into machine-readable and network-routable IP addresses, for example, `216.239.57.100`. DNS is a distributed application in that there is no single computer that holds translations for all possible hostnames. A domain registrar, for example, register.com, records that the domain servers for the google.com domain are at particular IP addresses. A user's local *name server* will query the name servers for google.com to find the translation for the hostname `www.google.com`. Note that there is nothing magic about "www"; it is merely a conventional name for a computer that runs a Web server. The procedure for translating a hostname such as `froogle.google.com` is the same as that applied for translating `www`.

Exercise 5: Settle on a Hostname

Working with your client, pick a hostname for the application that you'll be building this semester. If you're building something within MIT, for example, you'll probably want to pick `something.mit.edu`. You and your client will need to navigate the IT bureaucracy to register that hostname and map it to the IP address of your server. If you're building a service for a client who does not have an Internet domain, encourage them to come up with a good name and register it. The authors have had good experience with register.com, a service that includes bundled use of their DNS servers; the domain owner can edit the hostname-to-IP-address translations with a Web browser interface.

Exercise 6: Negotiate Intellectual Property Rights

One of the thing that distinguishes a professional software engineer is success in negotiating intellectual property rights. If you give away all rights to everything that you produce as a "work for hire," you won't have a personal toolkit of software that you can reuse on new projects. If you don't give away any rights, nobody will be able to run your software, which probably means that you won't be able to solve social or organizational problems. A good negotiator gives away things that are valuable to the other side, but that aren't valuable to his or her side.

During this course, for example, you will ideally want to retain ownership of all software that you produce. You will therefore be free to reuse the code in any way, shape, or form. The client, however, is going to be putting in a lot of time and effort working with you over a period of months and is thus entitled to some benefit. Your university tuition payments have probably drained away all of the cash in your bank account and, therefore, you won't be giving the client money as compensation for his or her time. What you can do is give the client a license to use your software. This obviously benefits the client, but it also benefits you. The more people that are out there happily running your software, the better your professional resume looks.

Should you try to limit what the client can do with your software? Generally, this isn't worthwhile. Any organization that comes to you for programming assistance is probably not an organization that will want to hang out a shingle and offer to develop software for others. If they do decide that it would make sense to adapt your software to another application within the company, it is very likely that they will call you first to offer a consulting fee in exchange for your assistance.

How about limiting your liability? Oftentimes software engineers are called upon to write programs whose failure would have catastrophic results. Suppose that you are offered $100,000 to write a trading program for an investment bank. That may seem like a great deal until the bank sues you for $100 million, alleging that a bug in your program cost them $100 million in lost profits. In the biomedical field a bug can be much more serious. There is the famous case of the Therac-25 radiation treatment machine, bugs in whose control software cost lives (see http://sunnyday.mit.edu/therac-25.html).

Disclaiming liability is difficult, even for trained lawyers, and hence this is best left to professionals. Nearly every commercial software license includes a disclaimer of warranty. Here's a snippet from the Microsoft End User License Agreement (EULA):

19. DISCLAIMER OF WARRANTIES. TO THE MAXIMUM EXTENT PERMITTED BY APPLICABLE LAW, MICROSOFT AND ITS SUPPLIERS PROVIDE THE SOFTWARE AND SUPPORT SERVICES (IF ANY) AS IS AND WITH ALL

FAULTS, AND HEREBY DISCLAIM ALL OTHER WARRANTIES AND CONDI-TIONS, WHETHER EXPRESS, IMPLIED, OR STATUTORY, INCLUDING, BUT NOT LIMITED TO, ANY (IF ANY) IMPLIED WARRANTIES, DUTIES OR CONDITIONS OF MERCHANTABILITY, OF FITNESS FOR A PARTICULAR PURPOSE, OF RELIABILITY OR AVAILABILITY, OF ACCURACY OR COM-PLETENESS OF RESPONSES, OF RESULTS, OF WORKMANLIKE EFFORT, OF LACK OF VIRUSES, AND OF LACK OF NEGLIGENCE, ALL WITH RE-GARD TO THE SOFTWARE, AND THE PROVISION OF OR FAILURE TO PRO-VIDE SUPPORT OR OTHER SERVICES, INFORMATION, SOFTWARE, AND RELATED CONTENT THROUGH THE SOFTWARE OR OTHERWISE ARISING OUT OF THE USE OF THE SOFTWARE. ALSO, THERE IS NO WARRANTY OR CONDITION OF TITLE, QUIET ENJOYMENT, QUIET POSSESSION, CORRE-SPONDENCE TO DESCRIPTION, OR NON-INFRINGEMENT WITH REGARD TO THE SOFTWARE.

20. EXCLUSION OF INCIDENTAL, CONSEQUENTIAL, AND CERTAIN OTHER DAMAGES. TO THE MAXIMUM EXTENT PERMITTED BY APPLICABLE LAW, IN NO EVENT SHALL MICROSOFT OR ITS SUPPLIERS BE LIABLE FOR ANY SPECIAL, INCIDENTAL, PUNITIVE, INDIRECT, OR CONSEQUEN-TIAL DAMAGES WHATSOEVER (INCLUDING, BUT NOT LIMITED TO, DAMAGES FOR LOSS OF PROFITS OR CONFIDENTIAL OR OTHER INFOR-MATION, FOR BUSINESS INTERRUPTION, FOR PERSONAL INJURY, FOR LOSS OF PRIVACY, FOR FAILURE TO MEET ANY DUTY INCLUDING OF GOOD FAITH OR OF REASONABLE CARE, FOR NEGLIGENCE, AND FOR ANY OTHER PECUNIARY OR OTHER LOSS WHATSOEVER) ARISING OUT OF OR IN ANY WAY RELATED TO THE USE OF OR INABILITY TO USE THE SOFTWARE, THE PROVISION OF OR FAILURE TO PROVIDE SUPPORT OR OTHER SERVICES, INFORMATION, SOFTWARE, AND RELATED CON-TENT THROUGH THE SOFTWARE OR OTHERWISE ARISING OUT OF THE USE OF THE SOFTWARE, OR OTHERWISE UNDER OR IN CONNECTION WITH ANY PROVISION OF THIS EULA, EVEN IN THE EVENT OF THE FAULT, TORT (INCLUDING NEGLIGENCE), MISREPRESENTATION, STRICT LIABILITY, BREACH OF CONTRACT, OR BREACH OF WARRANTY OF MICROSOFT OR ANY SUPPLIER, AND EVEN IF MICROSOFT OR ANY SUP-PLIER HAS BEEN ADVISED OF THE POSSIBILITY OF SUCH DAMAGES.

21. LIMITATION OF LIABILITY AND REMEDIES. NOTWITHSTANDING ANY DAMAGES THAT YOU MIGHT INCUR FOR ANY REASON WHATSO-EVER (INCLUDING, WITHOUT LIMITATION, ALL DAMAGES REFERENCED HEREIN AND ALL DIRECT OR GENERAL DAMAGES IN CONTRACT OR ANYTHING ELSE), THE ENTIRE LIABILITY OF MICROSOFT AND ANY OF ITS SUPPLIERS UNDER ANY PROVISION OF THIS EULA AND YOUR EX-CLUSIVE REMEDY HEREUNDER (EXCEPT FOR ANY REMEDY OF REPAIR OR REPLACEMENT ELECTED BY MICROSOFT WITH RESPECT TO ANY BREACH OF THE LIMITED WARRANTY) SHALL BE LIMITED TO THE

GREATER OF THE ACTUAL DAMAGES YOU INCUR IN REASONABLE RELIANCE ON THE SOFTWARE UP TO THE AMOUNT ACTUALLY PAID BY YOU FOR THE SOFTWARE OR U.S.\$5.00. THE FOREGOING LIMITATIONS, EXCLUSIONS, AND DISCLAIMERS SHALL APPLY TO THE MAXIMUM EXTENT PERMITTED BY APPLICABLE LAW, EVEN IF ANY REMEDY FAILS ITS ESSENTIAL PURPOSE.

This is so important to Microsoft that it is the only part of a twelve-page agreement that is printed in boldface and the only part that is presented in a French translation for Canadian customers as well.

If you don't want to cut and paste Microsoft's verbiage, which might expose you to a copyright infringement action from Redmond, consider employing a standard free software or open-source license, of which the GNU General Public License is the best-known example. Note that using a free software license doesn't mean that your software is now free to the world. You may have licensed one client under the GNU GPL, but whether or not you decide to offer anyone else a license is a decision for the future.

If you wish, you can use the sample contract at the end of this book as a starting point in negotiating rights with your client. And remember that old bromide of business: *You don't get what you deserve; you get what you negotiate.*

More

- "The case for on-line communities," *McKinsey Quarterly*, Shona Brown et al., 2002, Number 1, http://www.mckinseyquarterly.com/article_abstract .asp?ar=1143

To the Instructor

It is helpful during the second meeting of the class to bring clients on campus to give three-minute presentations pitching their projects. Here is a suggested outline to the client for the presentation:

1. introduce the speaker and the organization he or she represents (15 seconds)
2. explain who the users are and why they need to interact via an Internet application, i.e., what problem is this online community solving (1.5 minutes)

3. describe how users will be attracted to the site initially, e.g., is there a collection of magnet content that these people need that isn't available anywhere else? (30 seconds)

4. after the site has been up and running for a few months, what will a typical interaction look like for a new user? (30 seconds)

5. what will happen after the semester is over; how will the system be funded and sustained? (15 seconds)

The client should be prepared to answer questions for a minute or two after the presentation.

Time and Motion

This problem set involves a two-hour meeting with the client, perhaps two hours of discussion and Web surfing among the students, an hour to build the user-profile pages, two hours of writing. That's seven hours total, most of which requires the entire team to work together.

4　　Software Structure

Before embarking on a development project it is a good idea to sketch the overall structure of the system to be built.

Gross Anatomy

Any good online learning community will have roughly the same core structure:

1. user database
2. content database
3. user/content map
4. user/user map

As used above, "database" is an abstract term. The user database, for example, could be implemented as a set of SQL tables within a relational database management system. The tables for the user database need not be separated in any way from tables used to implement other modules, that is, they would all be owned by the same user and reside within the same tablespace. On the other hand, the user database might be external to the online learning community's core source of persistence. A common case in which the user database can become external is that of a corporation's knowledge-management system, where employees are authenticated by checking a central LDAP server.

A more modern example of how these core databases might become split up would be in the world of Web services. Microsoft Hailstorm, for example, offers to provide user database services to the rest of the Internet. A university might set up complementary communities, one for high school students and one for colleagues at other schools, both anchored by the same database of genomics content. The genomics content database might be running on a computer that is physically separate from the computer supporting the online communities and it might advertise its services via WSDL and provide those services via SOAP.

User Database

At a bare minimum the user database has to record the real name and email address of the user. Remember that the more identified, authenticated, and accountable people are, the better the opportunity for building a community out of an aggregate. An environment where anonymous users shout at each other from behind screen names isn't worth the programming and system administration effort. The user database should have a facility for recording the reliability of a user's name and email address since the name is likely to become more reliably known over time and the email address less likely.

To contribute to an accountable and identified environment the user database should be able to store a personal URL for each user. If this is a Yahoo! Geocities page it won't contribute too much to accountability and identification. On the other hand, if the URL starts with "http://research.hp.com/personal/" it will give other users some confidence. Since one of the sad features of the Web as architected in 1990 is that URLs rot, a user database needs an extra field to keep track of what has happened when a robot tries to visit the recorded URL. If a URL has not been reachable on several separate occasions over a one-week period, it is probably safe for a computer program to assume that the URL is out of date and stop displaying it publicly.

The user database should record privacy and contact preferences. Is Jane User willing to let you show her email address to the public? To other registered users? Is Joe User willing to let you spam him with news of the site?

Content Database

The content of an online learning community always includes questions and answers in a discussion forum. A programmer might start by building a table for discussion forum postings. Of the six required elements of online community, magnet content is listed first. Most online learning communities offer published articles that are distinguished from user-contributed questions. A programmer would therefore create a separate table to hold articles. Any well-crafted site that publishes articles provides a facility for users to contribute comments on those articles. This will be another separate table.

Is a pattern emerging here? We distinguish a question in the discussion forum table because it is an item of content that is not a response to any other discussion forum posting. We distinguish articles from comments because an article is an item of content that is not a response to any other content item. Perhaps the representation of articles, comments on articles, questions, answers, and so forth should be unified to the maximum extent possible. Each is a content item. Each has one or more authors. Each may optionally be a response to another content item.

Here are some services that it would be nice to centralize in a single-content repository within the content database:

- versioning of content
- whether an item of content is a reply to, a comment on, or an attachment to some other item
- whether an item of content has been approved or disapproved by the site moderators
- to whom may the content be shown? Is it only for members of a group, a particular user, or *le grand public* (as they say in France)
- who has the right to edit the content?
- who has the right to change who has the right to view or edit?
- who has the right to comment on an item? Who must review comments that have been posted before they go live?
- timing the content: When does it go live? When does it expire?
- quality or importance of the content: Should this be highlighted to users? Should it be withheld until it graduates from draft status?
- full-text indexing of the content
- summaries, descriptions, and keywords for the content
- a consistent site-wide taxonomy

plus some things that really belong in the user/content map below:

- who authored or contributed an item, with a distinction among publisher-authored, group-authored, and user-authored stuff
- who should be notified via email when a comment on or response to an item is posted
- whether a content item is rated of high interest by a user or low/no interest; given these stats, this implies the ability to pick out "new content that is likely to be of interest to User 17" (depends on text-processing software that can compute document similarity)

User/Content Map

An online learning community generally needs to be able to record the following statements:

- User 21 contributed Comment 37 on Article 529
- User 192 asked Question 512
- User 451 posted Answer 3 to Question 924
- User 1392 has read Article 456
- User 8923 is interested in being alerted when a change is made to Article 223
- User 8923 is interested in being alerted when an answer to Question 9213 is posted

We are careful to record authorship because attributed content contributes to our chances of building a real community. To offer users the service of e-mail notifications when someone responds to a question or comments on an article, it is necessary to record authorship.

Why record the fact that a particular user has read, or at least downloaded, a particular document? Consider an online learning community of professors and students at a university. It is necessary to record readership if one wishes to write a robot that sends out messages like the following:

```
To: Sam Student
From: Community Nag Robot
Date: Friday, 4:30 pm
Subject: Your Lazy Bones
```

```
Sam,

I notice that you have four assignments due on Monday and that you
have not even looked at two of them. I hope that you aren't planning
to go to a fraternity party tonight instead of studying.

Very truly yours,

Some SQL Code
```

Once an online learning community is recording the act of readership, it is natural to consider recording whether or not the act of reading proved worthwhile. In general, collaborative filtering is the last refuge of those too cowardly to edit. However, recording "User 7241 really liked Article 2451" opens up interesting possibilities for personalization.

Consider a corporate knowledge-management system. At the beginning the database is empty and there are only a few users. Scanning the titles of all contributed content would take only a few minutes. After five years, however, the database contains 100,000 documents and the 10,000 active users are contributing several hundred new documents every day (keep in mind that a question or answer in a discussion forum is a "document" for the purpose of this discussion). If Jane User wants to see what her coworkers have been up to in the last 24 hours, it might take her 30 minutes to scan the titles of the new content. Jane User may well abandon an online learning community that, when smaller, was very useful to her.

Suppose now that the database contains 100 entries of the form "Jane liked this article" and 100 entries of the form "Jane did not like this article." Before Jane has arrived at work, a batch job can compare every new article in the system to the 100 articles that Jane liked and the 100 articles that Jane said she did not like. This comparison can be done using most standard full-text search software, which will take two documents and score them for similarity based on words used. Each new document is given a score of the form

```
avg(similarity(:new_doc, all_docs_marked_as_liked_by_user(:user_id)))
-
avg(similarity(:new_doc, all_docs_marked_as_disliked_by_user(:user_id)))
```

The new documents are then presented to Jane ranked by descending score. If you're an Intel stockholder you'll be pleased to consider the computational implications of this personalization scheme. Every new document must be compared to every document previously marked by a user. Perhaps that is 200 comparisons. If there are 10,000 users, this scoring operation must be repeated 10,000 times. So that is 2,000,000 comparisons per day *per new document in the system*. Full-text comparisons generally are quite slow as they rely on looking up each word in a document to find its occurrence frequency in standard written English. A comparison of two documents can take one-tenth of a second of CPU time. We're thus looking at about 200,000 seconds of CPU time per new document added to the system, plus the insertion of 10,000 rows in the database, each row containing the personalization score of that document for a particular user. There are 86,400 seconds in a day. Thus we're talking roughly about enough work to keep a 3-CPU multiprocessor machine busy for an entire day. What if 500 documents are uploaded every day? We'll need 1500 CPUs to compute personalization scores.

User/User Map

Relationships among users become increasingly important as communities grow. Someone who is in a discussion forum with 100 others may wish to say "I am offended by User 45's perspective; I want the system to suppress his contributions in pages served to me or email alerts sent to me." The technical term for this is *bozo filtration* and it dates back at least to the early 1980s and the USENET (Netnews) distributed discussion forum system. Someone who is in a discussion forum with 100,000 others may wish to say "I am overwhelmed; I never want to see anything more from this forum *unless* User 67329 has contributed to a thread."

Grouping of users is the most fundamental operation within the User/User database. In a collaborative medical records system, you need to be able say "All of these users work at the same hospital and can have access to records for patients at that hospital." In a corporate knowledge-sharing system, you need to be able to say "All of these users work in the same department and therefore should have access to private departmental documents, a private discussion forum devoted to departmental issues, and should receive email notifications of departmental events."

Let's move on from the core data model to some tips for the software that you're soon to be building on top of the database.

Send SQL, Not Data, to the Database's SQL Parser

In the Basics chapter you might have written scripts that took user input, combined them with bits of SQL, and sent a final single string command to the relational database management system (RDBMS).

Here's a C# example stolen from one of our students:

```
string cmd = "Insert into quotations(author_name, category, quote)
              values ('" + txtAuthor.Text.Replace("'", "''") + "',
                     '" + ctg.Replace("'", "''") + "',
                     '" + txtQuotation.Text.Replace("'", "''") + "')";

UpdateDB(cmd); // ship that big string to SQL Server
```

There are several minor things wrong with this approach, which mixes SQL and string literals obtained from the user:

- the programmer must remember to escape any single quote characters in the uploaded string, replacing ' with '' [these are two single quotes, not one double quote]

- the statement might become too long for some RDBMS SQL parsers to handle and/or the string literals might exceed limits (Oracle 9.x imposes a 4,000-character limit on string literals) if the user is waxing expansive at the browser

- repeated invocations of this script will result in the RDBMS being fed versions of this SQL statement that are morphologically the same but differ in actual text; depending on how the RDBMS is implemented, this might prevent the query plan from being reused

Much more serious, however, is the possibility that a malicious user could craft a form submission that would result in destruction of data or violation of privacy. For example, consider the following code:

```
string EventQuery = "select *
                     from events
                     where event_id = " + EventIDfromBrowser;
```

Expecting a numeric event ID and knowing that numbers do not need to be wrapped in quotes like a string literal, the programmer does no processing on `EventIDfromBrowser`, a variable read from the open Internet.

Suppose that an evil-minded person submits a form with `EventIDfrom-Browser` set to `"42; select * from user_passwords"`. The semicolon near the beginning of this string could potentially terminate the first SELECT and the unauthorized "select * from user_passwords" query might then be executed. If the unauthorized query is well-crafted, the information resulting from it might be presented in a browser window. Another scary construct would be `"42; delete from customers"`.

You can solve all of these problems by separating SQL code and variable data. Here's a pseudo-code example of how it has been done using standard libraries going back to the late 1970s:

```
// associate the name "event_query" with a string of SQL
PrepareStatement("event_query","select * from events where event_id = :event_id");

// associate the bind variable :event_id with the particular value for this page
BindVar("event_query",":event_id",3722);

// ask the RDBMS to execute the completed query
ExecuteStatement("event_query");

... fetch results ...
```

Note that the structure of the SQL seen by the RDBMS is fixed as `"select * from events where event_id = :event_id"`, regardless of what input is received in the form. Only the value of `:event_id` changes.

This is an example of using *bind variables*, which is standard practice in most software that talks to an RDBMS.

Bind Variables in C#

```
using System;
using System.Configuration;
using System.Data;
using System.Data.SqlClient;

namespace ExecuteScalar
{
    ///
    /// An example of how to use named parameters in ADO.NET.
    ///
    class Class1
```

```csharp
{
    ///
    /// The main entry point for the application.
    ///
    [STAThread]
    static void Main(string[] args)
    {
        object objResult = null;
        string strResult = null;
        string strEmployeeID = "PMA42628M";

        //Initialize the database connection, command and parameter objects.
        SqlConnection conn = new SqlConnection(
            ConfigurationSettings.AppSettings["connStr"]
            );
        SqlCommand cmd = new SqlCommand(
            "select fname from employee where emp_id = @emp_id"
            );
        SqlParameter param = new SqlParameter("@emp_id",strEmployeeID);

        //Associate the connection with the command.
        cmd.Connection = conn;

        //Bind the parameter value to the command.
        cmd.Parameters.Add(param);

        //Connect to the database and run the command.
        try
        {
            conn.Open();
            objResult = cmd.ExecuteScalar();
        }
        catch (Exception e)
        {
            Console.WriteLine("Database error: {0}", e.ToString());
        }
        finally
        {
            //Clean up.
            if (!conn.State.Equals(ConnectionState.Closed))
            {
                conn.Close();
            }
        }
```

```
//Convert the query result to a string.
if (objResult == null)
{
    strResult = "[NULL]";
}
else
{
    strResult = objResult.ToString();
}
Console.WriteLine("Employee #{0}'s first name is: '{1}'", strEmployeeID,
strResult); Console.ReadLine();
        }
    }
}
```

Not too much to note here except that Microsoft seems to like `@emp_id` rather than Oracle's `:emp_id`, that is they use the at-sign rather than the colon to indicate that something is a bind variable.

Bind Variables in Java

Here's a code fragment showing the use of bind variables in Java:

```
PreparedStatement updateSales = con.prepareStatement(
        "UPDATE COFFEES SET SALES = ? WHERE COF_NAME LIKE ? ");
updateSales.setInt(1, 75);
updateSales.setString(2, "Colombian");
updateSales.executeUpdate():
```

Source: *The Java Tutorial* at http://java.sun.com/docs/books/tutorial/jdbc/basics/prepared.html.

Note that JDBC, the Java database connectivity library, uses "?" as a bind variable. It is up to the programmer to count the *n*th occurrence of the ? in a SQL string and bind a value to that. As you can imagine this process becomes error prone if the SQL statement contains fifteen or more variables, a very common situation in real applications. You can also imagine the possibilities for introducing subtle bugs if the SQL query is changed and the bind variable sequence numbers are not properly updated.

Supposedly this situation has been improved in JDBC 3.0, but this example of Java's inferiority to C interfaces from twenty years earlier should remind you to be skeptical of vendor claims for the advantages of new languages and development tools.

Configurable View Source Links

In the "Basics" chapter you added a hard-coded "View Source" link to every page that you built. It is important for the remainder of the course to continue making your source code available to colleagues. On the other hand, when the application launches to the public you wouldn't necessarily want everyone to see your dirty laundry. You probably want a single switch, somewhere on the server, that can turn on or off all the "view source" links on the site. This means that all of your scripts will have to be calling a single procedure to decide whether or not to offer a "View Source" link. In the long run, this procedure might decide based on IP address or logged-in user ID whether to serve a View Source link.

Get the Database Username and Password Out of the Page Scripts

Suppose that you have the following code in one of your page scripts:

```
dbconn = OpenDBConn("sysid=local,username=joestest,password=joerocks");
```

There are several problems with this approach to connecting to an RDBMS:

1. An evildoer reading this source code might be able to connect to the RDBMS running on your server and drop all of your tables.
2. Running this code against a test database, which will necessarily have a different database username, will require editing each and every page script.
3. Reusing this code on another project will require changing the database username and password.

Every good Web development environment has a means of pooling connections from the page scripts to the database so that the Web server need not reconnect and re-authenticate itself to the database millions of times per day. Generally the idea is that the Web server will open a handful of connections to the RDBMS and keep them open. When a page script needs to execute a query, it grabs one of the connections from the pool and uses it until page service is complete. The connection is then returned to the pool. This scheme is called *connection pooling*.

Often a good way to get the database username and password out of page scripts is to use the Web server's database connection pooling system.

Time and Motion

Teams should spend at least an hour together drawing a pen and paper sketch that identifies and locates the basic information that the system will process. Detailed data modeling is not necessary, as it will be covered in the next two chapters.

The work of figuring out bind variables, hiding the database password, and generalizing the view source code may be split among the team members. This ought to be doable within six to eight programmer-hours.

5   User Registration and Management

As noted in the "Software Structure" chapter, the more identified, authenticated, and accountable people are, the better the opportunity for building a
community out of an aggregate. Thus the user database should record as
much information as possible that might help Person A assess Person B's
credibility.

As you will see in the chapter on scaling, it may become important to facilitate occasional face-to-face meetings among subgroups of users. Thus it will be
helpful to record their country of residence and postal code (what Americans
call "Zoning Improvement Plan code" or "ZIP code").

Fat versus Skinny: The Ideas

Suppose that the system specifications start off with very simple requirements for the user database, one that can be handled by the following single
table:

```
create table users (
        user_id                 integer primary key,
        first_names             varchar(50),
        last_name               varchar(50) not null,
        email                   varchar(100) not null unique,
        -- we encrypt passwords using operating system crypt function
        password                varchar(30) not null,
        registration_date       timestamp(0)
);
```

Notice that the comment about password encryption is placed above, rather than below, the column name and that the primary key constraint is clearly visible to other programmers. It is good to get into the habit of writing data model files in a text editor and including comments and examples of the queries that you expect to support. If you use a desktop application with a graphical user interface to create tables you're losing a lot of important design information. Remember that the data model is the most critical part of your application. You need to think about how you're going to communicate your design decisions to other programmers.

After a few weeks online, someone says, "wouldn't it be nice to see the user's picture and hyperlink through to his or her home page?"

```
create table users (
        user_id                 integer primary key,
        first_names             varchar(50),
        last_name               varchar(50) not null,
        email                   varchar(100) not null unique,
        password                varchar(30) not null,
        -- user's personal homepage elsewhere on the Internet
        url                     varchar(200),
        registration_date       timestamp(0),
        -- an optional photo; if Oracle Intermedia Image is installed
        -- use the image datatype instead of BLOB
        portrait                blob
);
```

After a few more months . . .

```
create table users (
        user_id                 integer primary key,
        first_names             varchar(50),
        last_name               varchar(50) not null,
        email                   varchar(100) not null unique,
        password                varchar(30) not null,
        -- user's personal homepage elsewhere on the Internet
        url                     varchar(200),
        registration_date       timestamp(0)
        -- an optional photo; if Oracle Intermedia Image is installed
        -- use the image datatype instead of BLOB
        portrait                blob,
        -- with a 4 GB maximum, we're all set for Life of Johnson
        biography               clob,
        birthdate               date,
```

```
                              -- current politically correct column name would be "gender"
                              -- but data models often outlive linguistic fashion so
                              -- we stick with more established usage
              sex                         char(1) check (sex in ('m','f')),
              country_code                char(2) references country_codes(iso),
              postal_code                 varchar(80),
              home_phone                  varchar(100),
              work_phone                  varchar(100),
              mobile_phone                varchar(100),
              pager                       varchar(100),
              fax                         varchar(100),
              aim_screen_name             varchar(50),
              icq_number                  varchar(50)
      );
```

The table just keeps getting fatter. As the table gets fatter, more and more columns are likely to be NULL for any given user. With Oracle 9i you're unlikely to run up against the hard database limit of 1,000 columns per table. Nor is there a storage efficiency problem. Nearly every database management system is able to record a NULL value with a single bit, even if the column is defined `char(500)` or whatever. Still, something seems unclean about having to add more and more columns to deal with the possibility of a user having more and more phone numbers.

Medical informaticians have dealt with this problem for many years. The example above is referred to as a "fat data model." In the hospital world you'll very likely find something like this for storing patient demographic and insurance coverage data. But for laboratory tests, the fat approach begins to get ugly. There are thousands of possible tests that a hospital could perform on a patient. New tests are done every day that a patient is in the hospital. Some hospitals have experimented with a "skinny" data model for lab tests. The table looks something like the following:

```
create table labs (
        lab_id                      integer primary key,
        patient_id                  integer not null references patients,
        test_date                   timestamp(0),
        test_name                   varchar(100) not null,
        test_units                  varchar(100) not null,
        test_value                  number not null,
        note                        varchar(4000)
);
```

```
-- make it fast to query for "all labs for patient #4527"
-- or "all labs for patient #4527, ordered by recency"
create index labs_by_patient_and_date on labs(patient_id, test_date);

-- make it fast to query for "complete history for patient #4527 insulin levels"
create index labs_by_patient_and_test on labs(patient_id, test_name);
```

Note that this table doesn't have a lot of integrity constraints. If you were to specify `patient_id` as unique that would limit each hospital patient to having only one test done. Nor does it work to specify the combination of `patient_id` and `test_date` as unique because there are fancy machines that can do multiple tests at the same time on a single blood sample, for example.

We can apply this idea to user registration:

```
create table users (
        user_id                 integer primary key,
        first_names             varchar(50),
        last_name               varchar(50) not null,
        email                   varchar(100) not null unique,
        password                varchar(30) not null,
        registration_date       timestamp(0)
);

create table users_extra_info (
        user_info_id            integer primary key,
        user_id                 not null references users,
        field_name              varchar(100) not null,
        field_type              varchar(100) not null,
        -- one of the three columns below will be non-NULL
        varchar_value           varchar(4000),
        blob_value              blob,
        date_value              timestamp(0),
        check ( not (varchar_value is null and
                     blob_value is null and
                     date_value is null))
        -- in a real system, you'd probably have additional columns
        -- to store when each row was inserted and by whom
);

-- make it fast to get all extra fields for a particular user
create index users_extra_info_by_user on users_extra_info(user_id);
```

An example of how such a data model might be filled is shown in figure 5.1. Note that numbers are stored in a column of type VARCHAR. Won't this pre-

users table

user_id	first_names	last_name	email	password
1	Wile E.	Coyote	supergenius@yahoo.com	IFUx42bQzgMjE

users_extra_info table

user_info_id	user_id	field_name	field_type	varchar_value	blob_value	date_value
1	1	birthdate	date	--	--	1949-09-17
2	1	biography	blob_text	--	Created by Chuck Jones . . .	--
3	1	aim_screen_name	string	iq207	--	--
4	1	annual_income	number	35000	--	--

Figure 5.1 Example of a user record that is split between a skinny table and a second table.

clude queries such as "Find the average income of a registered user"? Not if you're using Oracle. Oracle is smart about automatically casting between character strings and numbers. It will work just fine to

```
select average(varchar_value)
from users_extra_info
where field_name = 'annual_income'
```

One complication of this kind of data model is that it is tough to use simple built-in integrity constraints to enforce uniqueness if you're also going to use the users_extra_info for many-to-one relations.

For example, it doesn't make sense to have two rows in the info table, both for the same user ID and both with a field name of "birthdate." A user can only have one birthday. Maybe we should

```
create unique index users_extra_info_user_id_field_idx on
users_extra_info (user_id, field_name);
```

(Note that this will make it really fast to fetch a particular field for a particular user as well as enforcing the unique constraint.)

If you're using a fancy commercial RDBMS and wish to make queries like this really fast, check out bitmap indices, often documented under "Data Warehousing." These are intended for columns of low cardinality, i.e., not too many distinct values compared to the number of rows in the table. You'd build a bitmap index on the `field_name` column.

But what about "home_phone"? Nothing should prevent a user from getting two home phone numbers and listing them both. If we try to insert two rows with the "home_phone" value in the `field_name` column and 451 in the `user_id` column, the RDBMS will abort the transactions due to violation of the unique constraint defined above.

How to deal with this apparent problem? One way is to decide that the `users_extra_info` table will be used only for single-valued properties. Another approach would be to abandon the idea of using the RDBMS to enforce integrity constraints and put logic into the application code to make sure that a user can have only one birthdate. A complex but complete approach is to define RDBMS triggers that run a short procedural program inside the RDBMS—in Oracle this would be a program in the PL/SQL or Java programming languages. This program can check that uniqueness is preserved for fields that indeed must be unique.

Fat versus Skinny: The Decision

Deciding between fat style and skinny style is an engineering judgement call. You can certainly build a working system using either approach, but how much guidance does that give you? You know that you can build a computer program in any Turing-complete computer language, but that doesn't make Assembler as practical as Basic, C#, Eiffel, Java, Lisp, or ML.

One argument in favor of fat style is maintainability and self-documentation. Fat is the convention in the database world. A SQL programmer who takes over your work will expect fat. He or she will sit down and start to understand your system by querying the *data dictionary*, the RDBMS's internal representation of what tables are defined. Here's how it looks with Oracle:

```
select table_name from user_tables;

describe users
 *** SQL*Plus lists the column names ***
```

```
describe other_table_name
  *** SQL*Plus lists the column names ***
describe other_table_name_2
  *** SQL*Plus lists the column names ***
...
```

Suppose that you were storing all of your application data in a single table:

```
create table my_data (
        key_id                  integer,
        field_name              varchar,
        field_type              varchar,
        field_value             varchar
);
```

This is an adequate data model in the same sense that a set of raw instructions for a Turing machine is an adequate programming language. Querying the data dictionary would be of no help toward understanding the purpose of the application. One would have to sample the contents of the rows of my_data to see what was being stored. Suppose, by contrast, you were poking around in an unfamiliar database and encountered this table definition:

```
create table address_book (
        address_book_id integer primary key,
        user_id         not null references users,
        first_names     varchar(30),
        last_name       varchar(30),
        email           varchar(100),
        email2          varchar(100),
        line1           varchar(100),
        line2           varchar(100),
        city            varchar(100),
        state_province  varchar(20),
        postal_code     varchar(20),
        country_code    char(2) references country_codes(iso),
        phone_home      varchar(30),
        phone_work      varchar(30),
        phone_cell      varchar(30),
        phone_other     varchar(30),
        birthdate       date,
        days_in_advance_to_remind       integer,
        date_last_reminded              date,
        notes                           varchar(4000)
);
```

Note the use of ISO country codes, constrained by reference to a table of valid codes, to represent country in the table above. You don't want records with "United States," "US," "us," "USA," "Umited Stares," etc. These are maintained by the ISO 3166 Maintenance agency, from which you can download the most current data in text format. See http://www.iso.ch/iso/en/prods-services/iso3166ma/index.html.

The author's source code comments have been stripped out, yet it is reasonably clear that this table exists to support an online address book. Moreover the purpose of each column can be inferred from its name. Quite a few columns will be NULL for each address book entry, but not so many that the table will be absurdly sparse. Because NULL columns take up so little space in the database, you shouldn't decide between skinny and fat based on presumed data storage efficiency.

Skinny is good when you are storing wildly disparate data on each user, such that you'd expect more than 75 percent of columns to be NULL in a fat data model. Skinny can result in strange-looking SQL queries and data dictionary opacity.

User Groups

One of the most powerful constructs in an online community is a user group. A group of users might want to collaborate on publishing some content. A group of users might want a private discussion forum. A group of users might be the only people authorized to perform certain actions or view certain files. The bottom line is that you'll want to be able to refer to groups of users from other objects in your database.

When building user groups you might want to think about on-the-fly groups. You definitely want to have a user group where each member is represented by a row in a table: "user 37 is part of user group 421." With this kind of data model, people can explicitly join and separate from user groups. It is also useful, however, to have groups generated on-the-fly from queried properties. For example, it might be nice to be able to say "this discussion forum is limited to those users who live in France" without having to install database triggers to insert rows in a user group map table every time someone registers a French address. Rather than denormalizing the data, it will be much cleaner to query for "users who live in France" every time group membership is needed.

A typical data model will include a USERS table and a USER_GROUPS table. This leads to a bit of ugliness in that many of the other tables in the system must include two columns, one for user_id and one for user_group_id. If the user_id column is not NULL, the row belongs to a user. If the user_group _id is not NULL, the row references a user group. Integrity constraints ensure that only one of the columns will be non-NULL.

Representing Membership in a Group (First Normal Form)

Suppose that you have a USERS table and a USER_GROUPS table. How do you represent the fact that User 234 is a member of Groups 17 and 18? It might seem that the simplest way to do this is with a data structure stored in a column within the USERS table:

```
create table users (
        user_id                 integer primary key,
        ...
        -- a space-separated list of group IDs
        group_memberships       varchar(4000),
        ...
);
```

In this case, we'd store the string "17 18" in the group_memberships column. This is known as a *repeating group* or a *multivalued column* and it has the following problems:

- you might not have enough space if the number of values in the column grows larger than anticipated

- the combination of table name, column name, and key value no longer specifies a datum

- the basic INSERT, UPDATE, and SELECT operations are not sufficient to manipulate multivalued columns

- programmers' brains will have to adapt simultaneously to unordered data in table rows and ordered data inside a multivalued column

- design opacity: If you use multivalued columns even once, people will never know what to expect when they look under the hood of your design; did you use multiple tables to express a many-to-one relation or multivalued columns?

To get the data model into *First Normal Form,* in which there are no multi-valued columns, you'd create a mapping table:

```
create table user_group_map (
        user_id          not null references users;
        user_group_id    not null references user_groups;
        unique(user_id, user_group_id)
);
```

Note that in Oracle the unique constraint results in the creation of an index. Here it will be a concatenated index starting with the user_id column. This index will make it fast to ask the question, "To which groups does User 37 belong?" but will be of no use in answering the question, "Which users belong to Group 22?"

A good general rule is that representing a many-to-one relation requires two tables: *Things A* and *Things B*, where many Bs can be associated with one A. Another general rule is that representing a many-to-many relation requires three tables: *Things A*, *Things B*, and a mapping table to associate arbitrary numbers of As with arbitrary numbers of Bs.

Derivable Data

Storing users and groups in three tables seems as though it might be inefficient and ugly. To answer the question "To which groups does Norman Horowitz belong" we must JOIN the following tables: users, user_groups, user_group_map:

```
select user_groups.group_name
from users, user_groups, user_group_map
where users.first_names = 'Norman' and users.last_name = 'Horowitz'
and users.user_id = user_group_map.user_id
and user_groups.user_group_id = user_group_map.user_group_id;
```

To answer the question "Is Norman Horowitz part of the Tanganyikan Ciclid interest group and therefore entitled to their private page" we must execute a query like the following:

```
select count(*)
from user_group_map
where user_id = (select user_id
                 from users
                 where first_names = 'Norman'
                 and last_name = 'Horowitz')
and user_group_id = (select user_group_id
                     from user_groups
                     where group_name = 'Tanganyikans')
```

If this is a popular group, there is a temptation among new database programmers to *denormalize* the data model by adding a column to the users table, for example, `tanganyikan_group_member_p`. This column will be set to "t" when a user is added to the Tanganyikans group and reset to "f" when a user unsubscribes from the group. This feels like progress. We can answer our questions by querying one table instead of three. Historically, however, RDBMS programmers have been bitten badly any time that they stored *derivable data*, that is, information in one table that can be derived by querying other, more fundamental, tables. Inevitably a programmer comes along who is not aware of the unusual data model and writes application code that updates the information in one place but not another.

Note the use of the _p suffix to denote a boolean column. Oracle does not support a boolean data type and therefore we simulate it with a CHAR(1) that is restricted to "t" and "f." The "p" in the suffix stands for "predicate" and is a naming convention that dates back to Lisp programmers circa 1960.

What if you really need to simplify queries? Use a view:

```
create view tanganyikan_group_members
as
select * from users
where exists (select 1
              from user_group_map, user_groups
              where user_group_map.user_id = users.user_id
              and user_group_map.user_group_id = user_groups.user_group_id
              and group_name = 'Tanganyikans');
```

What if you know that you're going to need this information almost every time that you query the USERS table?

```
create view users_augmented
as
select
  users.*,
  (select count(*)
   from user_group_map ugm, user_groups ug
   where users.user_id = ugm.user_id
   and ugm.user_group_id = ug.user_group_id
   and ug.group_name = 'Tanganyikans') as tanganyikan_group_membership
from users
where exists (select 1
                from user_group_map, user_groups
                where user_group_map.user_id = users.user_id
                and user_group_map.user_group_id = user_groups.user_group_id
                and group_name = 'Tanganyikans');
```

This results in a virtual table containing all the columns of users plus an additional column called `tanganyikan_group_membership` that is 1 for users who are members of the group in question and 0 for users who aren't. In Oracle, if you want the column to bear the standard ANSI boolean data type values, you can wrap the DECODE function around the query in the select list:

```
decode(select count(*) ..., 1, 't', 0, 'f') as tanganyikan_group_membership_p
```

Notice that we've added an "_p" suffix to the column name, harking back to the Lisp programming language in which functions that could return only boolean values conventionally had names ending in "p."

Keep in mind that data model complexity can always be tamed with views. Note, however, that views are purely syntactic. If a query is running slowly when fed directly to the RDBMS, it won't run any faster simply by having been renamed into a view. Were you to have 10,000 members of a group, each of whom was requesting one page per second from the group's private area on your Web site, doing three-way JOINs on every page load would become a substantial burden on your RDBMS server. Should you fix this by denormalizing, thus speeding up queries by perhaps 5X over a join of indexed tables? No. Speed it up by 1,000X by caching the results of authorization queries in the virtual memory of the HTTP server process.

Clean up ugly queries with views. Clean up ugly performance problems with indices. If you're facing Yahoo! or Amazon levels of usage, look into unloading the RDBMS altogether with application-level caching.

Access Control and Approval

Suppose that you are building a corporate knowledge-sharing site. You might decide to place the server on the public Internet to facilitate employee access while at home or traveling. Perhaps some close collaborators within other organizations will be allowed access. However, you won't want random people registering at the site and getting immediate access. Each new user should probably have to be approved by an administrator.

Or perhaps you're building a public online learning community. You want users to be identified and accountable at the very least to their Internet Service Provider. So you'll want to limit access to only those registrants who've verified receipt of an email message at the address that they supplied upon registering. You may also want to reject registration from users whose only email address is at hotmail.com or a similar anonymous provider.

A community may need to change its policies as the membership grows.

One powerful way to manage user access is by modeling user registration as a finite-state machine, such as the one shown in figure 5.2. Rather than checking

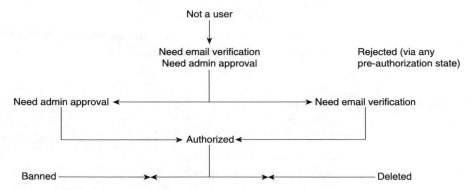

Figure 5.2 A finite-state machine approach to user registration. A reader starts in the "not a user" state. After filling out a registration form, he progresses to the "Need Email Verification/Need Admin Approval" state. After responding to an email message from the server he is moved into the "Need Admin Approval" state. Suppose that on this site we have a rule that anyone whose email ends in "mit.edu" is automatically approved. In that case the reader is moved to the "Authorized" state, which is where he will stay unless he decides to leave the service ("Deleted") or is deemed to be an unreasonable burden on moderators ("Banned").

columns `admin_approved_p`, `email_verified_p`, `banned_p`, `deleted_p` in the `users` table on every page load, this approach allows application code to examine only a single `user_state` column.

The authors built a number of online communities with this same finite-state machine and for each one made a decision with the publisher as to whether or not any of these state transitions could be made automatically. The Siemens Sharenet knowledge-sharing system, despite being inaccessible from the public Internet, elected to require administrator approval for every new user. By contrast, on photo.net users would go immediately from "Not a user" to "Authorized."

Exercise 1: Data Model

Define an SQL data model to represent users and user groups. Before proceeding to Exercise 2, discuss this data model with your teaching assistant.

Questions: Do you store users' passwords in the database encrypted or non-encrypted? What are the advantages and disadvantages of encryption? What columns in your tables will enable your system to handle the query "Find me users who live within 50 kilometers of User 37"?

Make sure that your data model and answers are Web accessible and easy to find from your main documentation directory, perhaps at the URL `/doc/`.

Multi-Page Design and Flow

This book defers discussion of individual page design until the "Content Management" chapter, but we need to think about page flow design right now. Why? The bad design of a single page will offend a user; the bad design of the page-to-page flow of a site will defeat a user.

One of the things that users love about the Web is the way in which computation is *discretized*. A desktop application is generally a complex miasma in which the state of the project is only partially visible. Despite software vendors having added multiple-level Undo commands to many popular desktop programs, the state of those programs remains opaque to users.

The first general principle of multi-page design is therefore: *Don't break the browser's Back button.* Users should be able to go forward and back at any time in their session with a site. For example, consider the following flow of pages on a shopping site:

- choose a book
- enter shipping address
- enter credit card number
- confirm
- thank you

A user who notices a typo in the shipping address on the confirm page should be able to return to the shipping address entry form with the Back button or the "click right" menu attached to the Back button, correct the address, and proceed from there. See the "Choosing between GET and POST" section later in this chapter.

A second general principle is: *Have users pick the object first and then the verb.* For example, consider the customer service area of an e-commerce site. Assume that Jane Consumer has already identified herself to the server. The merchant can show Jane a list of all the items that she has ever purchased. Jane clicks on an item (picking the object) and gets a page with a list of choices, for example, "return for refund" or "exchange." Jane clicks on "exchange" (picking the verb) and gets a page with instructions on how to schedule a pickup of the unwanted item and pages offering replacement goods.

How original is this principle? It is lifted straight from the Apple Macintosh, circa 1984, and is explicated clearly in *Macintosh Human Interface Guidelines* (Apple Computer, Inc. [Addison-Wesley, 1993]; full text available online at http://developer.apple.com/documentation/mac/HIGuidelines/HIGuidelines-2 .html). In a Macintosh word processor, for example, you select one word from the document with a double-click (object). Then from the pull-down menus you select an action to apply to this word, for example, "put it into italics" (verb). Originality is valorized in contemporary creative culture, but it was not a value for medieval authors and it does not help users. The Macintosh was enormously popular to begin with, and its user interface was copied by the developers of Microsoft Windows, which spread the object-then-verb idea to tens of millions of people. Web publishers can be sure that the vast majority of their users will be intimately familiar with the "pick the object then the verb" style of interface. Sticking with a familiar user interface cuts down on user time and confusion at a site.

These principles are especially easy to apply to user administration pages, for example. The administrator looks at a list of users and clicks on one to select it. The server produces a new page with a list of possible actions to apply to that user.

Exercise 2: Page Flow

Start by sketching the page flow for user registration and administration. There should be one circle or box for every URL in the system and one arc for every possible transition from URL A to URL B. If you have a lot of URLs that are form targets and perform database updates, but redirect to other pages in the system for display, you may want to distinguish those URLs with a light or dashed outline.

Ideally this drawing should be scanned and made available in your online documentation.

Figure 5.3 is an example of the kind of drawing we're looking for.

Choosing between GET and POST

Following an ordinary hyperlink on an HTML page results in a GET request to the server under the HTTP protocol. When programming a page with an HTML form, you have a choice between using METHOD=GET and METHOD=POST. A heavy reliance on POST will result in a site that breaks the browser Back button. An attempt to go back to a page that was the result of a POST will generally bring up a "Page Expired" error message and possibly a dialog box asking whether the user wishes to resubmit information by using the "Refresh" button.

Some of our students asked for further guidance on how to choose between GET and POST and here's the response from Ben Adida, part of the course's teaching staff in fall 2003:

Most of you may be wondering, why GET vs. POST in submitting forms? Oftentimes, one will use POST just to keep pretty URLs (without ?var=val&var=val). But that's the wrong way to think about it.

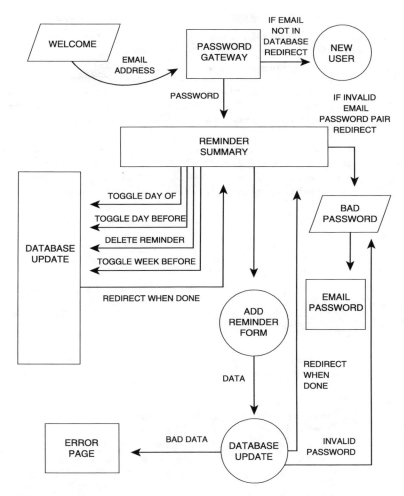

Figure 5.3 Page flow documentation for a stand-alone birthday reminder service. Email reminders are sent out either the day of, the day before, or one week before the date each year. For more info on this application, see chapter 15 of *Philip and Alex's Guide to Web Publishing* at http://philip.greenspun.com/panda/.

A *GET* implies that you are getting information. You can resubmit a GET any number of times: you are just querying information, not performing any actions on the back-end.

A *POST* implies that you are performing some action with side-effect: inserting a row, updating a row, launching a missile, etc... That's why when you try to reload a POST page, your browser warns you: are you sure you want to launch another missile?

In general, you should strive to respect the above principles. Here are two key examples:
- searching users or content. That should be a GET.
- Inserting a user or updating a profile. That should be a POST.

Of course, HTML and HTTP have some restrictions that complicate things:

   a) GET forms are limited in length by how much your browser can send in a URL field. This can be a problem for very complicated search forms, though probably not an issue at this stage. If you do hit that limit though, then it's okay to use a POST.

   b) POST forms can only be performed by having an HTML button, or by using JavaScript to submit a form. JavaScript is not ideal. Thus, sometimes you want to have a link that is effectively an action with side-effect (e.g. "ban user"), but you make it a GET.

You can use redirects (HTTP return code 302) to make your life easier. The nice thing about correct 302s is that the URL that issues a 302 is never kept in a browser's history, so it is never queried twice unless the user does something really conscious (like click back and actively resubmit the form). Specifically:

   1) when you POST data for an insert or update, have your script process the POST, then redirect to a thank-you page. That way, if the user clicks "reload", they are simply reloading the thank-you page, which is just a GET and won't cause side-effects or warnings. You can also redirect to something more meaningful, perhaps the list of recently registered users once you've edited one.

   2) when you use a GET link to actually perform an action with side-effect, you can also have that target script perform its action

then immediately redirect to a script with no side effects. This will prevent the accidental repetition of an action.

Scripts that have side effects should not be reachable at URLs that may enter the cache and be randomly re-requested by the browser. The one exception is if the POST causes some kind of error: it's mostly okay for the script that processes the POST to display the error instead of redirecting to some kind of error-displaying page (which would be clunky to build anyways).

.NET folks: when you use ASP.NET and postback, you have no choice of method: it's always POST. Remember to follow the above rule for POST: you can have your handler method perform the side-effects but it should then redirect somewhere else instead of returning content.

I hope this helps in making your sites more usable. Let me know if you have any questions.

—Ben

PS: None of the above solves the "double-click" problem which is what happens if a user double-submits a form quickly (especially those users who don't know the difference between single and double clicking). We'll talk about double-click protection later.

Exercise 3

Build the basic user registration and login pages. Use HTTP cookies to make the rest of the semester's work easier.

Questions: Can someone sniffing packets learn your user's password? Gain access to the site under your user's credentials? What happens to a user who forgets his or her password?

Exercise 4

Build the site administrator's pages for working with users. The site administrator should be able to (1) see recently registered users, (2) look up a particular user, (3) exclude a user from the site, and (4) see current and historical statistics on user registration.

Questions: How can the administrator control who is permitted to register and use the site? What email notification options does the site administrator have that relate to user registration?

Exercise 5

Look at your tables again for referential integrity constraints and query performance. How long will it take to look up a user by email address? What if this email address is capitalized differently from what you've stored in the database? Is it possible to have two users with the same email address? (Note that by Internet standards a lowercase email address or hostname is the same as an uppercase email address or hostname.)

Many Web applications contain content that can be viewed only by members of a specific user group. With your data model, how many table rows will the RDBMS have to examine to answer the question "Is User 541 a member of Group 90"? If the answer is "every row in a big table," that is, a *sequential scan*, what kind of index could you add to speed up the query?

More

- *SQL for Web Nerds*, data modeling chapter, at http://philip.greenspun.com/sql/data-modeling
- for a discussion of indices, see *SQL for Web Nerds*, tuning chapter, at http://philip.greenspun.com/sql/tuning
- Normal forms: Chapter 4 of Steve Roman, *Access Database Design & Programming* (O'Reilly, 1999), available online at http://www.oreilly.com/catalog/accessdata2/chapter/ch04.html and chapter 1 of Kevin Kline et al., *Transact-SQL Programming* (O'Reilly, 1999), available online at http://www.oreilly.com/catalog/wintrnssql/chapter/ch01.html
- "Reverse Engineering a Data Model" by Eve Andersson at http://eveandersson.com/writing/data-model-reverse-engineering is useful for understanding how to work with the Oracle Data Dictionary.

Time and Motion

The data modeling, page flow sketching, and questions about query performance will probably be done by the team as a group and require approximately three hours. Implementing the page scripts could be divided up among team members, but in any case should be doable in ten programmer-hours.

6   Content Management

There are two fundamental elements to content management: (1) storing stuff in a *content repository*, and (2) supporting the workflow of a group of people engaged in putting stuff into that repository. This chapter will treat the storage problem first and then the workflow support problem. We'll also look at version control for both content and software, at look and feel design for individual pages, and at navigation design and information architecture.

Part of the art of content management for an online learning community is reducing the number of types of content. For example, consider a community where the publisher says "I want articles [magnet content], comments from users on articles, news from the publisher, comments on news from users, questions from users, and answers to questions." A naive implementation from these specifications would result in the creation of six database tables: `articles, comments_on_articles, news, comments_on_news, questions, answers`. From the RDBMS's perspective, there is nothing overwhelming about six tables. But consider that every new table defined in the RDBMS implies roughly twenty Web scripts. Ten of these scripts will constitute a user experience: view a directory of content in Table A, view one category, view one item, view the newest items, grab a form to insert an item, confirm insertion, request an e-mail alert of comments on an item. Ten of these scripts will constitute an administrator's experience: view a directory of content in Table A, view one category, view one item, view the newest items, approve an item, disapprove an item, delete an item, confirm deletion of an item, and so on. It will be a bit tough to code these twenty scripts in a general fashion because the SQL statements will differ in at least the table names used.

Consider further that to offer a complete index of site content, you'll have to write a program that pulls text from at least six tables into a single index.

Figure 6.1   Parco dei Mostri. Bomarzo, Italy. Photo copyright Philip Greenspun.

How different are these six kinds of content, really? We'll look at the tables that we need to define for storing articles, then proceed to the other types of content.

A Simple Data Model for Articles

Here's a very basic data model for storing articles:

```
create table articles (
        article_id              integer primary key,
        -- who contributed this and when
        creation_user           not null references users,
        creation_date           not null date,
        -- what language is this in?
        -- visit http://www.w3.org/International/O-charset-lang
        -- to see the allowable 2-character codes (en is English, ja is Japanese)
        language                char(2) references language_codes,
```

```
-- could be text/html or text/plain or some sort of XML document
mime_type                varchar(100) not null,
-- will hold the title in most cases
one_line_summary         varchar(200) not null,
-- the entire article; 4 GB limit
body                     clob
);
```

Should all articles in the database be shown to all users? Perhaps it would be nice to have the ability to store an article and hold it for editorial examination:

```
create table articles (
        article_id               integer primary key,
        creation_user            not null references users,
        creation_date            not null date,
        language                 char(2) references language_codes,
        mime_type                varchar(100) not null,
        one_line_summary         varchar(200) not null,
        body                     clob,
        editorial_status         varchar(30)
          check (editorial_status in
('submitted','rejected','approved','expired'))
);
```

Do you trust all the programmers in your organization to remember to include a where editorial_status = 'approved' clause in every script on the site? If not, perhaps it would be better to rename the table altogether and build a view for use by application programmers:

```
create table articles_raw (
        article_id               integer primary key,
        ...
        editorial_status         varchar(30)
          check (editorial_status in
('submitted','rejected','approved','expired'))
);

create view articles_approved
as
select *
from articles_raw
where editorial_status = 'approved';
```

If you change your mind about how to represent approval status, you won't need to update dozens of Web scripts; you need only change the definition of the `articles_approved` view. (See the views chapter of *SQL for Web Nerds* at http://philip.greenspun.com/sql/views for more on this idea of using SQL views as a means of programming abstraction.)

Comments on Articles

Recall the six required elements of online community:

1. magnet content authored by experts
2. *means of collaboration*
3. powerful facilities for browsing and searching both magnet content and contributed content
4. means of delegation of moderation
5. means of identifying members who are imposing an undue burden on the community and ways of changing their behavior and/or excluding them from the community without them realizing it
6. means of software extension by community members themselves

A facility that lets a user post an alternative perspective to a published article is a means of collaboration that distinguishes a one-way publishing site from an online community. More interestingly, the facility lifts the Internet application out of the constraints of the literate culture within which Western culture has operated ever since Gutenberg (1452). A literate culture produces such works as the *Michelin Green Guide to Italy*: "Extending below the town is the park of the 16th-century Villa Orsini (Parco dei Mostri) which is a Mannerist creation with a series of fantastically shaped sculptures" (Michelin Travel Publications, 2003). Compare that description to the images in figure 6.2 showing just a tiny portion of the Parco dei Mostri ("Park of Monsters"). If a friend of yours came back from this place and showed these slides, you'd expect to hear something much richer and more interesting than the *Michelin Guide's* sentence. A literate culture operates with the implicit assumption that knowledge is closed, that Italian tourism can fit into a book. Perhaps the 350 pages of the *Green Guide* aren't enough, but some quantity of writers and pages would suffice to encapsulate everything worth knowing about Italy.

Comments are often the most interesting material on a site. Here's one from http://philip.greenspun.com/humor/bill-gates:

I must say, that all of you who do not recognize the absolute genius of Bill Gates are stupid. You say that bill gates stole this operating system. Hmm.. i find this interesting. If he stole it from steve jobs, why hasn't Mr. Jobs relentlessly sued him and such. Because Mr. Jobs has no basis to support this. Macintosh operates NOTHING like Windows 3.1 or Win 95/NT/98. Now for the mac dissing. Mac's are good for 1 thing. Graphics. Thats all. Anything else a mac sucks at. You look in all the elementary schools of america.. You wont see a PC. Youll see a mac. Why? Because Mac's are only used by people with undeveloped brains.

—Allen (chuggie@geocities.com), August 10, 1998

Oral cultures do not share this belief. Knowledge is open ended. People may hold differing opinions without one person being wrong. There is not necessarily one truth; there may be many truths. Though he didn't grow up in an oral culture, Shakespeare knew this. Watch *Troilus and Cressida* and its five perspectives on the nature of a woman's love and try to figure out which perspective Shakespeare thinks is correct.

Feminists, chauvinists, warmongers, pacifists, Jew-haters, inclusivists, cautious people, heedless people, misers, doctors, medical malpractice lawyers, atheists, and the pious are all able to quote Shakespeare in support of their beliefs. That's because Shakespeare uses the multiple characters in each of his plays to show his culture's multiple truths.

In the 400 years since Shakespeare we've become much more literate. There is usually one dominant truth. Sometimes this is because we've truly figured something out. It is tough to argue that a physics textbook on Newtonian mechanics should be an open-ended discussion (though a user comment facility might still be very useful in providing clarifying explanations for confusing sections). Yet even in the natural sciences, one can find many examples in which the culture of literacy distorts discourse.

Academic journals of taxonomic botany reveal disagreement on whether Specimen 947 collected from a particular field in Montana is a member of species X or species Y. But the journals imply agreement on the taxonomy, that is, on how to build a categorization tree for the various species. If you were to eavesdrop on a cocktail party in a university's department of botany, you'd discover that even this agreement is illusory. There is widespread disagreement on what constitutes the correct taxonomy. Hardly anyone believes

Figure 6.2   Parco dei Mostri. Bomarzo, Italy. Photo copyright Philip Greenspun.

that the taxonomy used in journals is correct, but botanists have to stick with it for publication because otherwise older journal articles would be rendered incomprehensible. Taxonomic botany based on an oral culture or a computer system capable of showing multiple views would look completely different.

The Internet and computers, used competently and creatively, make it much easier and cheaper to collect and present multiple truths than in the old world of print, telephone, and snail mail. Multiple-truth Web sites are much more interesting than single-truth Web sites and, per unit of effort and money invested, much more effective at educating users.

Figure 6.2 (continued)

Implementing Comments

Comments on articles will be represented in a separate table:

```
create table comments_on_articles_raw (
        comment_id              integer primary key,
        -- on what article is this a comment?
        refers_to               not null references articles,
        creation_user           not null references users,
```

```
                    creation_date          not null date,
                    language               char(2) references language_codes,
                    mime_type              varchar(100) not null,
                    one_line_summary       varchar(200) not null,
                    body                   clob,
                    editorial_status       varchar(30)
                       check (editorial_status in
            ('submitted','rejected','approved','expired'))
            );

            create view comments_on_articles_approved
            as
            select *
            from comments_on_articles_raw
            where editorial_status = 'approved';
```

This table differs from the `articles` table only in a single column: `refers_to`. How about combining the two:

```
create table content_raw (
        content_id              integer primary key,
        -- if not NULL, this row represents a comment
        refers_to               references content_raw,
        -- who contributed this and when
        creation_user           not null references users,
        creation_date           not null date,
        -- what language is this in?
        -- visit http://www.w3.org/International/O-charset-lang
        -- to see the allowable 2-character codes (en is English, ja is Japanese)
        language                char(2) references language_codes,
        -- could be text/html or text/plain or some sort of XML document
        mime_type               varchar(100) not null,
        one_line_summary        varchar(200) not null,
        -- the entire article; 4 GB limit
        body                    clob,
        editorial_status        varchar(30)
           check (editorial_status in ('submitted','rejected','approved','expired'))
);

-- if we want to be able to write some scripts without having to think
-- about the fact that different content types are merged

create view articles_approved
as
select *
```

```
from content_raw
where refers_to is null
and editorial_status = 'approved';

create view comments_on_articles_approved
as
select *
from content_raw
where refers_to is not null
and editorial_status = 'approved';

-- let's build a single full-text index on both articles and comments
-- using Oracle Intermedia Text (formerly known as "Context")

create index content_ctx on content_raw (body)
indextype is ctxsys.context;
```

What Is Different about News?

What is so different about news that we need to have a separate table? Often-times news has an expiration date, after which it is no longer interesting and should be pushed into an archive. "Pushing into an archive" does not necessarily mean that the item must be moved into a different table. It might be enough to program the presentation scripts so that unexpired news items are on the first page and expired items are available by clicking on "archives."

Often a company's press release will be tagged "for release Monday, April 17." If a publisher wants to continue receiving press releases from this company, it will respect these dates. This implies the need for a `release_time` column in the news data model.

Other than these two columns (`expiration_time` and `release_time`), it would seem that a news story needs more or less the same columns as articles: a place for a one-line summary, a place for the body of the story, a way to indicate authorship, a way to indicate approval within the editorial workflow.

Upon further reflection, however, perhaps these columns could be useful for all site content. An article on upgrading from Windows 2000 to Windows XP probably should be set to expire in 2006. If a bunch of authors and editors are working on a major site update, perhaps it would be nice to synchronize the release of the new content for Tuesday at midnight. Let's go back to `content_raw`:

```
create table content_raw (
        content_id                integer primary key,
        refers_to                 references content_raw,
        creation_user             not null references users,
        creation_date             not null date,
        release_time              date,    -- NULL means "immediate"
        expiration_time           date,    -- NULL means "never expires"
        language                  char(2) references language_codes,
        mime_type                 varchar(100) not null,
        one_line_summary          varchar(200) not null,
        body                      clob,
        editorial_status          varchar(30)
           check (editorial_status in
('submitted','rejected','approved','expired'))
);
```

How do we find news stories among all the content rows? What distinguishes a news story with a scheduled release time and expiration date from an article on the Windows 2003 operating system with a scheduled release time and expiration date? We'll need one more column:

```
create table content_raw (
        content_id                integer primary key,
        content_type              varchar(100) not null,
        refers_to                 references content,
        creation_user             not null references users,
        creation_date             not null date,
        release_time              date,
        expiration_time           date,
        language                  char(2) references language_codes,
        mime_type                 varchar(100) not null,
        one_line_summary          varchar(200) not null,
        body                      clob,
        editorial_status          varchar(30)
           check (editorial_status in
('submitted','rejected','approved','expired'))
);

create view news_current_and_approved
as
select *
from content_raw
where content_type = 'news'
and (release_time is null or sysdate >= release_time)
and (expiration_time is null or sysdate  <= expiration_time)
and editorial_status = 'approved';
```

Notice the explicit checks for NULL in the view definition above. You'd think that something simpler such as

```
and sysdate between release_time and expiration_time
```

would work. The problem here is SQL's three-valued logic. For the RDBMS to return a row, all of the AND clauses must return true. NULL is not true. Any expression or calculation including a NULL evaluates to NULL. Thus

```
where sysdate >= release_time
```

will exclude any rows where `release_time` is NULL.

What Is Different about Discussion?

It seems that we've managed to treat four of the six required content types with one table. What's more, we've done it without having a long list of NULLed columns for a typical item. For an article, `refers_to` will be NULL. For content that is not temporal, the release and expiration times will be NULL. Otherwise, most of the columns will be filled most of the time.

What about questions and answers in a discussion forum? If there is only one forum on the site, we can simply add rows to the `content_raw` table with a `content_type` of "forum_posting" and query for the questions by checking `refers_to is null`. On a site with multiple forums, we'd need to add a `parent_id` column to indicate under which topic a given question falls. Within a forum with many archived posts, we'll also need some way of storing categorization, for example, "this is a Darkroom question." See http://www.photo .net/bboard/ for a running example of a multi-forum system in which older postings are categorized. The "Discussion" chapter of this book treats this subject in more detail.

Why Not Use the File System?

Let's step back for a moment and ask ourselves why we aren't making more use of the hierarchical file system on our server. What would be wrong with having articles stored as .html files in directories? This is the way that most Web sites were built in the 1990s and it is certainly impossible to argue with the performance and reliability of this approach.

One good thing about the file system is that there are a lot of tools for users with different levels of skill to add, update, remove, and rename files. Programmers can use text editors. Designers can use Web design tools and FTP the results. Page authors can use HTML editors such as Microsoft Front Page.

One bad thing about giving many people access to the file system is the potential for chaos. A designer is supposed to upload a template, but ends up removing a script by mistake. Now users can't log into the site anymore. The standard Windows and Unix file systems aren't versioned. It isn't possible to go back and ask "What did this file look like six months ago?" The file system does not by itself support any workflow (see below). You authorize someone to modify a file or not. You can't say "User 37 is authorized to update this article on aquarium filters, but the members shouldn't see that update until it is approved by an editor."

The deepest problem with using the file system as a cornerstone of your content management system is that files are outside of the database. You will need to store a lot of references to content in the database, for example, "User 960 is the author of Article 231," "Comment 912 is a comment on Article 529," and so on. It is very difficult to keep a set of consistent references to things outside the RDBMS. Suppose that your RDBMS tables are referring to file system files by file name. Someone renames a file. The database doesn't know. The database's referential integrity constraint mechanisms cannot be invoked to protect against this circumstance. It is much easier to keep a set of data structures consistent if they are all within the RDBMS.

Static .html files also have the problem of being, well, static. Suppose that you want a standard header and footer on every page. You can cut and paste these into every .html file on the system. But what if you want to change "Copyright 2003" to "Copyright 2006" in the site-wide footer? You may have to update thousands of files. Suppose that you want the header to include a "Login" link if the request comes in with no user authorization cookie and a "Logout" link if the request comes in from a registered user.

Some of the problems with publisher maintenance of static .html files can be solved by periodically writing and running clever Perl scripts. Deeper problems with the user experience remain, however. First and foremost is the fact that with a static .html file every person who views the page thinks that he or she might be the only person ever to have viewed the page. This makes for a very lonely Internet experience and, generally speaking, not a very profitable one for the publisher.

A sustainable online business will typically offer some sort of online community interaction anchored by its content and will offer a consistently personalized user experience. These requirements entail some sort of computer program executing on every page load. So you might as well take this to its logical conclusion and build every URL in your application the same way: a script in the file system executes and pulls content from the RDBMS.

Exercise 1

Develop a data model for the content that you'll be storing on your site. Note that at a bare minimum your content repository needs to be capable of handling a discussion forum since we'll be building that in a later chapter.

You might find that, in making the data model precise with SQL table definitions, questions for the client arise. You realize that your earlier discussions with the client were too vague in some areas. This is a natural consequence of building a SQL data model. Pick up the phone and call your client to get clarifications. Email with several alternative concrete scenarios. Get your client accustomed to fielding questions in a timely manner.

Show the draft data model to your teaching assistant and discuss with other students before proceeding.

How the Workflow Problem Arises

It is easy to build and maintain a Web site if

- one person is publisher, author, and programmer
- the site comprises only a few pages
- nobody cares whether these few pages are formatted consistently
- nobody cares about retrieving old versions or figuring out how a version got to be the way that it is

Fortunately for companies and programmers that hope to make a nice living from providing content management "solutions," the preceding conditions seldom obtain at better-financed Web sites. What is more typical are the following conditions:

- labor is divided among publishers, information designers, graphic designers, authors, and programmers
- the site contains thousands of pages
- pages must be consistent within sections and sections must have a unifying theme
- version control is critical

The publisher decides what major content sections are available, when a content section goes live, and the relative prominence to be assigned each content section. The information designer decides what navigational links are available from every document on the page, how to present the available content sections, and what graphic design elements are required. The graphic designer contributes drawings, logos, and other artwork in service of the information designer's objectives. The graphic designer also produces mock-up templates (static HTML files) in which these artwork elements are used. The programmer builds production templates and computer programs that reflect the instructions of publisher, information designer, and graphic designer. Editors approve content and decide when specific pages go live. Editors assign relative prominence among pages within sections. In keeping with their relative financial compensation, we consider the needs and contributions of authors second to last. Authors stuff fragments of HTML, plain text, photographs, music, and sound, into the database. These authored entities will be viewed by users only through the templates developed by the programmers.

Below is an example workflow that we used to assign to students at MIT:

Your "practice project" will be a content management system to support a guide to Boston, along the lines of the AOL City Guide at http://home.digitalcity.com/boston/. You will need to produce a design document and a prototype implementation. The prototype implementation should be able to support the following scenario:

1. log in as publisher and visit /admin/content-sections/
2. build a section called "movies" at /movies
3. build a section called "dining" at /dining
4. build a section called "news" at /news
5. log out
6. log in as information designer and visit /cm and specify navigation. From anywhere in dining, readers should be able to get to movies. From movies, readers should be able to get to dining or news.

7. log out

8. log in as programmer and visit /cm

9. make two templates for the movie section, one called movie_review and one called actor_profile; make one template for the dining section called restaurant_review

10. log out

11. log in as author and visit /cm

12. add two movie reviews and two actor profiles to the movies section and a review of your favorite restaurant to the dining section

13. log out

14. log in as editor and visit /cm

15. approve two of the movie reviews, one of the actor profiles, and the restaurant review

16. log out

17. without logging in (i.e., you're just a regular public Web surfer now), visit the /movies section and, ideally, you should see that the approved content has gone live

18. follow a hyperlink from a movie review to the dining section and note that you can find your restaurant review

19. log in as author and visit /cm

20. edit the restaurant review to reflect a new and exciting dessert

21. log out

22. visit the /dining section and note that the old (approved) version of the restaurant review is still live

23. log in as editor and visit /cm and approve the edited restaurant review

24. log out

25. visit the /dining section and check that the new (with dessert) version of the restaurant review is being served

A Workflow Problem without Any Work

The preceding section dealt with the problem of supporting the standard publishing world. You know all the authors. They know what they're supposed to write. In an online learning community, especially a non-commercial one, the workflow problem arises before any work has been done or assigned. For example, suppose that the publishers behind the photo.net community decide that they want the following articles:

- Basic black and white darkroom photography
- Basic color darkroom (color negative)
- Making Ilfochrome prints
- Hardcore black and white printmaking
- Platinum prints

Among the 300,000 people who visit photo.net every month, surely there are people capable of writing each of the preceding articles. We want a system where

1. Joe User can transactionally sign up to write "Platinum prints," thus marking the article "assignment requested pending editorial approval," and supplies a brief outline and commits to completing a draft by July 1.
2. Jane Editor can approve the outline and schedule, thus generating an email alert back to Joe.
3. Joe User gets periodic email reminders of what he has signed up to do and by when.
4. Jane Editor is alerted when Joe's first draft is submitted on July 17 (Joe is unlikely to be the first author in the history of the world to submit work on time).
5. Joe User gets an email alert asking him to review Jane's corrected version and sign off his approval.
6. The platinum printing article shows up at the top of Jane Editor's workspace page as "signed off by author" and she clicks to push it live.

Notice the intricacies of the workflow and also the idiosyncracies. The *New York Times* and the *Boston Globe* put out very similar-looking products. They are owned by the same corporation. What do you think the chances are that software that supports one newspaper's workflow will be adequate to support the other's?

Exercise 2

Lay out the workflow for each content item that will be user visible in your online learning community. For each workflow step, specify (1) who needs to give approval, (2) what e-mail alerts are generated, (3) what happens if approval is given, and (4) what happens if approval is denied.

Tip: we recommend modeling workflow as a finite-state machine in which a content item can be in only one state at a time and that single state tells you everything that you need to know about the item. In other words, your software can take action without ever needing to go back and look to see what states the article was in previously.

Version Control (for Content)

Anyone involved in the administration and editing of an online learning community ought to be able to fetch an old version of a content item. If an author complains that a paragraph was dropped, the editors should be able to retrieve the first draft of the article from the content management system. Old versions are sometimes useful for public users as well. For example, on photo.net in the mid-1990s we had a lot of classified ads whose subject lines were of the form "Reduced to $395!" A check through the server logs revealed that the ad had been posted earlier that day with a price of $400, then edited a few hours later. So technically the subject line was true, but it was misleading. Instead of hiring additional administrators to notice this kind of problem, we changed the software to store all previous versions of a classified ad. When presenting an ad that had been edited, the new scripts offered a link to view old versions of the ad. The practice of screaming "Reduced!" stopped.

Version control becomes critical for preventing lost updates when people are working together. Here's how a lost update can happen:

- Ira grabs Version A of a document at 9:00 A.M. from the Web site in order to fix a typo. He fixes it at 9:01 A.M., but forgets to write the document back to the Web site.

- Shoshana grabs Version A at 10:00 A.M. and spends six hours adding a chapter of text, writing it back at 4:00 P.M. (call this Version B).

- Ira notices that he forgot to write his typo correction back to the server and does so at 5:00 P.M. (call this Version C).

Unfortunately, Version C (the typo fix) is what future users will see; all of Shoshana's work was wasted.

Programmers and technical writers at large companies are familiar with the problem of lost updates when multiple people are editing the same document. File-system based version control systems were developed to help coordinate multiple contributors. These systems include the original Walter Tichy's Revision Control System (RCS; early 1980s), Dick Grune and Brian Berliner's Concurrent Versions System (CVS; 1986), and Marc Rochkind's Source Code Control System (SCCS; 1972). These systems require more training than is practical for casual users. For example, RCS mandates explicit check-out and check-in. While a file is checked out by User A it is locked and nobody but User A can check it back in. Suppose that User A goes out to lunch, but there is some important news that absolutely must be put on the site. What if User A leaves for a two-week vacation and forgets to check a bunch of files back in? These problems can be worked around manually, but it becomes a challenge when the collaborators are on opposite sides of the globe and cannot see "Oh, Schlomo's coat is still on the back of his chair so he's not yet left for the day."

For distributed authorship of Web content by geographically distributed casually connected users, the most practical system turns out to be one in which check-in is allowed at any time by any authorized person. However, all versions of every document are kept in the database so that one can always revert to an earlier version or pull a section out of an earlier version. This implies that your content management system will have an *audit trail*: a record of past values held by row-column intersections in a database table, who was responsible for any changes in those values, and when the values were changed.

There are two classical ways to implement an audit trail in an RDBMS. The first is to set up separate audit tables, one for each production table. Every time an update is made to a production table, the old row is written out to an audit table, with a time stamp. This can be accomplished transparently via RDBMS triggers, which are described in the "Triggers" chapter of *SQL for Web Nerds* at http://philip.greenspun.com/sql/triggers and demonstrated in practice in an open-source audit trail package documented at http://philip.greenspun .com/seia/examples-content-management/audit-acs-doc. The second classical approach is to keep current and archived information in the same table. This is more expensive in terms of computing resources required because the information that you want for the live site is interspersed with seldom-retrieved archived information. But it is easier if you want to program in the capability to show the site as it was on a particular day. Your templates won't have to query a different table, they will merely need a different WHERE clause.

Michael Stonebraker, a professor at University of California Berkeley, looked at this problem around 1990 and decided to build an RDBMS with, among other advanced features, native support for versioning. This became the PostgreSQL open-source RDBMS. The original PostgreSQL had a "no-overwrite architecture" in which a change to a row resulted in a complete new version of that row being written out to the disk. Thus the hard disk drive contained all previous versions of every row in the table. A programmer could `select * from content_table['epoch','1995-01-01']` ... to get all versions from the beginning of time ("epoch") until January 1, 1995. This innovation made for some nice articles in academic journals, but execrable transaction processing performance. The modern PostgreSQL scrapped this idea in favor of Oracle-style write-ahead logging in which only updates are written to the hard drive (see the "Write-Ahead Logging" chapter of the PostgreSQL documentation at http://www.postgresql.org/docs/current/static/wal.html).

Second Normal Form

Suppose that you decide to keep multiple versions in a single content repository table:

```
create table content_raw (
        content_id              integer primary key,
        content_type            varchar(100) not null,
        refers_to               references content_raw,
        creation_user           not null references users,
        creation_date           not null date,
        release_time            date,
        expiration_time         date,
        -- some of our content is geographically specific
        zip_code                varchar(5),
        -- a lot of our readers will appreciate Spanish versions
        language                char(2) references language_codes,
        mime_type               varchar(100) not null,
        one_line_summary        varchar(200) not null,
        -- let's use BLOB in case this is a Microsoft Word doc or JPEG
        -- a BLOB can also hold HTML or plain text
        body                    blob,
        editorial_status        varchar(30)
          check (editorial_status in
('submitted','rejected','approved','expired'))
);
```

If this table were to contain seven versions of an article with a Content ID of 5657 that would violate the primary key constraint on the `content_id` column. What if we remove the primary key constraint? In Oracle this prevents us from establishing referential integrity constraints pointing to this ID. With no integrity constraints, we will be running the risk, for example, that our database will contain comments on content items that have been deleted. With multiple rows for each content item, our pointers become ambiguous. The statement "User 739 has read Article 5657" points from a specific row in the users table into a set of rows in the `content_raw`. Should we try to be more specific? Do we want a comment on an article to refer to a specific version of that article? Do we want to know that a reader has read a specific version of an article? Do we want to know that an editor has approved a specific version of an article? It depends. For some purposes, we probably do want to point to a version, for example, for approval, and at other times we want to point to the article in the abstract. If we add a `version_number` column, this becomes relatively straightforward.

```
create table content_raw (
        -- the combination of these two is the key
        content_id              integer,
        version_number          integer,
        ...
        primary key (content_id, version_number)
);
```

Retrieving information for a specific version is easy. Retrieving information that is the same across multiple versions of a content item becomes clumsy and requires a GROUP BY, since we want to collapse information from several rows into a one-row report:

```
-- note the use of MAX on VARCHAR column; this works just fine

select content_id, max(zip_code)
from content_raw
where content_id = 5657
group by content_id
```

We're not really interested in the largest ZIP code for a particular content item version. In fact, unless there has been some kind of mistake in our application code, we assume that all ZIP codes for multiple versions of the same content item are the same. However, GROUP BY is a mechanism for collapsing information from multiple rows. The SELECT list can contain column names only for those columns that are being GROUPed BY. Anything else in the SELECT list must be the result of aggregating the multiple values for columns that aren't GROUPed. The choices with most RDBMSes are pretty limited: MAX, MIN, AVERAGE, SUM. There is no "pick any" function. So we use MAX.

Updates are similarly problematic. The U.S. Postal Service periodically redraws the ZIP code maps. Updating one piece of information, for example, "20016" to "20816," will touch more than one row per content item.

This data model is in First Normal Form. Every value is available at the intersection of a table name, column name, and key (the composite primary key of `content_id` and `version_number`). However, it is not in Second Normal Form, which is why our queries and updates appear strange.

In Second Normal Form, all columns are functionally dependent on the whole key. Less formally, a Second Normal Form table is one that is in First Normal Form with a key that determines all non-key column values. Even less formally, a Second Normal Form table contains statements about only one kind of thing.

Our current `content_raw` table contains some information that depends on the whole key of `content_id` and `version_number`, for example, the body and the language code. But much of the information depends only on the `content_id` portion of the key: author, creation time, release time, ZIP code.

When we need to store statements about two different kinds of things, it makes sense to create two different tables, that is, to use Second Formal Form:

```
-- stuff about an item that doesn't change from version to version
create table content_raw (
        content_id              integer primary key,
        content_type            varchar(100) not null,
        refers_to               references content_raw,
        creation_user           not null references users,
        creation_date           not null date,
        release_time            date,
        expiration_time         date,
        mime_type               varchar(100) not null,
        zip_code                varchar(5)
);

-- stuff about a version of an item
create table content_versions (
        version_id              integer primary key,
        content_id              not null references content_raw,
```

```
        version_date              date not null,
        language                  char(2) references language_codes,
        one_line_summary          varchar(200) not null,
        body                      blob,
        editorial_status          varchar(30)
          check (editorial_status in
('submitted','rejected','approved','expired')),
        -- audit the person who made the last change to editorial  status
        editor_id                   references users,
        editorial_status_date   date
);
```

How does one query into the versions table and find the latest version? A first try might look something like the following:

```
select *
from content_versions
where content_id = 5657
and editorial_status = 'approved'
and version_date = (select max(version_date)
                         from content_versions
                         where content_id = 5657
                         and editorial_status = 'approved')
```

Is this guaranteed to return only one row? No! There is no unique constraint on `content_id, version_date`. In theory, two editors or authors could submit new versions of an item within the same second. Remember that the date data-type in Oracle is precise only to within one second. Even more likely is that an editor doing a revision might click on an editing form submit button twice with the mouse or perhaps use the Reload command impatiently. Here's a slight improvement:

```
select *
from content_versions
where content_id = 5657
and editorial_status = 'approved'
and version_id = (select max(version_id)
                       from content_versions
                       where content_id = 5657
                       and editorial_status = 'approved')
```

The `version_id` column is constrained unique, but we're relying on unstated knowledge of our application code, that is, that `version_id` will be larger for later versions.

Some RDBMS implementations have extended the SQL language so that you can ask for the first row returned by a query. A brief look at the Oracle manual would lead one to try

```
select *
from content_versions
where content_id = 5657
and editorial_status = 'approved'
and rownum = 1
order by version_date desc
```

but a deeper reading of the manual would reveal that the rownum pseudo-column is set before the ORDER BY clause is processed. An accepted way to do this in one query is the nested SELECT:

```
select *
from (select *
      from content_versions
      where content_id = 5657
      and editorial_status = 'approved'
      order by version_date desc)
where rownum = 1
```

Another common style of programming in SQL that may seem surprising is taking the following steps:

1. open a cursor for the SQL statement

```
select *
from content_versions
where content_id = 5657
and editorial_status = 'approved'
order by version_date desc
```

2. fetch one row from the cursor (this will be the one with the max value in version_date)

3. close the cursor

Third Normal Form

An efficiency-minded programmer might look at the preceding queries and observe that a content version is updated at most ten times per year, whereas the public pages may be querying for and delivering the latest version ten times per second. Wouldn't it make more sense to compute and tag the most current approved version at insertion/update time?

```
create table content_versions (
        version_id              integer primary key,
        content_id              not null references content_raw,
        version_date            date not null,
        ...
        editorial_status        varchar(30)
          check (editorial_status in
('submitted','rejected','approved','expired')),
        current_version_p       char(1) check(current_version_p in ('t','f')),
        ...
);
```

The new `current_version_p` column can be maintained via a trigger that runs after insert or update and examines the `version_date` and `editorial_status` columns.

Querying for user pages can be simplified with the following view:

```
create view live_versions
as
select *
from content_versions
where current_version_p = 't';
```

Modern commercial **RDBMS** implementations offer a feature via which rows in a table can be spread across different tablespaces, each of which is located on a physically separate disk drive. In Oracle, this is referred to as *partitioning*:

```
create table content_versions (
        version_id              integer primary key,
        content_id              not null references content_raw,
        version_date            date not null,
        ...
        editorial_status        varchar(30)
          check (editorial_status in
('submitted','rejected','approved','expired')),
        current_version_p       char(1) check(current_version_p in ('t','f')),
        ...
)
partition by range
```

```
(current_version_p)
(partition old_crud values less than 's'
 tablespace slow_extra_disk_tablespace
 partition live_site values less than(maxvalue)
 tablespace fast_new_disk_tablespace)
;
```

All of the rows for the live site will be kept together in relatively compact blocks. Even if the ratio of old versions to live content is 99:1 it won't affect performance or the amount of RAM consumed for caching database blocks from the disk. As soon as Oracle sees a "WHERE CURRENT_VERSION_P =" clause it knows that it can safely ignore an entire tablespace and won't bother checking any of the irrelevant blocks.

Have we reached Nirvana? Not according to the database eggheads, whose relational calculus formulae do not embrace such factors as how data are spread among physical disk drives. The database theoretician would note that our data model is in Second Normal Form, but not in Third Normal Form. In a table that is part of a Third Normal Form data model, all columns are directly dependent on the whole key. The column current_version_p is not dependent on the table key, but rather on two other non-key columns (editorial_status and version_date). SQL programmers refer to this kind of performance-enhancing storage of derivable data as "denormalization."

If you want to serve ten million requests per day directly from an RDBMS running on a server of modest capacity, you may need to break some rules. However, the most maintainable production data models usually result from beginning with Third Normal Form and adding a handful of modest and judicious denormalizations that are documented and justified.

Note that any data model in Third Normal Form is also in Second Normal Form. A data model in Second Normal Form is also in First Normal Form.

Version Control (for Computer Programs)

Note that a solution to the version control problem for site content (stuff in the database) still leaves you, as an engineer, with the problem of version control for the computer programs that implement the site. These are most likely in the operating system file system and are edited by a handful of professional software developers. During this class you may decide that it is not worth the effort to set up and use version control, in which case your *de facto* version control system becomes backup tapes, so make sure that you've got daily backups. However, in the long run you need to learn about approaches to version control for Internet application development.

Throughout this section, keep in mind that a project with a very clear publishing objective, specs that never change, and one very smart developer, does not need version control. A project with evolving objectives, changing specifications, and multiple contributors needs version control.

Classical Solution: One Development Area per Developer

Classically, version control is used by C developers with each C programmer working from his or her own directory. This makes sense because there is no persistence in the C world. Code is compiled. A binary runs that builds data structures in RAM. When the program terminates, it doesn't leave anything behind. The entire "tree" of software is checked out from a version control repository into the file system of the development computer. Changed files are checked back into the repository when the programmer is satisfied.

A shallow objection to this development method in the world of database-backed Internet applications is that it becomes very tedious to make a small change. The programmer checks out the tree onto a development server. The programmer installs an RDBMS, then creates an RDBMS user and a tablespace. The programmer exports the RDBMS from the production site into a dump file, transfers that dump file over the network to the development machine, and imports it into the RDBMS installation on the development server. Keep in mind that for many Internet applications the database may approach one terabyte in size, and therefore it could take hours or days to transfer and import the dump file. Finally, the programmer finds a free IP address or port and sets up an HTTP server rooted at the development tree. Ready to code!

A deeper objection to applying this development method to our world is that it is an obstacle to collaboration. In the Internet application business, developers always work with the publisher and users. Those collaborators need to know, at all times, where to find the latest running version of the software so that they can offer criticism and advice. If there are ten software developers on a service it is not reasonable to ask the publishers and users to check ten separate development sites.

A Solution for Our Times

1. three HTTP servers (they can be on one physical computer)
2. two or three RDBMS users/tablespaces (they can be in one RDBMS instance)
3. one version control repository

Let's go through these item by item.

Item 1: Three HTTP Servers

Suppose that a publisher's overall objective is to serve an Internet application accessible at "foobar.com." This requires a production server, rooted in the file system at /web/foobar/ (**Server 1**). It is too risky to have programmers making changes on the live production site. This requires a development server, rooted at /web/foobar-dev/ (**Server 2**). Perhaps this is enough. When everyone is happy with the way that the development server is functioning, declare a code freeze, test a bit, then copy the development code over to the production directory and restart.

What's wrong with the two-server plan? Nothing if the development and testing teams are the same, in which case there is no possibility of simultaneous development and testing. For a complex site, however, the publisher may wish to spend a week testing before launching a revision. It isn't acceptable to idle authors and developers while a handful of testers bangs away at the development server. The addition of a staging server, rooted at /web/foobar-staging/ (**Server 3**) allows development to proceed while testers are preparing for the public launch of a new version.

Here's how the three servers are used:

1. developers work continuously in /web/foobar-dev/
2. when the publisher is mostly happy with the development site, a named version or branch is created and installed at /web/foobar-staging/
3. the testers bang away at the /web/foobar-staging/ server, checking fixes back into the version control repository, but only into the staging branch

4. when the testers and publishers sign off on the staging server's performance, the site is released to /web/foobar/ (production)

5. any fixes made to the staging branch of the code that have not already been fixed by the development team are merged back into the development branch in the version control repository

Item 2: Two or Three RDBMS Users/Tablespaces

Suppose that the publisher has a working production site running version 1.0 of the software. One could connect the development server rooted at /web/foobar-dev/ to the production database. After all, the raison d'être of the RDBMS is concurrency control. It will be happy to handle eight simultaneous connections from a production Web server plus two or three from a development server. The fly in this ointment is that one of the developers might get sloppy and write a program that sends `drop table users` rather than `drop table users _experimental_extra_table` to the database. Or, less dramatically, a junior developer might leave out a WHERE clause in an SQL statement and inadvertently request a result set of 10^9 rows, thus slowing down the production site.

So it would seem that this publisher will need at least one new database. Here are the steps:

1. create a new database user and tablespace; if this is on a separate physical computer from your production RDBMS server it will protect your production server's performance from inadvertent denial-of-service attacks by sloppy development SQL statements

2. export the production database into a file system file, which is a good periodic practice in any case as it will verify the integrity of the database

3. import the database export into the new development database

4. every time that a developer alters a table, adds a table, or populates a new table, record the operation in a "patches.sql" file

5. when ready to move code from staging to production, hastily apply all the data model modifications from patches.sql to the production RDBMS

Should there be three databases, that is, one for development, one for staging, and one for production? Not necessarily. Unless one expects radical data model evolution, it may be acceptable to use the same database for development and staging. Keep in mind that adding a column to a relational database table seldom breaks old queries. This was one of the objectives set forth by E. F. Codd in 1970 in "A Relational Model of Data for Large Shared Data Banks" (http://www.acm.org/classics/nov95/toc.html) and certainly modern implementations of the relational model have lived up to Codd's hopes in this respect.

Item 3: One Version Control Repository

The function of the version control repository is to

- remember what all the previous checked-in versions of a file contained
- show the difference between what's in a checked-out tree and what's in the repository
- help merge changes made simultaneously by multiple authors who might have been unaware of each other's work
- group a snapshot of currently checked-in versions of files as, e.g., "Release 2.1" or "JuneIssue"

An example of a system that meets the preceding requirements is Concurrent Versions System (CVS), which is free and open source. CVS uses a single file system directory as its repository or "CVS root." CVS can run over the Internet so that the repository is on Computer A and development, staging, and production servers are on Computers B, C, and D. Alternatively, you can run everything in separate file system directories on one physical computer.

Good things about this solution Let's summarize the good things about the version control (for computer programs) solution proposed here:

- if something is screwy with the production server, one can easily revert to a known and tested version of the software
- programmers can protect and comment their changes by explicitly checking files in after significant changes
- teams of programmers and testers can work independently

Further reading: *Open Source Development With CVS* (Karl Fogel and Moshe Bar [Coriolis, 2001]), a portion of which is available online at http://cvsbook.red-bean.com/cvsbook.html.

Exercise 3: Version Control

Write down your answers to the following questions:

- What is your system for versioning content?
- What is your system for versioning the software behind your application, including data model and page scripts?
- What kind of answer can your system produce to the question "Who is responsible for the content on this current user-visible page?"

Note that generally most teams must write some additional SQL code to complete this exercise, augmenting the data model that they built in Exercise 1.

Exercise 4: Skeletal Implementation

Build enough of the pages so that a group of users can cooperate to put a few pieces of content live on your server. Focus your efforts on the primary kinds of publisher-authored content that you expect to have in your online learning community. For most projects, this will be articles and navigation pages to those articles.

After you've got a few articles in, step back and ask the following questions:

- Is this data model working?
- Is it taking a reasonable number of clicks to get some content live?
- Do the people who need to approve new content have an easy way of figuring out what needs approval and what has been approved or rejected already? Must those editors come to the site every few hours and check or will they get email alerts when new content needs review?

A skeletal implementation should have stable and consistent URLs, that is, the home page should be just the hostname of the server and filenames should be consistent. If you haven't had a chance to make abstract URLs work (see the "Basics" chapter), this is a good time to do it. Every page should have a descriptive title so that the browser's Back button and bookmarks ("favorites") are fully functional. Every page should have a "View Source" link at the bottom and a way to contact the persons responsible for page function and content. Some sort of consistent navigation system should be in place (also see below). The look and feel of a skeletal implementation will be plain, but it need not be ugly or inconsistent. Look to Google for inspiration, not the personal home pages of fellow students at your university.

Look and Feel

At this point you have some content on your server. It is thus possible to begin experimenting with the look and feel of HTML pages. A good place to start is with the following issues:

- space
- time
- words
- color

Screen Space

In the 1960s a computer user could tap into a 1/100th share of a computer with 1 MB of memory and capable of executing 1 million instructions per second, viewing the results on a 19-inch monitor. In 2005, a computer user gets a full share of a computer with 2000 MB of memory (2 GB) and capable of executing 4 billion instructions per second. This is roughly a 400,000-fold improvement in available computing capability. How does our modern computer user view the results of his or her computations? On a 19-inch monitor.

Programmers of most applications no longer need concern themselves too much with processor and memory efficiency, which were obsessions in the 1960s. CPU and RAM are available in abundance. But screen real estate is as precious as ever. Look at your page designs. Is the most important information available without scrolling? (In the newspaper business, the term for this is "above the fold.") Are you making the best use of the screen space that you have? Are there large swaths of empty space on the page? Could you be using HTML tables to present two or three columns of information at the same time?

One particularly egregious waste of screen space is the use of icons. Typically, users can't understand what the icons mean so they need to be supplemented with plain language annotation. Generally the best policy is to *let the information be the interface*, for example, display a list of article categories (the information) where clicking on a category is the way to navigate to a page showing articles within that category.

Time

Most people prefer fast to slow. Most people prefer consistent service time to inconsistent service time. These two preferences contribute substantially to the popularity of McDonald's restaurants worldwide. When people are done with their lunch they bring those same preferences to computer applications: fast is better than slow; response time should be consistent from session to session.

Computer and network speeds will change over the years, but human beings will evolve much more slowly. Thus we should start by considering limits derived from the humanity of our users. The experimental psychologists will tell us that short-term memory is good for remembering only about seven things at once (George A. Miller, "The Magical Number Seven, Plus or Minus Two: Some Limits on Our Capacity for Processing Information," *Psychological Review* 63 [1956]: 81–97; http://www.well.com/user/smalin/miller.html) and that this memory is good for only about twenty seconds. It is thus unwise to build any computer application in which users are required to remember too much from one page to another. It is also unwise to build any computer application where the interpage delay is more than twenty seconds. People might forget what task they were trying to accomplish!

IBM Corporation carried out some studies around 1970 and discovered the following required computer response times:

- 0.1 seconds for direct manipulation, e.g., moving objects around on a screen with a pointer
- 1 second for maximum productivity in screen-click-screen systems such as they had on the IBM 3270 terminal back in 1970 and we have on the Web in 2005
- less than 10 seconds to hold the full attention of a user; when response times extended beyond 10 seconds users would try to engage in another task, such as reading a magazine, while also using the computer application

A reasonable goal to strive for in an Internet application is sub-second response time. This goal is based partly on IBM's research, partly on the inability to achieve (in 2005) the 0.1-second mark at which direct manipulation becomes possible, and partly on what is being achieved by the best practitioners. Your users will have used Amazon and Yahoo! and eBay. Any service that is slower than these is going to set off alarm bells in the user's mind: maybe this site is going to fail altogether? Maybe I should try to find a competitive site that does the same job but is faster?

One factor that affects page-loading time is end-to-end bandwidth between your server and the user. You can't do much about this except measure and average. Some Web servers can be configured or reprogrammed to log the total time spent serving a page. By looking at the times spent serving large photographs, for example, you can infer average bandwidth available between your server and the users. If the tenth percentile users are getting 50 Kbits per second, you know that, even if your server were infinitely fast at preparing pages, you should try to make sure that your pages, with graphics, are either no larger than 50 Kbits in size or that the HTML is designed such that the page will render incrementally. (A page that is one big TABLE is bad; a page in which any images have WIDTH and HEIGHT tags is good because the text will be rendered immediately with blank spaces that will be gradually filled in as the images are loaded.)

You can verify your decisions about page layout and graphics heaviness by comparing your pages to those of the most successful Internet service operators such as eBay, Yahoo!, and Amazon.

Remember that in the book and magazine world every page design loads at the same speed, which means that page design is primarily a question of aesthetics. In the Internet world page design and application speed are inextricably linked, which makes page design an engineering problem.

Words

As a programmer, there are two kinds of text that you will be putting into the services that you build: instructions and error messages.

For instructions, you can choose active or passive voice and first, second, or third person. Instructions should be second person imperative. Leave out the pronouns, for example, "Enter departure date" rather than "Enter your departure date."

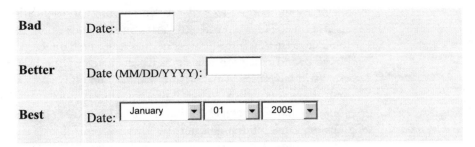

Figure 6.3 Different ways of asking the user to specify a date. Generally it is best to ask in such a way that the user cannot possibly make a mistake and necessitate the serving of an error page reading "date not properly formatted," "invalid date," or "date in the past."

Oftentimes you can build a system such that error messages are unnecessary. The best user interfaces are those where the user can't make a mistake. For example, suppose that an application needs to prompt for a date. One could do this with a blank text entry box and no hint, expecting the user to type MM/DD/YYYY, for example, 09/28/1963 for September 28, 1963. If the user's input did not match this pattern or the date did not exist, for example, 02/30/2002, the application returns a page explaining the requirements. A minor improvement would be to add a note next to the box: "MM/DD/YYYY." If the application logs showed that the number of error pages served was reduced, but not eliminated, perhaps defaulting the text entry box to today's date in MM/DD/YYYY format would be better. Surf over to your favorite travel site, however, and you'll probably find that they've chosen "none of the above." Users are asked to pick a date from a JavaScript calendar widget or pull down month and day from HTML menus.

Sadly, you won't be able to eliminate the need for all error messages. Thus you'll have to make a choice between terse or verbose and between lazy or energetic. A lazy system will respond "syntax error" to any user input that won't work. An energetic system will try to autocorrect the user's input or at least figure out what is likely to be wrong.

Studies have shown that it is worthwhile to develop sophisticated error-handling pages, e.g., ones that correct the user's input and serve a confirmation page. At the very least, it is worth running some regular expressions against the user's offending input to see if its defects fall into a common pattern that can be explained on an error page. It is best to avoid anthropomorphism—the computer shouldn't say "I didn't understand what you typed."

Color

The natural world is too green and badly lit.
—Francois Boucher, 18th-century painter

Text is most readable when it is black against a white or off-white background. It is best to avoid using color as part of your interface with the exception of sticking with conventions such as "blue text = hyperlink; purple text = visited hyperlink." If you limit your creativity to `<body bgcolor=white text=black>`, the browser will treat your users kindly with familiar link colors. By this sparing use of color in your interface, you'll have most of the color spectrum available for presenting information: charts, graphs, photos. Compare www.britneyspears .com and http://britneyspears.ac/physics/basics/basics.htm, for example, to see these principles at work.

Be a bit careful with medium gray tones at the very top of Web pages. Many Web browsers use various shades of gray for the backgrounds of menu and button bars at the top of windows. If a Web page has a solid gray area at the top, a user may have trouble distinguishing where the browser software ends and the page content begins. Notice that pages on Yahoo! and Amazon include a bit of extra white space at the top to separate their page content from the browser location and menu bars.

Whatever scheme you choose, keep it consistent site wide. In 1876 MIT agreed on cardinal and gray for school colors. See how the agreement is holding up by visiting www.mit.edu, click on "Administration" and then look at the subsites for four departments: IS, Medical, Arts, Disabilities Service.

For an excellent discussion of the use of color, see *Macintosh Human Interface Guidelines*, available online at http://developer.apple.com/documentation/ mac/HIGuidelines/HIGuidelines-2.html. Basically the messages are the following: (1) use color sparingly, (2) make sure that a colorblind person can make full use of the application, and (3) avoid red because of its association with alerts and danger.

Navigation

As with page design, the best strategy for navigation is to copy the most successful and therefore familiar-to-your-users Internet applications. Best practice for a site home-page circa 2005 seems to boil down to the following elements:

1. a navigation directory to the rest of the site

2. news and events

3. a single text input box for site-wide search

4. a quick form targeting the most frequently requested service on the site, e.g., on an airline site, a quick fare/schedule finder with form inputs for cities and dates

In building the navigation directory, look at www.yahoo.com. Note that Yahoo! does not use icons for category navigation. To get to the photography category, underneath Arts & Humanities, you click on the word "Photography." *The information is the interface.* This principle is articulated in Edward Tufte's classic *Visual Explanations* (Graphics Press, 1997). Tufte notes that if you were to have icons you'd also need a text explanation underneath. Why not let the text alone be the interface? Tufte also argues for broad and flat presentation of information; a user shouldn't have to click through eight screens each with only a handful of choices.

On interior pages, it is important to answer the following questions:

- Where am I?
- Where have I been?
- Where can I go?

To answer "Where am I?" relative to other sites on the Internet, you can include a logo graphic or font-distinguished site name in the upper left corner of each page, hyperlinked to the site home-page. See the interior pages at amazon.com for how this works. To answer "Where am I?" relative to other pages on the same site, you can include a site map with the current page highlighted. On a complex site, this won't scale very well: better to use the Yahoo-style navigation bar, also known as "hierarchical path" or "bread crumbs." For example, http://dir.yahoo.com/Arts/Visual_Arts/Photography/Panoramic/ contains the following navigation bar:

Home > Arts > Visual Arts > Photography > Panoramic

Note that this bar grows in size as O[log N] where N is the number of pages on the site. Showing a full site map or top tabs results in linear growth.

To answer "Where have I been?," start by making sure not to instruct the browser to change the standard link colors. The user will thus be cued by the browser for any links that have already been visited. If you're careful with your programming and consistent with your page titles, the user will be able to right-click on the Back button and optionally return to any previous place on your service. Note further that the Yahoo-style navigation bar is effective at answering "Where have I been?" for users who have actually clicked down from the home page.

To answer "Where can I go?" you need ... links! Let the browser default to standard colors so that users will perceive the links as links. It is generally a bad idea to use rollovers, select boxes, or graphics. These controls won't work the same from site to site and therefore users may not understand how to use them. These controls don't have the property that visited links turn a different color; they generally can't or don't tap into the browser's history database. Finally, these controls aren't effective at showing the user where he or she can go because many of the choices are hidden.

Exercise 5: Criticism

Take or get a tour of the other projects being built by your classmates in this course. For each project make sure that you familiarize yourself with the overall service objectives and the data model. Then register as a user and author an article. (If you get stuck on any of these steps, contact the team members behind the project by phone and email and ask them to add links or hints to their server.)

Working with your project team members, write a plain-text critique of each project that you review. Look for situations in which the client's requirements, as expressed in the planning exercise solutions, can't be fulfilled with the data model that you see. Look for opportunities to provide constructive criticism. Remember that your classmates don't need a self-esteem boost; they need the benefit of your engineering skills.

Here are some suggested areas where it might be easy to find improvements:

- page flows in user registration and content authoring—could the number of clicks to accomplish a task be reduced?
- look, feel, and navigation referenced to the standards outlined above
- version control and audit trail
- where do/should attachments go, e.g., is there a place to store a JPEG photo attached to a comment on an article?
- categorization and presentation hints—can the content be presented within a clear information architecture?
- is there a place to store keywords, i.e., hand-authored collections of words associated with a content item (to aid full-text search)
- can the content repository store an arbitrary data type, e.g., a video, an audio clip, or a photograph?

Sign the critique with the name of your project team and also the names of all team members.

Email your critique to the team members whose work you've just reviewed. Archive these in a file and make them available at http://yourservername/doc/critiques/cm-sent.txt. Watch your own inbox for critiques coming in from the rest of the class. Please assemble these into one file and make them available at http://yourservername/doc/critiques/cm-received.txt.

Information Architecture: Implicit or Explicit?

Suppose that there are 1,000 content items on a site. The manner of organizing, labeling, and presenting these 1,000 items to a user is referred to as the *information architecture* of the site. For the sake of simplicity, let's start by assuming that we will be presenting all 1,000 items on one page. For the sake of concreteness, we'll assume that all the content is related to photography. Even this degenerate one-page user experience requires some information architecture decisions. Here are a few possibilities:

- sort from newest to oldest (good for experienced users)
- sort from highest quality to lowest quality (might be good for first-time users)

- categorize by what's in front of the camera and present the items separated by subheadlines, e.g., "Portraits," "Architecture," "Wedding," "Family," "Animals"

- categorize by type of camera used and present items separated by subheadlines such as "Digital point and shoot," "Digital SLR," "35mm point and shoot," "35mm SLR," "Medium Format," "Large Format"

Information architecture decisions have a strong effect on the percentage of users who say "I got my questioned answered." Most studies of corporate Web sites, all of which owe their tested form to hundreds of thousands of dollars in design work, find that users have less than a 50 percent chance of finding the answer to questions that are in fact answerable from documents present on the site. We redid the information architecture on the photo.net site, a change that touched only about six top-level pages, and the number of new users registering each day doubled.

One reason that the information architecture on a typical site is so ill suited to the user is that the architecture is implicit in scripts and HTML pages. To test an alternative would involve expensive hand-manipulation of computer programs and HTML markup. To offer an individual user or class of user a custom information architecture would be impossible.

What if we represented information architecture explicitly in database tables? These tables would hold the following information:

- information about information architectures: who made them, when, which ones are current and for whom

- whether items underneath a category or subcategory, within a given information architecture (IA), should be presented in-line on one page or merely summarized with links down to separate pages for each item

- where a content item fits in a given IA: what subcategory (category can be inferred from the subcategory), what presentation order ("sort key") compared to other items at the same level

- how a content item or category should be described

With such a large part of the user experience driven from database tables, testing an alternative is as easy as inserting some rows into the database from the information architecture admin pages. If during a site's conceptualization people can't agree on the best categorization of content, it becomes possible to launch with two alternatives. Half the users see IA 1 and half see IA 2. If users who've experienced IA 1 are more likely to register and return, we can assume that IA 1 is superior, at least for first-time users.

For the application that you build in this course, it is acceptable to take the expedient path of pounding out scripts with an implicit information architecture. However, we'd like you to be aware of the power for development and testing that can be gained from an explicit information architecture.

Exercise 6: The Lived-In Look

A skeletal prototype has one big limitation: it is skeletal. Incorporating the feedback that you've gotten from other students (in Exercise 5) and from instructors, beef up your content management system while simultaneously pouring in enough content that your application has a "lived-in" look. This will ensure that your system truly is powerful enough to handle the users' basic needs.

If your client has an existing site, use that as a source of content and minimum requirements. Also look at a couple of sites run by organizations with comparable missions and sizes. For example, if you're building something for an academic group you might look at Harvard University's Department of Molecular and Cellular Biology's Web site at http://www.mcb.harvard.edu/. This site illustrates the basic requirements for a medium-sized organization's Web site. An "overview" section describes the department's purpose and history. A "news" section offers press releases. A "faculty" section explains who works there and what their specialties are. There are also sections for prospective undergraduates and graduate students, that is, the potential customers for this organization. If you're building something for a small non-profit organization, look at the Web sites for Sustainable Harvest (www.sustainableharvest .org) and the Southern Animal Rescue Association (www.sarasanctuary.org). If you're working for a small manufacturing company, look at www.cirrusdesign .com, the Web site for Cirrus Design Corporation, a Duluth, Minnesota maker of small airplanes.

What if you can't reach your client in time to complete the assignment? Or if you can't get content from your client? Use content from their existing site or a site operated by a similar organization. Make sure that at a minimum there is a lived-in look for a reader who comes to see the "About," "News," and "Contact Us" sections. During the remainder of the course, you'll have an opportunity to replace the placeholder content with content from your client.

Note that before embarking on this you may want to read at least the "Separating the Designers and the Programmers" section on templates in the "Software Modularity" chapter.

Exercise 7: Client Signoff

Ask your client to register as a user and try out the "lived-in" site. Most people have a difficult time designing on a blank sheet of paper. You'll get new and different insights from your client by showing them a partially finished site than you did at the beginning of the project.

Record your client's answers to the following questions:

1. What changes would you like to see in the plan, now that you've tried out the prototype?

2. What will be the fastest way to fill this site with real content?

3. Are we collecting the right amount of information on initial user registration?

Presenting Your Work

If you're enrolled in a course using this textbook, you'll probably be asked at this point to give a four-minute presentation of your work on the content management system and skeletal implementation of the site.

Four minutes isn't very long so you'll need to rehearse and you'll want to make sure that all team members know what they're supposed to do. As a general rule, the person speaking should be addressing the audience, not typing at a computer. Team Member A talks; Team Member B drives. Perhaps at some point in the presentation they switch, but nobody is ever talking and driving a computer at the same time.

Open with an "elevator pitch," that is, the kind of thirty-second explanation that you'd give to someone you met during an elevator ride. The pitch should explain what problem you're solving and why your system will be better than existing mechanisms available to people.

Create one or more users ahead of time so that you don't have to show your user registration pages. Everyone who has used the Internet has registered at sites. They'll assume that you copied the best practices from amazon.com and other popular sites. If you did, the audience will be bored. If you didn't, the audience will be appalled by your sloppiness. Either way it is best to log in as already-registered users. In fact, sometimes you can arrange to prepare two browsers, for example, Mozilla and MSIE, one of which is logged in as a new user of the service and one of which is logged in as a site administrator or some other role that you want to demonstrate.

It is best not to refer to "users" during your talk. Instead talk about the roles by name. If, for example, you are building a service around flying, you could say "A student pilot logs in [your teammate logs in], finds an article on flight schools in San Francisco [your teammate navigates to this article], and posts a comment at the bottom about how much he likes his particular instructor." Then perhaps swap positions and your teammate comes up to say "The site editor [you switch browsers to the one logged in as a site admin], clicks on the new content page [you click], sees that there are some new comments pending approval, reads this one from a student pilot, and approves it [you click]." You return the browser to the public page where the comment may now be seen in the live site.

Close by parking the browser at a page that reveals as much of the site's overall structure as possible. Don't despair if you weren't able to show every feature of what you've built. Computer applications are all about the tasks that can be accomplished. If you've made the audience believe that it will be easy to complete a few clearly important tasks, you will have instilled confidence in them.

Exercise 8 (For the Instructor)

Call up each team's clients and ask how strongly they agree with the following statements:

1. I believe that my student team understands my problem.
2. I understand what my student team is planning to accomplish and by what dates, right through the end of the course.
3. My student team has been well-prepared for our meetings.
4. My student team is responsive.
5. I believe that the content management system my student team has built will be adequate to support the types of documents on my site and the workflow required for publishing those documents.

6. I think it is easy for users to register at my site, to recover a lost password, and that users are being asked all the required personal information.

7. I like the user administration pages that my student team has built.

8. My student team has made it easy for me to check on their progress myself.

9. My student team has kept me well informed of their progress.

10. I am impressed by the clarity and thoroughness of the documentation prepared so far.

Score this exercise by adding scores from each question: 0 for "disagree" or wishy-washy agreement (clients won't want to say bad things about young volunteers), 1 for "agree," 2 for "strongly agree."

Time and Motion

The data modeling, workflow, and version control exercises are intended to be done by the entire team working together. They should take about three hours. Many projects will need to do little more than adapt data models and policies from this chapter and put them in their own server's /doc directory.

The skeletal implementation may be challenging depending on how ambitious the goals of the content management system are, but perhaps 10 to 20 programmer-hours of work.

Criticizing other teams' work should take about 15 minutes per project criticized or about two hours total in a class with 8 to 10 projects. This could be done as a group or divided and conquered.

Achieving a lived-in look by pouring in real content shouldn't take more than two hours and ought to be divisible among team members.

Talking to the client will probably take about one hour.

7   Software Modularity

At this point in the course, you've built enough software that things may be starting to get unwieldy. What will life be like for those who maintain your code? Will they be able to figure out what modules you've written? Will they be able to find your documentation? Will it be simple to make small changes site wide?

This chapter is about ways to group all the code for a module, to record the existence of documentation for that module, to publish APIs to other parts of the system, and methods for storing configuration parameters.

Grouping Code

Each module in your system will contain the following kinds of software:

- RDBMS table definitions
- stored procedures that run in the database (in Oracle these would be PL/SQL or Java programs)
- procedures that run inside your Web or application server program that are shared by more than one page (we'll call these *shared procedures*)
- scripts that generate individual pages
- (possibly) templates that work in conjunction with page scripts
- documentation explaining the objectives of the module

Here are some examples of the modules that might be behind a large online community:

- user registration
- articles and comments
- discussion forum (shares the same tables with articles, but has radically different workflow for moderation and different presentation scripts)
- chat (separate tables from other content, optimized for extremely rapid queries, custom JavaScript client software)
- adserver for selling, placing, and logging banner advertisements
- calendar (personal, group, and site-wide events)
- classified ads and auctions
- e-commerce (catalogue of products, table of orders, presentation of product pages with reviews from community members, billing and accounting)
- email, server-based email (like Hotmail) for community members
- survey (opinion polls and other types of surveys among the members)
- weblog, private blogs for each community member who wants one, possibly sharing tables with articles, but different editing, approval workflow, and presentation interfaces plus RSS feeds, trackback, and the rest of the machine-to-machine interfaces that are expected in the blog world
- (trouble) ticket tracker for bug and feature request tracking

Good software developers might disagree on the division into modules. For example, rather than create a separate classified ads module, a person might decide that classifieds and discussion are so similar that adding `price` and `bid` columns to an existing content table makes more sense than constructing new tables and that adding a lot of IF statements to the scripts that present discussion questions and answers makes more sense than writing new scripts.

If the online community is used to support a group of university students and teachers, additional specialized modules would be added, for example, for recording which courses are being taught by whom and when, which students are registered in which courses, what handouts are associated with each class, what assignments are due and by when, and what grades have been assigned and by which teachers.

Recall that the software behind an Internet service is frequently updated as the community grows and new ideas are developed. Frequently updated software is going to have bugs, which means that the system will be frequently debugged, oftentimes at 2:00 A.M. and usually by a programmer other than the one who wrote the software. It is thus important to publish and abide by conventions that make it easy for a new programmer to figure out where the relevant source code files are. It might take only fifteen minutes to figure out what is wrong and patch the system. But if it takes three hours to find the source code files to begin with, what would have been an insignificant bug becomes a half-day project.

Let's walk through an example of how the software is arranged on the photo .net service. The server is configured to operate multiple Internet services. Each one is located at `/web/service-name/` which means that all the directories associated with photo.net are underneath `/web/photonet/`. The page root for the site is `/web/photonet/www/`. The Web server is configured to look for "library" procedures (shared by multiple pages) in `/web/photonet/tcl/`, a name derived from the fact that photo.net is run on AOLserver, whose default extension language is Tcl.

RDBMS table, index, and stored procedure definitions for a module are stored in a single file in the `/doc/sql/` directory (directory names in this chapter are relative to the Web server page root unless specified as absolute). The name for this file is the module name followed by a `.sql` extension, for example, `chat.sql` for the chat module. Shared procedures for all modules are stored in the single library directory `/web/photonet/tcl/`, with each file named "modulename-defs.tcl," for example, `chat-defs.tcl`.

Scripts that generate individual pages are parked at the following locations: `/module-name/` for the user pages; `/module-name/admin/` for the moderator pages, for example, where a user with moderator privileges would go to delete a posting; `/admin/module-name/` for the site administrator pages, for example, where the service operator would go to enable or disable a service, delegate moderation authority to another user, and so forth.

A high-level document explaining each module is stored in `/doc/module-name.html` and linked from the index page in `/doc/`. This document is intended as a starting point for programmers who are considering using the module or extending a feature of the module. The document has the following structure:

1. Where to find all the software associated with this module (site-wide conventions are nice, but it doesn't hurt to be explicit).

2. Big picture information: Why was this module built? Why aren't/weren't existing alternatives adequate for solving the problem? What are the high-level good and bad features of this module? What choices were considered in developing the data model?

3. Configuration information: What can be changed easily by editing parameters?

4. Use and maintenance information.

For an example of such a document, see http://philip.greenspun.com/seia/ examples-software-modularity/chat.

Shared Procedures versus Stored Procedures

Even in the simplest Web development environments, there are generally at least two places where procedural abstractions, that is, fragments of programs that are shared by multiple pages, can be developed. Modern relational database management systems can interpret Turing-complete imperative programming languages such as C#, Java, and PL/SQL. Thus any computation that could be performed by any computer could, in principle, be performed by a program running inside an RDBMS such as Microsoft SQL Server, Oracle, or PostgreSQL. In other words, you don't need a Web server or any other tools, but could implement page scripting and an HTTP server within the database management system in the form of *stored procedures*.

As we'll see in the "Scaling Gracefully" chapter, there are some performance advantages to be had in splitting off the presentation layer of an application into a set of separate physical computers. Thus our page scripts will most definitely reside outside of the RDBMS. This gives us the opportunity to write additional software that will run within or close to the Web server program, typically in the same computer language that is used for page scripting, in the form of *shared procedures*. In the case of a PHP script, for example, a shared procedure could be an include file. In the case of a site where individual pages are scripted in Java or C#, a shared procedure might be some classes and methods used by multiple pages.

How do you choose between using shared procedures and stored procedures? Start by thinking about the multiple applications that may connect to the same database. For example, there could be a public Web server, a nightly program that pulls out all new information for analysis, a maintenance tool for administrators built on top of Microsoft Excel or Access, and so on.

If you think that a piece of code might be useful to those other systems that connect to the same data model, put it in the database as a stored procedure. If you are sure that a piece of code is only useful for the particular Web application that you're building, keep it in the Web server as a shared procedure.

Documentation

As we enter the 21st century we find that rifle marksmanship has been largely lost in the military establishments of the world. The notion that technology can supplant incompetence is upon us in all sorts of endeavors, including that of shooting.
—Jeff Cooper in *The Art of the Rifle* (Paladin Press, 1997)

Given a system with 1,000 procedures and no documentation, the typical manager will lay down an edict to the programmers: you must write a "doc string" for every procedure saying what inputs it takes, what outputs it generates, and how it transforms those inputs into outputs. Virtually every programming environment going back to the 1960s has support for this kind of thinking. The fancier "doc string" systems will even parse through directories of source code, extract the doc strings, and print a nice-looking manual of 1,000 doc strings.

How useful are doc strings? Useful, but not sufficient. The programmer new to a system won't have any idea which of the 1,000 procedures and corresponding doc strings are most important. The new programmer won't have any idea why these procedures were built, what problem they solve, and whether the whole system has been deprecated in favor of newer software from another source. Certainly the 1,000 doc strings aren't going to convince any programmers to adopt a piece of software. It is much more important to present clear English prose that demonstrates the quality of your thinking and design work in attacking a real problem. The prose does not have to be more than a few pages long, but it needs to be carefully crafted.

Separating the Designers and the Programmers

Criticism and requests for changes will come in proportion to the number of people who understand that part of the system being criticized. Very few people are capable of data modeling or interaction design. Although these are the only parts of the system that deeply affect the user experience or the utility of an information system to its operators, you will thus very seldom be required to entertain a suggestion in this area. Only someone with years of relevant experience is likely to propose that a column be added to an SQL table or that five tables can be replaced with three tables. A much larger number of people are capable of writing Web scripts. So you'll sometimes be derided for your choice of programming environment, regardless of what it is or how state-of-the-art it was supposed to be at the time you adopted it. Virtually every human being on the planet, however, understands that mauve looks different from fuchsia and that Helvetica looks different from Times Roman. Thus the largest number of suggestions for changes to a Web application will be design related. Someone wants to add a new logo to every page on the site. Someone wants to change the background color in the discussion forum section. Someone wants to make a headline larger on a particular page. Someone wants to add a bit of white-space here and there.

Suppose that you've built your Web application in the simplest and most direct manner. For each URL there is a corresponding script, which contains SQL statements, some procedural code in the scripting language (IF statements, basically), and static strings of HTML that will be combined with the values returned from the database to form the completed page. If you break down what is inside a Visual Basic Active Server Page or a Java Server Page or a Perl CGI script, you always find these three items: SQL, IF statements, HTML.

Development of an application with this style of programming is easy. You can see all the relevant code for a page in one text editor buffer. Maintenance is also straightforward. If a user sends in a bug report saying "There is a spelling error on http://www.yourcommunity.org/foo/bar" you know that you need only look in one file in the file system (/foo/bar.asp or /foo/bar.jsp or /foo/bar.pl or whatever) and you are guaranteed to find the source of the user's problem. This goes for SQL and procedural programming errors as well.

What if people want site-wide changes to fonts, colors, headers and footers? This could be easy or hard depending on how you've crafted the system. Suppose that default colors are read from a configuration parameter system and headers, footers, and per-page navigation aids are generated by the page script calling shared procedures. In this happy circumstance, making site-wide changes might take only a few minutes.

What if people want to change the wording of some annotation in the static HTML for a page? Or make a particular headline on one page larger? Or add a bit of white space in one place on one page? This will require a programmer because the static HTML strings associated with that page are embedded in a file that contains SQL and procedural language code. You don't want someone to bring a section of the service down because of a botched attempt to fix a typo or add a hint.

The Small Hammer

The simplest way to separate the programmers from the designers is to create two files for each URL. File 1 contains SQL statements and some procedural code that fills local variables or a data structure with information from the RDBMS. The last statement in File 1 is a call to a procedure that will fetch File 2, a template file that looks like standard HTML with simple references to data prepared in File 1.

Suppose that File 1 is named `index.pl` and is a Perl script. By convention, File 2 will be named `index.template`. In preparing a template, a designer needs to know (a) the names of the variables being set in index.pl, (b) that one references a variable from the template with a dollar sign, for example, `$standard_navbar`, and (c) that to send an actual dollar sign or at-sign character to the user it should be escaped with a backslash. The merging of the template and local variables established in index.pl can be accomplished with a single call to Perl's built-in `eval` procedure, which performs standard Perl string interpolation, that is, replacing `$foo` with the value of the variable `foo`.

The Medium Hammer

If the SQL/procedural script and the HTML template are in separate files in the same directory, there is always a risk that a careless designer will delete, rename, or modify a computer program. It may make more sense to establish a separate directory and give the designers permission only on that parallel tree. For example on photo.net you might have the page scripts in `/web/photonet/www/` and templates underneath `/web/photonet/templates/`. A script at `/ecommerce/checkout.tcl` finishes by calling the shared procedure `return_template`. This procedure first invokes the Web server API to find out what URI is being served. A configuration parameter specifies the start of the templates tree. `return_template` uses the URL plus the template tree root to probe in the file system for a template to evaluate. If found, the template, in AOLserver ADP format (same syntax as Microsoft ASP), is evaluated in the context of `return_template`'s caller, which means that local variables set in the script will be available to the ADP file.

The "medium hammer" approach keeps programmers and designers completely separated from a file system permissioning point of view. It also has the advantage that the shared procedure called at the end of every script can do some poking around. Is this a user who prefers text-only pages? If so, is there a text-only template available? Is this a user who prefers a language other than the site's default? If so, is there a template available in which the annotation is in the user's preferred language?

The SQL Hammer

If a system already has extensive RDBMS-backed facilities for versioning and permissioning, it may seem natural to store templates in a database table. These templates can then be edited from a browser, and changes to templates can be managed as part of a site's overall publishing workflow. If the information architecture of a site is represented explicitly in RDBMS tables (see the "Content Management" chapter), it may be natural to keep templates and template fragments in the database along with content types, categories, and subcategories.

The Sledgehammer

Back in 1999, Karl Goldstein was the sole programmer building the entire information system for a commercial online community. The managers of the community changed their minds about fifteen times about how the site should look. Every page should have a horizontal navbar. Maybe vertical would be better, actually. But move the navbar on every page from the left to the right. After two or three of these massive changes in direction, Goldstein developed an elegant and efficient system:

- every page script would have a corresponding template, e.g., `register.tcl` would look for `register.template`
- nearly all templates would include a "master" tag indicating that the template was only designed to render a portion of the page
- the server would look for a `master.template` file in the same directory as the script; if found, the content rendered by the page script and its corre-

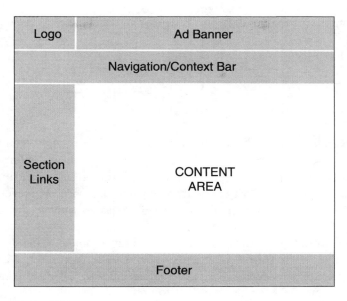

Logo	Ad Banner
	Navigation/Context Bar
Section Links	CONTENT AREA
	Footer

Figure 7.1

sponding template would be substituted for the `<slave>` tag in the master template and the result of evaluating the master template returned to the user

- when a master template was not found in the same directory as the script, the server would search at successively higher levels in the file system until a master template was found, then apply that one

Figure 7.1 is an example of how what the user viewed would be divided by master and slave templates. Content in gray is derived from the master template. Note that doesn't mean that it is static or not page specific. If a template is an ASP or JSP fragment, it can execute arbitrarily complex computer programs to generate what appears within its portion of the page. Content in white comes from the per-page template.

This sounds inefficient due to the large number of file system probes. However, once a system is in production, it is easy for the Web server to cache, per-URL, the results of the file system investigation. In fact, the Web server could cache all of the templates in its virtual memory for maximum speed. The reason that one wouldn't do this during development is that it would make debugging difficult. Every time you changed a template you'd have to restart the Web server or clear the cache in order to view the results of the change.

Intermodule APIs

Recall from the "User Registration and Management" chapter that we want people to be accountable for their actions within an online community. One way to enhance accountability is by offering a "user contributions" page that will show all contributions from a particular user. Wherever a person's name appears within the application it will be a hyperlink to this user contributions page.

Given that all site content is stored in relational database tables, the most obvious way to start writing the user contributions page script is by looking at the SQL data models for each individual module. Then we can write a program that queries a few dozen tables to find all contributions by a particular user.

A drawback to this approach is that we now have code that may break if we change a module's data model, yet this code is not within that module's subdirectory, and this code is probably being authored by a programmer other than the one maintaining the individual module.

Let's consider a different application: email alerts. Suppose that your community offers a discussion forum and a classified ad system, coded as separate modules. A user wishes to get a daily summary of activity in both areas. Each module could offer a completely separate alerts mechanism. However, this would mean that the user would get two email messages every night when a single combined email was desired. If we build a combined email alert system, however, we have the same problem as with the user history page: shared code that depends on the data models of individual modules.

Finally, let's look at the site administrator's job. The site administrator is probably a busy volunteer. He or she does not want to waste twenty mouse clicks to see today's new content. The site administrator ought to be able to view recently contributed content from all modules on a single page. Does that mean we will yet again have a script that depends on every table definition from every module?

Here's a hint at a solution. On the photo.net site each module defines a "new stuff" procedure, which takes the following arguments:

- `since_when`—the date of the earliest content we're interested in
- `only_from_new_users_p`—a boolean indicating whether or not we want to limit the report to contributions from new users (useful for site administration because new users are the ones who don't understand community standards and norms)
- `purpose`—"admin," "email_summary," or "user"; this controls delivery of unapproved content, inclusion of links to administration options such as approval/disapproval, and the format of the report

The output of such a procedure can be simple: HTML for a Web page or plain text for an email message. The output of such a procedure can be a data structure. The output of such a procedure could be an XML document, to be rendered with an XSL style sheet. The important thing is that pages interested in "new stuff" site wide need not be familiar with the data models of individual modules, only the name of the "new stuff" procedure corresponding to each module. This latter task is made easy on photo.net: as each module is loaded by the Web server, it adds its "new stuff" procedure name to a site-wide list. A page that wants to display site-wide new stuff loops through this list, calling each named procedure in turn.

Configuration Parameters

It is possible, although not very tasteful, to build a working Internet application with the following items hard-coded into each individual page:

- RDBMS username and password
- email addresses of site administrators who wish notifications on events such as new user registration or new content posting
- the email address of a sysadmin to notify if the Web server can't connect to the RDBMS or in case of other errors
- IP addresses of users we don't like
- legacy URLs and the new URLs to which requests for the old ones should be redirected
- the name of the site
- the names of the editors and publishers

- the maximum attachment size that the site is willing to accept (maybe you don't want a user uploading an 800 MB TIFF image as an attachment to a bboard posting)
- whether or not to serve a link offering the source code behind the page

The ancient term for this approach to building software is "putting magic numbers in the code." With magic numbers in the code, it is tough to grab a few scripts from one service and apply them to another application. With magic numbers in the code, it is tough to know how many programs you have to examine and modify after a personnel change. With magic numbers in the code, it is tough to know if rules are being enforced consistently site wide.

Where should you store parameters such as these? Except for the database username and password, an obvious answer would seem to be "in the database." There are a bunch of keys (the parameter names) and a bunch of values (the parameters). This is the very problem for which a database management system is ideal.

```
-- use Oracle's unique key generator
create sequence config_param_seq start with 1;

create table config_param_keys (
        config_param_key_id      integer primary key,
        key_name                 varchar(4000) not null,
        param_comment            varchar(4000)
);

-- we store the values in a separate table because there might
-- be more than one for a given key
create table config_param_values (
        config_param_key_id      not null references config_param_keys,
        value_index              integer default 1 not null,
        param_value              varchar(4000) not null
);

-- we use the Oracle operator "nextval" to get the next
-- value from the sequence generator
insert into config_param_keys
values
(config_param_seq.nextval, 'view_source_link_p', 'damn 6.171 instructor is
making me do this');

-- we use the Oracle operator "currval" to get the last
-- value from the sequence generator (so that rows inserted in this transaction
```

```
-- will all have the same ID)
insert into config_param_values
values
(config_param_seq.currval, 1, 't');

commit;

insert into config_param_keys
values
(config_param_seq.nextval, 'redirect', 'dropping the /wtr/ directory');

insert into config_param_values
values
(config_param_seq.currval, 1, '/wtr/thebook/');

insert into config_param_values
values
(config_param_seq.currval, 2, '/panda/');

commit;
```

At the end of every page script we can query these tables:

```
select cpv.param_value
from config_param_keys cpk, config_param_values cpv
where cpk.config_param_key_id = cpv.config_param_key_id
and key_name = 'view_source_link_p'
```

If the script gets a row with "t" back, it includes a "View Source" link at the bottom of the page. If not, no link.

Recording a redirect required the storage of two rows in the config_param_values table, one for the "from" and one for the "to" URL. When a request comes in, the Web server will want to query to figure out if a redirect exists:

```
select cpk.config_param_key_id
from config_param_keys cpk, config_param_values cpv
where cpk.config_param_key_id = cpv.config_param_key_id
and key_name = 'redirect'
and value_index = 1
and param_value = :requested_url
```

where :requested_url is a bind variable containing the URL requested by the currently connected Web client. Note that this query tells us only that such a redirect exists; it does not give us the destination URL, which is stored in a separate row of `config_param_values`. Believe it or not, the conventional thing to do here is a three-way join, including a self-join of `config_param_values`:

```
select cpv2.param_value
from
  config_param_keys cpk,
  config_param_values cpv1,
  config_param_values cpv2
where cpk.config_param_key_id = cpv1.config_param_key_id
and cpk.config_param_key_id = cpv2.config_param_key_id
and cpk.key_name = 'redirect'
and cpv1.value_index = 1
and cpv1.param_value = :requested_url
and cpv2.value_index = 2

-- that was pretty ugly; maybe we can encapsulate it in a view

create view redirects
as
select cpv1.param_value as from_url, cpv2.param_value as to_url
from
  config_param_keys cpk,
  config_param_values cpv1,
  config_param_values cpv2
where cpk.config_param_key_id = cpv1.config_param_key_id
and cpk.config_param_key_id = cpv2.config_param_key_id
and cpk.key_name = 'redirect'
and cpv1.value_index = 1
and cpv2.value_index = 2

-- a couple of Oracle SQL*Plus formatting commands
column from_url format a25
column to_url format a30

-- let's look at our virtual table now
select * from redirects;

FROM_URL                  TO_URL
------------------------- ------------------------------
/wtr/thebook/             /panda/
```

N-way joins notwithstanding, how tasteful is this approach to storing parameters? The surface answer is "extremely tasteful." All of our information is in the RDBMS where it belongs. There are no magic numbers in the code. The parameters are amenable to editing from admin pages that have the same form as all the other pages on the site: SQL queries and SQL updates. After a little more time spent with this problem, however, one asks "Why are we querying the RDBMS one million times per day for information that changes once per year?"

Questions of taste aside, an extra five to ten RDBMS queries per request is a significant burden on the database server, which is the most difficult part of an Internet application to distribute across multiple physical computers (see the "Scaling" chapter) and therefore the most expensive layer in which to expand capacity.

A good rule of thumb is that Web scripts shouldn't be querying the RDBMS to figure out what to do; they should query the RDBMS only for content and user data.

For reasonable performance, configuration parameters should be accessible to Web scripts from the Web server's virtual memory. Implementing such a scheme with a threaded Web server is pretty straightforward because all the code is executing within one virtual memory space:

- look in the server API documentation to find a mechanism for saying "run this bit of code at server startup time"
- build an in-memory hash table where the parameter keys are the hash table keys
- load the parameter values associated with a key into the hash table as a list
- document an API to the hash table that takes a key as an input and returns a value or a list of values as an output

A hash table is best because it offers O[1] access to the data, that is, the time that it takes to answer the question "what is the value associated with the key 'foobar'" does not grow as the number of keys grows. In some hobbyist computer languages, built-in hash tables might be known as "associative arrays."

If you expect to have a lot of configuration parameters, it might be best to add a "section" column to the `config_param_keys` table and query by section and key. Thus, for example, you can have a parameter called "bug_report_email" in both the "discussion" and "user_registration" sections. The key to the hash table then becomes a composite of the section name and key name.

With Microsoft .NET

Configuration parameters are added to IIS/ASP.NET applications in the Web .config file for the application.

For example, if you place the following in `c:\Inetpub\wwwroot\Web .config` (assuming default IIS installation)

```
<configuration>
 <appSettings>
  <add key="publisherEmail"
   value="marketing@mycompany.com" />
 </appSettings>
</configuration>
```

you will be able to access publisherEmail in a VB .aspx page as follows

```
<%

Dim publisherEmail as String
publisherEmail = ConfigurationSettings.AppSettings( "publisherEmail"
)

%>

<html>
<body>

...

For further information please contact us at <%= publisherEmail %>

...

</body>
</html>
```

By default, configuration settings apply to a directory and all its subdirectories. Also by default, these settings can be overridden by settings in Web.config files in the subdirectories. More elaborate rules for scoping and override behavior can be established using the <location> tag.

More:

- "ASP.NET Configuration" from *.NET Framework Developer's Guide* at http://msdn.microsoft.com/library/default.asp?url=/library/en-us/cpguide/html/cpconaspnetconfiguration.asp (note that the MSDN guys haven't figured out how to do abstract URLs and they also haven't converted to .aspx yet!)

With Java Server Pages

The following is Jin S. Choi's recommendation for storing and accessing configuration parameters when using Java Server Pages.

Specify Parameter tags within the Context specification for your application in conf/server.xml. Example:

```
<Context path="/myapp" docBase="myapp" debug="0"
        reloadable="true" crossContext="true">
  <Parameter name="companyName" value="My Company, Inc."
            override="false"/>
</Context>
```

You can also specify the parameter in the WEB-INF/web.xml file for your application:

```
<context-param>
  <param-name>companyName</param-name>
  <param-value>My Company, Inc.</param-value>
</context-param>
```

The "override" attribute in the first example specifies that you do not want this value to be overridden by a context-param tag in the web.xml file. The default value is "true" (allow overrides).

To retrieve parameters from a servlet or JSP, you can call:

```
getServletContext().getInitParameter("companyName");
```

More:

- documentation for Context: http://jakarta.apache.org/tomcat/tomcat-4.0-doc/config/context.html
- javadoc for ServletContext: http://jakarta.apache.org/tomcat/tomcat-4.0-doc/servletapi/javax/servlet/ServletContext.html

Exercise 1

Create a `/doc/` directory on your team server. Create an index page in this directory that links to a development standards document (`/doc/development-standards` would be a reasonable URL, but you can use whatever you like so long as it is clearly linked from `/doc/`).

In this development standards document, cover at least the following issues:

1. naming of URLs: abstract versus non-abstract (bleah), dashes versus underscores (hard for many users to read), spelled out or abbreviated

2. naming of URLs used in forms and form processing—will these be at the same URL or will a user working through a sequence of forms proceed `/foo/bar`, `/foo/bar-1`, `/foo/bar-2`, etc.

3. RDBMS used

4. computer languages used for Web scripts and procedural code within the RDBMS

5. means of connecting to the RDBMS (libraries, bind variables, etc.)

6. variable-naming conventions

7. how to document a module

8. how to document a shared procedure

9. how to document a Web script (author, valid inputs)

10. how Web form inputs are validated by scripts

11. templating strategy chosen (if any)

12. how to add a configuration variable and how to name it so that at least all parameters associated with a particular module can be identified quickly

Step back from your document before moving on to the next exercise. Ask yourself "If a new programmer joined this project tomorrow, and I asked her to build a surveys module, would she be able to be an effective consistent developer in my environment without talking to me?" Remember that a surveys module will require an extensive administrative interface for creation of surveys, questions, and possible answers, both admin and user interfaces for looking at results, and a user interface for answering surveys. If the answer to the question is "Gee, this new programmer would have to ask me a lot of questions," go back and make your development standards document more explicit and add some more examples.

Exercise 2

Document your team's intermodule API within the /doc/ directory, perhaps at /doc/intermodule-API, linked from the doc index page. Your strategy must be able to handle at least the following cases:

- production of a site administrator's page containing all content going back a selectable number of days, with administration links next to each item *without the page script having any dependence on any module's data model*

- production of a user-level page showing new content site wide

- a centralized email alert system in which a user gets a nightly summary combining new content from multiple modules

Protecting Users from Each Other's HTML

Fundamentally, the job of the server behind an online community is to take text from User A and display it to User B. Unfortunately, there is a security risk inherent in this activity. Suppose that User A is malicious and includes tags such as <SCRIPT> in a comment body? When User B visits the page containing this comment, suddenly JavaScript may be executing on his machine, downloading objectionable images from various locations around the Internet, playing music, popping up new windows, and ultimately forcing the user's browser to visit a page of User A's choosing.

The most obvious solution would seem to be disallowing all HTML tags. Any uploaded text is scanned for the characters "<" and ">" and, if those are present, the posting is rejected with an explanation. This wouldn't work out that well in a site for mathematicians! Maybe they need to use greater-than and less-than signs in their postings.

The beginning of a workable solution is a procedure, perhaps named something such as quoteHTML, that takes a user-uploaded text string and performs the following conversions:

- < characters to <.
- > characters to >.
- & characters to &.

If your page scripts call this procedure any time they are writing user-uploaded content out to a browser, no browser will ever interpret user-uploaded data as an HTML tag.

That works great for fields such as `first_names`, `last_name`, `street_address`, subject summary lines, and so forth, where there is no value to having an HTML tag. For some longer documents obtained from users, however, it might be nice to enable them to use a restricted set of HTML tags such as B, I, EM, P, BR, UL, LI, and so on. If you're going to store HTML in the database once and serve it back out thousands of times per day, it is better to check for legal tags at upload time. The problem with checking for disallowed tags such as SCRIPT, DIV, and FONT is that HTML keeps getting extended in de jure and de facto ways. Unless you want the responsibility of keeping current with all of the ways in which new HTML tags can make browsers behave, it may be better to check for approved tags. Either way, you'll want the allowed or disallowed tags list to be kept in an easy-to-modify configuration file. Further, you probably want to perform a bit of validation on the use of allowed tags such as B or I. A user who makes a mistake and forgets to close one of these tags might render 100 comments underneath in an unusual font style.

Exercise 3

Document your team's approach to preventing one user from attacking other users with malicious HTML. Your documentation of this infrastructure should include procedure names and examples of how those procedures are to be used.

Time and Motion

All of the exercises in this chapter are intended to be done by the team as a whole. A team that takes the assignment seriously should spend about 3 hours together agreeing to and documenting standards. They then might decide to re-work some of their older code to conform to these standards, which could take another 5 or 10 programmer-hours. The second step is optional, though by the end of the course we would expect all the projects to be internally consistent.

8   Discussion

A discussion forum is one of the most basic tools for computer-supported co-operation among human beings. User A can post a question. User B can post an answer. User C can view both question and answer and learn from the exchange. In a *threaded* forum, User D has the choice of posting a response to User A's question or to User B's response. In a *Q&A format* forum, Users D, E, and F can post responses to User A's question, and the responses will simply be presented in the order that they were submitted. With minor tweaks to the presentation layer, a discussion forum system can function as a personal commentable weblog.

In this chapter you'll prototype a discussion forum, conduct a usability test, and then refine your system based on what you learned from observing the users.

Discussion Forum as Community?

A well-designed discussion forum can by itself fulfill all of the requirements for a sustainable online learning community. Recall that these elements are the following:

1. magnet content authored by experts
2. means of collaboration
3. powerful facilities for browsing and searching both magnet content and contributed content
4. means of delegation of moderation

5. means of identifying members who are imposing an undue burden on the community and ways of changing their behavior and/or excluding them from the community without them realizing it

6. means of software extension by community members themselves

An early example of the forum-as-community is USENET, which was started in 1979 and is also known to old people as "NetNews" and to young people as "Google Groups." Each newsgroup is a more or less self-contained community of people interested in a particular topic, collaborating through a threaded discussion forum. A good example is `rec.aviation.soaring`, where people talk about flying around in airplanes without engines.

Aviation in itself is not inherently dangerous. But to an even greater degree than the sea, it is terribly unforgiving of any carelessness, incapacity or neglect.

—Captain A. G. Lamplugh, 1930s

In a USENET group the magnet content can be any longish posting from a recognized expert. Keep in mind that the number of people using a group such as `rec.aviation.soaring` is fairly small—most people get nervous in little planes and even more nervous in a little plane with no engine. An analysis of October 2004's activity by Marc Smith's Netscan service (netscan.research .microsoft.com) shows that the group had only 174 "Returnees." Thus it will be fairly straightforward for these core users to recognize each other by name or e-mail address. A typical magnet content posting in a newsgroup is the FAQ or frequently asked questions summary in which each question has an agreed-upon-by-the-group-experts answer.

The means of collaboration in the USENET group is the ability for any member to start a new thread or reply to a message within an existing thread. In the early days of USENET, the means of browsing and searching were reasonably good for recent messages, but terrible or nonexistent for learning from older exchanges. Starting in the mid-1990s, Web-based search engines such as DejaNews provided fast and easy access to old messages.

USENET has traditionally been weak on the fourth required element ("means of delegation of moderation"). Not enough people have volunteered to moderate, software to divide the effort of moderating a single forum among multiple moderators was nonexistent, and the news protocols had security holes that let commercial spam messages through even on moderated groups. For an overview of the circa 2001 state of the art, read http://www.landfield.com/ usenet/moderators/handbook/. For a discussion of spam in history, see "Origin of the term 'spam' to mean net abuse" by Brad Templeton at http://www .templetons.com/brad/spamterm.html, a site that contains a lot of other interesting articles on the history of Internet.

Where USENET has fallen tragically short is element 5: "Means of excluding burdensome people." Most USENET clients include "bozo filters" that enable an individual user to filter out messages from a persistently troublesome poster. But there is no collective way for a group to exclude a person who consistently starts irrelevant threads, spams the group, abuses others, or otherwise becomes unwelcome.

With regard to element 6, software extension by community members themselves, USENET has done remarkably well. USENET servers and clients tend to be monolithic C programs where small modifications can have catastrophic consequences. On the other hand, the average user of the early Internet was a skilled software developer. So if not every USENET user was a programmer of USENET tools, it was at least safe to say that every programmer of USENET tools was a user of USENET.

If the engine stops for any reason, you are due to tumble, and that's all there is to it!
—Clyde Cessna

Beyond USENET

If the online learning community that you build is only as good as USENET, congratulate yourself. The Google USENET archive contains 700 million messages from twenty years. Hundreds of thousands of people have gotten the answers to their questions, as shown in figure 8.1.

When building our own database-backed discussion forum system, there are some simple improvements that we can add over the traditional USENET system:

- an optional "mail me when a response is posted" field
- email summaries or instant alerts
- up-to-the-second full text indexing (assuming your RDBMS supports it)

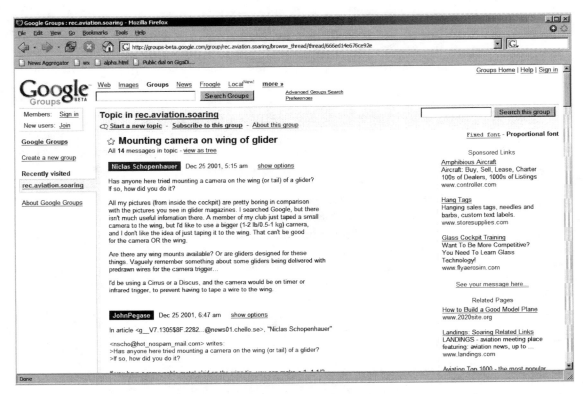

Figure 8.1 A December 25, 2001 USENET exchange in the group rec.aviation.soaring regarding mounting a camera on the wing of a glider. Notice that the first answer comes less than two hours after the question was posted. See http://groups.google.com/group/rec.aviation.soaring/browse_thread/thread/666ed14e676ce92e.

- secure transmission of data to and from the bboard via SSL
- collaborative moderation via admin pages to delete stale/ugly/whatever messages
- older postings browsable by category

More dramatic improvements can be obtained with attention to element 5: "Means of excluding burdensome people." Your software can do the SQL query "show me users who've submitted questions that were deleted by a moderator as redundant" and then automatically welcome those users back to the forum with an interstitial page explaining how to search and browse archived threads. If the online community is short on moderator time, it will make a lot of sense to query for those users whose postings have resulted in moderator intervention. If it turns out that 0.1 percent of the users consume 50 percent of the moderators' time, perhaps it is better to ban those handful of users and thereby double the community's available moderation resources.

As the semester proceeds, you'll discover another advantage of building your own discussion forum, which is that it becomes an integrated part of your service. All of a user's contributions in different areas, including the discussion forum, are queryable from a single database and viewable on a single page.

Flying is inherently dangerous. We like to gloss that over with clever rhetoric and comforting statistics, but these facts remain: gravity is constant and powerful, and speed kills. In combination, they are particularly destructive.

—Dan Manningham

Exercise 1

Visit five sites on the public Internet with discussion forums, one of which can be the Medium Format Digest forum at photo.net (http://www.photo.net/bboard/q-and-a?topic_id=35). For each site gather the following statistics:

- given an already-registered user, the number of clicks required to post a message
- the number of clicks required to go from the top-level forum page to a single thread
- if there are 20 postings within a thread, the number of clicks required to view all the text within all of the postings
- the number of clicks required to view the subject lines of all archived postings in a particular category

List the user interface and customer service features that you think are the best from these five sites and give a brief explanation of why each feature is good.

One Forum or Many?

How many forums should a site have? Let's consider a site for music lovers. Would one forum be enough? Maybe not. Will the classical music lovers be interested in a discussion of Pat Boone's cover of AC-DC's "It's a Long Way to the Top (If You Wanna Rock 'N' Roll)"? So it will be a good idea to split the discussion into at least two forums: Classical and Pop. Let's say that a Pat Boone fan comes into the Pop forum one day and encounters a discussion of the lyrics from Ice Cube's *Death Certificate* or an MP3 from Prodigy's *Fat of the Land*? We'll clearly need to split up the Pop forum into Christian Pop, Techno, and Rap. We're expecting a lot of Beatles fans as well. Which of these forums would they gravitate toward? Maybe we need a '60s Rock forum. On the classical side, there are a lot of grand opera nuts who won't want to be distracted by discussions about authentic instrument performances of Baroque music. Sophisticated modern music fans discussing John Cage's "Four Minutes, Thirty-three Seconds" won't want to waste time discussing the fossils of the eighteenth and nineteenth centuries. And if we turn our attention to the many styles of Jazz . . .

I certainly had no feeling for harmony, and Schoenberg thought that that would make it impossible for me to write music. He said, "You'll come to a wall you won't be able to get through." So I said, "I'll beat my head against that wall."

—John Cage

If something is boring after two minutes, try it for four. If still boring, then eight. Then sixteen. Then thirty-two. Eventually one discovers that it is not boring at all.

—John Cage

It would be easy to justify the creation of 100 separate forums on our music site. And indeed USENET contains more than 50 rec.music.* groups, including `rec.music.beatles.moderated`, for example. That turns out to be the tip of the iceberg, for the alternative hierarchy sports more than 700 alt.music.* groups, including `alt.music.celine-dion` and `alt.music.j-s-bach`. If USENET can support nearly 1,000 discussion forums, surely a popular comprehensive music site ought to have at least 100.

Maybe not.

When discussion is fragmented, it is hard for a community to get off the ground. If there are 50 users and 100 forums, how will those users find each other? The average visit will result in a user concluding that the community isn't active. Such a user is unlikely to return or refer a friend to the site. Even when a community is large enough to support numerous forums, presenting discussion in a fragmented manner leads to extra work for the user whose interests are diverse. Suppose that a music scholar comes to USENET looking to see if there has been any recent discussion of Bach's "Schubler Chorales" and their influence on later composers. That's as simple as visiting `alt.music.j-s-bach`. If that scholar wants to check up on recent postings concerning Celine Dion's "My Heart Will Go On," he or she will have to scan `alt.music.celine-dion` separately.

A good example of a thriving community with a single discussion forum is slashdot.org. It is very easy to find the topics being actively discussed on slashdot: look at the front page.

It is possible to take the "one forum" and "many forum" approaches on the same site at the same time. For example, look at http://www.photo.net/bboard/ (static copy at http://philip.greenspun.com/seia/images-discussion/photonet-bboard-original.htm). There are separate Medium Format, Nature Photography, and Photo Critique forums. For a user to browse the new postings in these three forums will require seven mouse clicks: down into this page, down into Medium Format, back, down into Nature, back, down into Critique. With a different SQL query, however, postings from all these very same forums can be combined on one page, as in http://www.photo.net/bboard/unified/ (static copy at http://philip.greenspun.com/seia/images-discussion/photonet-bboard-unified.htm). Postings from particular forum topics may be distinguished with a special publisher-chosen color or icon. Suppose that the user finds the Photo Critique forum overwhelming and uninteresting. These postings can be excluded from his or her personalized unified view via clicking on the "Customize forums" link at the top (static copy at http://philip.greenspun.com/seia/images-discussion/unified-forum-personalization.htm) and unchecking those forums that are no longer of interest.

She had a voice like the New Jersey State Anthem played on an electric razor.

—*Bright Lights, Big City* by Jay McInerney

Exercise 2: Design the User Experience

Figure out whether your service should have one forum, one forum with categories, several forums, several forums each with categories, or something else. Document the page flow for your users (recall the example page flow diagram from the "User Registration" chapter).

Exercise 3: Document the Data Model

Document how you intend to spread the discussion forum data among the content repository tables that you defined in the "Content Management" chapter.

Exercise 4: Build the User Pages

Implement the user experience that you designed in Exercise 2.

Exercise 5: Build the Admin Pages

Design a set of admin pages. In this case it is usually better to start with a required list of tasks that must be accomplished. Then try to build a page flow that will let the administrator accomplish those tasks in as few clicks as possible.

Recall from the "User Registration" chapter an important user interface principle to keep in mind: it is more natural for most computer users to pick the noun first and then the verb. For example, the forum moderator might first click on a message's subject line to select it and then, on a subsequent page, select an action to perform to this message: delete, approve, rate, categorize, and so forth. It is technically feasible to build a system in which the moderator is first asked "Would you like to delete some messages?" and then is prompted for the messages to be deleted. However, this is not how the Apple Macintosh was designed, and therefore anyone who has used the Macintosh user interface or its derivatives, notably Microsoft Windows, will be accustomed to the noun-verb order.

This is your community and these are your users. So in the long run only you can know what administrative actions are most needed. At a minimum, however, you should support the following:

- find the most active contributors
- select a contributor to become a co-moderator (presumably from the above list)
- approve or disapprove a posting or a thread (this might be handled by more general pages from your content management system, though remember that moderating a discussion forum ought to be a very streamlined process); note that these functions could be worked into the user pages, but only enabled for those logged-in users who have moderator privileges

In-Class Presentations

At this point we recommend that teams present their functioning discussion forum implementations. So that the audience can evaluate the workability of the interface, the forums should be preloaded with questions and answers of realistic length, with material copied from Google Groups if necessary.

A suggested outline for the presentation is the following:

- explain the kinds of people who are expected to use the discussion subsystem, e.g., it might be only the site administrators (30 seconds)
- without logging in or logged in as a casual visitor, demonstrate the pages that show all the forums (if more than one), questions within a forum, and questions and answers within a single thread (1 minute)
- demonstrate responding to an existing question/adding to an existing thread (30 seconds)
- demonstrate asking a new question/starting a new thread (30 seconds)
- log in as a forum moderator or site administrator (15 seconds)
- demonstrate disapproving or moderating down a posting (30 seconds)
- demonstrate viewing statistics on forum usage and participation level by user (1 minute)
- show the source code for the page that shows a single thread (one question, many answers), with the SQL query (or queries) highlighted (1 minute)

- show the execution plan for that query or those queries, i.e., the output of whatever SQL performance-tracing tool is available in the RDBMS chosen for this project (1 minute)

The presentation should be accompanied by a handout that shows (a) the data model that supports discussion, (b) any SQL code invoked by the URL that displays one thread of discussion (pulled out of whatever imperative language scripts it is imbedded in), and (c) the results of the query trace.

Usability

At this point your discussion forum should work. Users can register. Users can ask questions. Users can post answers. Is it usable? Well, consider that most computer programs were considered perfect at one time by their creator(s). It is only in encounters with real users that most problems become evident.

These encounters between freshly minted Internet applications and first users have become increasingly startling for all parties. One reason is the large and growing *user experience gap*. In 1994 the average Web user was a researcher with a Unix machine on his or her desk. Very likely the user knew how to write at least simple computer programs. The average Web page was straight HTML 2.0 with no scripts or other active components. All Web pages worked the same: you read the black text, you clicked on the blue text, you were reminded by the purple text that you'd already visited a link. Once you learned how to use your first Web site, you knew how to use all subsequently visited sites.

The user experience gap has grown larger because the users are less sophisticated while the applications have grown more complex. In 2005 the average Web user is a first-time computer user and the Web browser may be the only application that he or she knows how to use. Despite the manifest inability of these users to cope with a complex user interface, Web sites have been tarted up with JavaScript, ActiveX, Java, Flash, to the point where they are as hard to use and different from each other as old Unix applications. Users unable or unwilling to deal with the horrors of custom user interfaces have voted with their mice. They buy at Amazon. They search at Google. They get their information from Yahoo! and nytimes.com.

Idiosyncratic ideas make sense for magazine and television advertisements. Different is good when it takes the user the same 30 seconds to absorb the message. But different is bad if it means the user needs extra time or extra clicks to

Figure 8.2   "Think of others, you could be a user yourself" and "It is an offense not to flush the toilet after use." Men's room interior, Singapore. Photo copyright Philip Greenspun.

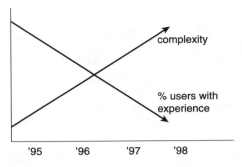

Figure 8.3 As the Internet gets older, applications become more complex and difficult to use while the average user becomes less and less experienced. Source: Mark Hurst, www.goodexperience.com.

get to the desired task. Some studies show that on each extra click there is a 50 percent chance that a user will abandon the site altogether. In mid-2000, Webvan purchased HomeGrocer, a competing grocery delivery company, and converted the old HomeGrocer users to the new Webvan user interface. Orders fell by more than half. The HomeGrocer business went from breaking even to losing lots of cash simply because of the inferior usability of the Webvan software. Ultimately Webvan went bankrupt, taking with it $1.2 billion in invested cash.

How is it possible that people follow what they imagine to be their own good taste instead of either copying the successful Internet services (e.g., Yahoo!, Amazon, Google) or listening to the users? And that people continue to believe in the value of their own ideas even as the red ink starts to dominate their financial reports? Justin Kruger and David Dunning, experimental psychologists at Cornell University, wondered the same thing and wrote up their findings in "Unskilled and Unaware of It: How Difficulties in Recognizing One's Own Incompetence Lead to Inflated Self-Assessments" (*Journal of Personality and Social Psychology* 77, no. 6 [1999]: 1121–1134; http://www.phule.net/mirrors/unskilled-and-unaware.html). Kruger and Dunning found that people in the 12th percentile of skill estimated themselves to be in the 62nd. Furthermore, these incompetent people failed to recalibrate themselves when shown the range of performance by their peer group. The authors concluded that "those with limited knowledge in a domain suffer a dual burden: Not only do they reach mistaken conclusions and make regrettable errors, but their incompetence robs them of the ability to realize it."

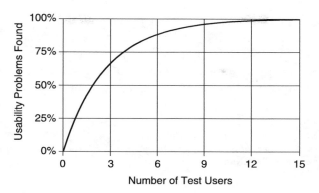

Figure 8.4   Source: "Why You Only Need to Test With 5 Users" by Jakob Nielsen; http://www.useit.com/alertbox/20000319.html.

As an aid to deciding whether to spend your future as an engineer or go on to business school, note that Webvan CEO George Shaheen ran the company into the ground, then resigned shortly before the bankruptcy filing, collecting a $375,000-per-year for life retirement package.

Exercise 6: The Usability Test

An ideal usability test involves the following elements:

1. a test subject whose experience with computers and the Internet is comparable to what you expect for your average user

2. a set of tasks that you want the subject to try to accomplish

3. a quiet comfortable environment for the test subject

4. no assistance from the product developers

5. observation of the test subject through a one-way mirror

6. videotaping of the test subject's experience for later study

Conduct a usability test of your discussion forum software, incorporating elements 1–4 from the list above. You should find at least four testers from among your friends—*do not pick anyone who is taking this course* (classmates will have too many subconscious expectations). Run your usability test subjects in series, one after the other, with your entire team observing and writing down what happens. Ask your subjects to voice their thoughts aloud. How long does it take the subject to complete a task? Does the subject get stuck on any step? Does the subject indicate confusion as to the appropriate next step at any time?

A scientist is someone who measures her results against Nature. An engineer is someone who measures her results against human needs. A computer scientist is someone who doesn't measure his results.

—us

Use the following script of tasks (cut and paste these into a separate document, and print it out, after filling in the bracketed sections), with no extra hints:

1. starting as an unregistered user at the site home page, find the area on the site where one would ask questions of other users (if you can't accomplish this task, or any other task on this page, within 3 minutes, just move on)

2. read through the existing questions and answers to determine whether or not [*some question that has been asked already*] has been asked and answered already; if not, post a question on that subject (registering if necessary)

3. read through the existing questions and answers to determine whether or not [*some question that has not been asked already*] has been asked and answered already; if not, post a question on that subject

4. log out

5. log in with the existing username/password of [*user/password*] and try to find all the unanswered questions in the discussion forum

6. answer the question(s) that you yourself posted a few minutes earlier, pretending to be this other user

7. log out

8. log in with the existing username/password of [*admin user/password*] and find the administrator's pages

9. delete the discussion forum thread(s) that you created earlier

10. log out

In between test subjects, clean up any rows that they may have left in database tables. If your first subject has a disastrous experience, consider taking a few hours off to fix your software, add links and annotation, and so on, before proceeding with the second subject.

Stand as far away from the subject as you possibly can while still being able to see the computer screen and hear the subject's comments. Force yourself to remain absolutely silent. If the subject is completely confused and clicking around randomly, let the subject continue until he or she figures it out. Keep track of the number of seconds each subject requires to complete each task.

Post a report on your team server at `/doc/testing/discussion-usability`. This report will contain a summary of what you learned from this test with average task times and average total time (we can use these to compare the efficiency of various teams' solutions). The report should contain hyperlinks to subpages that contain transcripts of individual user sessions, what each test subject said, and what happened. Link to your report from your main documentation index page.

Discussion for Education

Recall from the introduction that our goal in working through this text is to build an online *learning* community. An active discussion forum might be evidence of a tremendous amount of member-to-member education or it could merely be a place where loudmouths enjoy seeing their name in print. Moderation is the first line of defense against postings that aren't responsive to the original question or helpful to the would-be learners.

Building more structure into a discussion forum is an option worth considering, especially if your discussion forum is supporting an organized class. The Berkman Center at Harvard Law School (HLS) was a pioneer in this area. The teachers at HLS weren't happy with the bias in favor of early responders inherent in a standard discussion forum system. The first response to a question gets the most readers because it is near the top of the page, so it might be more ego-gratifying to be first than to spend more time crafting a thoughtful response. This shortcoming was addressed by writing what they call a *semisynchronous* discussion forum. Responses are collected for a period of time, but not made public until the deadline for responses is reached. The system is called the Rotisserie.

An additional capability of the Rotisserie is the ability to randomly assign participants to respond to postings. For example, every student in a class will be required to post an essay in response to a question. After a deadline lapses, those essays are made public. The Rotisserie then assigns to each participant the task of responding to a particular essay. Every student must write an essay. Every essay gets a response. A particularly good or controversial essay might get additional responses. A particularly loudmouthed participant might elect to respond to many essays.

See http://h2o.law.harvard.edu for more information about the Rotisserie, to try it out, or to download the software.

Suppose that your online learning community is more open and fluid. You can't insist that particular people respond at all or that people respond on any kind of schedule. Is there anything that can be done with software to help ensure that all questions get answered appropriately? Yes! Build *server-mediated mentoring*.

Server-mediated mentoring requires, at a minimum, two things: (1) a mechanism for novice members (mentees) to be connected with more experienced members (mentors), and (2) asking people who post questions whether or not their question has been adequately answered. To make the service as effective as possible, you'll probably want to add at least the following: (3) automated reminders from the server to mentors who have left mentees hanging, and (4) rewards, rankings, and distinguishing typography to recognize community members who are answering a lot of questions and mentoring a lot of novices.

Imagine the following interaction:

- Joe Novice, never having kept an aquarium before, visits a local pet store and finds himself attracted to the intelligent colorful fish in the African Cichlid tank.

- Joe Novice, after a Google search, visits world-o-cichlids.org, reads the articles on fish that live in Lake Malawi, and finds that it raises additional questions, which he posts in the discussion forum.

- Lured by email notifications of replies to his questions, Joe returns to world-o-cichlids.org to sift through them. As soon as Joe logs in, his "workspace" page shows all of the questions that he has asked, all of which are initially marked "open." Having some difficulty sorting out conflicting responses, Joe clicks on the "get a mentor page," explaining that he is a complete beginner with the goal of keeping African Cichlids.

- Jane Experienced visits the "be a mentor page" and browsing through the requests sees that most people asking for help want to keep South American Cichlids, with which she has no experience. However, Jane has had an African tank for five years and feels confident that she can help Joe. She agrees to mentor Joe.

- Jane's "workspace" page now contains a subsection relating to her mentoring of Joe and lists his currently open questions. Jane clicks on a question title and, seeing that none of the current responses are truly adequate, posts her own authoritative answer.

- A week later Joe returns to world-o-cichlids.org and finds that his list of "open" questions has gotten quite long and that in fact many of these questions are no longer relevant for him. He clicks on the "close" button next to a question, and the server asks him "Which of the responses actually answered the question for you." Joe clicks on a response from Ned Malawinut, and the database records (1) that the question has been adequately answered and should no longer appear in a mentor's workspace, and (2) that Ned Malawinut has contributed an answer that was seen as useful by another member.

- Joe has a question that he thinks might be ridiculous and is afraid to try it out on the community at large. When posting he checks the "initially show only to my mentor" option, and the question gets sent via email to Jane and appears in her workspace.

- Jane returns to the server and decides that Joe's question is not so easy to answer. She marks it for release to the general membership.

- Two weeks later Jane gets an email from the world-o-cichlids.org server. A summary of some discussion threads that she has been following constitutes the bulk of her email, but right at the top is a note "You haven't logged in for more than a week and Joe, whom you're supposed to be mentoring, has accumulated three questions that haven't been adequately answered after five days." (This prodding mechanism addresses the issue revealed when a large management consulting firm surveyed its employees asking "Whom are you mentoring?" and "Who is mentoring you?" When matching the responses, there was surprisingly little overlap!)

How can you estimate the effort required in building the full user experience example? Start by looking at the number of new tables and columns that you'd be adding to the system and the number of new URLs to which the server would be responding. Then try to find a subsystem that you've already built for this project with a similar number of tables and page scripts. The implementation effort should be comparable.

Let's start with the data model first. To support requests for and assignment of mentors, you'll need at least one table, `mentor_mentee_map` with the following columns: `mentee`, `mentor` (NULL, if not assigned), `date_of_request`, `date_of_assignment`, `mentee_goal`. To support the query "who is the currently connected member mentoring" and build the workspace subsection page for Jane, you'll want to add an index on the `mentor` column. To support the query "are there any mentors who should be notified about a message posted by a member," you would add an index on the `mentee` column. If you were to make this a concatenated index on `mentee, mentor`, it would help the database identify outstanding requests for mentors (`mentor is NULL`) efficiently for the "be a mentor page."

Attempting to support the open/closed question status display and the query "Which members have answered a lot of questions well?" might make you regret some of the data model decisions that you made in the preceding exercises and/or in the "Content Management" chapter exercises. In the "Content Management" chapter, we have a headline asking "What Is Different about Discussion?" above the suggestion that the `content_raw` table can be used to support forum questions and answers. If you went down that route and were implementing the mentoring user experience, this is where discussion would diverge a bit from the rest of the content on the site. You need a way to represent in the database management system whether a discussion forum question is open or closed. If you add a `discussion_forum_question_status` column to the `content_raw` table, you'll have a NULL column value whenever the content item is not a discussion forum question. That's not very clean. You may also be adding a `closed_question_p` boolean column to indicate that a forum posting had been identified by the original questioner as having answered the question. This will be NULL for more than 99 percent of content items. That's not a storage efficiency problem, but it is sort of ugly.

An alternative to adding columns is to build some sort of bag-on-the-side table recording which questions are open and closed and which answers closed them. To decide whether or not this is a reasonable approach, it is worth starting by asking "In what percentage of queries will the helper table need to be JOINed in?" When presenting articles and comments, you wouldn't need the table. When presenting the discussion forum to a public user, that is, someone who wasn't logged in, the discussion forum page scripts wouldn't need the table data. You might need these data only when serving workspace pages to members and when serving an individual discussion forum thread to a logged-in member. It might be worth considering a table of the following form:

```
-- content_id is the primary key here; it is possible to have at most
-- one row in this table for a row in the content_raw table

create table discussion_question_status (
        content_id    not null primary key references content_raw,
        status        varchar(10) check (status in ('open', 'closed')),
        -- if the question is closed the next column will contain
        -- the content_id of the posting that closed it
        closed_by     references content_raw
);

-- make it fast to figure out whether a posting closed a question
create index discussion_question_status_by_closed_by on
discussion_question_status(closed_by);
```

As the community gains experience with this system, it will probably eventually want to give greater prominence to responses from members with a history of writing good answers. In a fully normalized data model, for each answer displayed, the server would have to count up the number of old answers from the author and query the `discussion_question_status` table to figure out what percentage of those were marked as closing the question. In practice, you'd probably want to maintain a denormalized metric as an extra column or columns in the `users` table, perhaps columns for `n_answers_posted` and `n_answers_closing`, counts maintained by nightly batch updates or database triggers.

Supporting the "initially show only to my mentor" option for new content would require the addition of a `show_only_to_mentor` column to the `content_raw` table, where it could be used for discussion forum postings, comments on articles, and any other content item. Rather than changing all of the pages that use the content tables, it would be easier to update the SQL views that those tables use, for example, `articles_approved`, so as to exclude content that should be shown only to a mentor.

Some new page scripts would be required, at least the following:

- /workspace—a page or sidebar providing a logged-in member with links to previously asked questions and possibly other information as well, e.g., new content since last visit, recent content by members previously marked as interesting, etc. A mentor viewing this page would also be offered links to content marked "show only to my mentor" by the author.

- /mentoring/request-form—a page whereby a member can sign up to request a mentor
- /mentoring/request-confirm—a script that processes the preceding form and adds a row to the `mentor_mentee_map` table
- /mentoring/sign-up—a page that shows members who are requesting mentors, with at least the first 200 characters of their request underneath
- /mentoring/request-detail—a click-down page showing more details of a member's request for a mentor
- /mentoring/sign-up-confirm—a script that accepts a member's agreement to serve as a mentor, updating a row in the `mentor_mentee_map` table
- /mentoring/admin/—a page showing summary statistics for the service

Modifications would likely be required to the following pages:

- buttons would be added to the page that shows a discussion forum question-and-answer exchange to "mark this answer as closing the thread," to be displayed only to the user who asked the question and only when the question has not previously been marked as closed
- the page that displays a community member's profile would be augmented with information as to the number of members mentored and the number of question-closing responses submitted

For the purposes of this course, you need not implement all of these grand ideas, and indeed some of them don't make sense when a community is just getting started because the number of members is so small. If, however, some of these ideas strike you as interesting, consider adding them to your project implementation plan.

Exercise 7: Refinement Plan

Prepare a plan for how you're going to improve your discussion forum system, including any changes to data model, page flow, navigation links, page layout, annotation (help text), and so on. Place this plan on your team server at /doc/

`planning/YYYYMMDD-discussion`. (If you name files with year-month-day in the beginning, they will sort in order of creation.)

Exercise 8: Client Signoff

Ask your client to visit the discussion forum user and admin pages. Ask your client to review your usability test results and refinement plan. This is a good chance to impress your client with the soundness of your methodology. If your client responds via email, make that your answer to this exercise. If your client responds orally, make notes from that conversation your answer.

Exercise 9: Execute

After consultation with your teaching assistant, execute your planned improvements.

Time and Motion

One programmer who has mastered the basics of Web/db scripting can usually whip out a basic question-and-answer forum in 8 hours. The team together will need to spend about one hour preparing a good in-class presentation. The team together will generally require 3 hours to conduct and write up the user test. Talking to the client and refining the forum will generally take at least as long as the initial development effort.

9   Adding Mobile Users to Your Community

Among the principles of sustainable online community in the "Planning" chapter of this textbook, notice that the following are not mentioned:

7. means of waiting for machines to boot up
8. means of chaining users to their desks
9. means of producing repetitive strain injury

Though the alternatives vary in popularity from country to country as we write this chapter (February 2005), there is no reason to believe that desktop computer programs such as Mozilla Firefox and Microsoft Internet Explorer are the best way of participating in online communities.

In this chapter you'll learn how to open your community to users connecting from small mobile devices.

Be the User

If you were to close your eyes and visualize a person participating in your community, what would this participation look like? The users you've considered thus far would probably be sitting at a desk with their hands keyboarding sixty words per minute and their gazes set upon a twenty-inch screen. By contrast, a mobile user might be walking along a busy street or looking down from a mountain top. Their screen will be a few inches across, and they may be able to type only five or ten words per minute. What kinds of content and means of participation will best suit this class of users?

Exercise 1

Either using your phone or one of the emulators discussed later in this chapter, use the mobile Internet to

- find the weather forecast for your city
- get a stock quote for IBM
- look up "ineluctable" in the dictionary
- order a book from amazon.com (at least up to the final checkout page)
- visit www.photo.net and find the latest question that has been asked

For each task, write down how long it takes you to accomplish the task. Then repeat the tasks with a desktop HTML browser and write down how long each task takes.

Exercise 2

Come up with a list of two or three services from your learning community that will be valuable to mobile users. You may find the following guidelines useful:

- **Timeliness.** A community is sustained by the active participation of its members. Though the members will often be separated in time, anyone who has participated in a heated bulletin board debate, an online auction, or a chat session can appreciate the value of timely interaction. Mobile browsers are particularly well suited to this type of interaction because they allow the user to stay connected in a wide variety of settings.

- **Brevity.** Users with small screens will have a difficult time receiving, reading, and entering large amounts of content.

- **Native applications.** Mobile browsers are commonly bundled with cellular telephones. Until phone companies provide General Packet Radio Service (GPRS) in your users' region, it is impossible to deliver an application that simultaneously uses voice and hypertext. However, it is possible to produce a hypertext document that provides one-click dialing to a publisher-specified phone number.

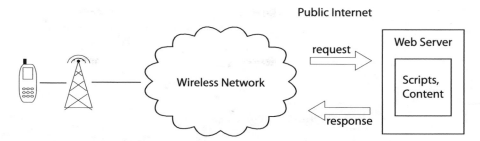

Figure 9.1 Content to mobile devices goes from an HTTP server on the public Internet via TCP/IP and is sometimes translated into proprietary formats and protocols within a phone company's wireless network before reaching the handset.

Standards

Though the bits may be transported through a proprietary network, anyone can serve content to mobile devices with a standard Web server (figure 9.1). As illustrated in figure 9.1, the cell phone connects to your server through the service provider's wireless network. Depending on the phone and network, the "Wireless Network" cloud may contain standard Internet Protocol (IP) routing, a standard HTTP proxy, or a WAP gateway. In the last case, the gateway and phone communicate using a special set of protocols that, among other things, compresses data before transmission over the wireless network. The net effect is that the phone's browser (sometimes called a *microbrowser*) looks to a public HTTP server like a standard Web browser issuing HTTP GETs and POSTs.

The mobile industry is consuming markup languages at a rapid rate. The progression has taken us from the Handheld Device Markup Language (HDML; 1997) to the Wireless Markup Language (WML; 1998) to the current recommendation, XHTML Mobile Profile (XHTML-MP; 2001). We can take heart from the fact that XHTML-MP is derived from XHTML, the World Wide Web Consortion recommendation for standard browsers. Gone are the bad old days when a developer had to learn a new markup language, and servers had to be configured to send new `Content-Type` headers, in order to deliver mobile content. We expect that XHTML-MP will thereby enjoy wider adoption and greater stability.

Content is delivered in "XHTML Mobile Profile," a strict subset of XHTML, which is an XML-conformant version of HTML. Here's a shell session resulting in the return of an XHTML-MP document short enough to print in its entirety:

```
XHTML-MP Example Document

% telnet philip.greenspun.com 80
Trying 216.127.244.134...
Connected to philip.greenspun.com.
Escape character is '^]'.
GET /seia/mobile/ex1.html HTTP/1.0

HTTP/1.0 200 OK
MIME-Version: 1.0
Content-Type: text/html

<?xml version="1.0" encoding="UTF-8"?>
<!DOCTYPE html PUBLIC "-//WAPFORUM//DTD XHTML Mobile 1.0//EN"
    "http://www.wapforum.org/DTD/xhtml-mobile10.dtd">

<html xmlns="http://www.w3.org/1999/xhtml" xml:lang="en">

  <head>
    <title>
     XHTML-MP Example
    </title>
  </head>

  <body>
    <p>We're not in the 1970s anymore.</p>
  </body>

</html>

Connection closed by foreign host.
```

The text in bold (above) is what the programmer types, simulating a micro-browser request. The exchange looks a lot like what we'd see for a regular HTML browser. The main differences are the inclusion of the XML declaration and document-type definition in the first two lines of the document, and the use of the namespace attribute, `xmlns`, in the opening `html` tag.

A server wishing to distinguish between desktop and mobile users could search the contents of the HTTP `Accept` header for the string `application/xhtml+xml; profile="http://www.wapforum.org/xhtml,"` which is supposedly required by the XHTML Mobile Profile specification (http://www.openmobilealliance.org/tech/affiliates/wap/wap-277-xhtmlmp-20011029-a.pdf). By contrast, a desktop browser, if it lists XHTML among the formats that it accepts, will generally not refer to the mobile profile. Here's what Microsoft Internet Explorer 6.0 supplies as an Accept header:

```
image/gif, image/x-xbitmap, image/jpeg, image/pjpeg, application/
vnd.ms-excel, application/vnd.ms-powerpoint, application/msword,
application/x-shockwave-flash, */*
```

Mozilla 1.4a (the open-source Netscape Navigator) does promise to accept XHTML:

```
text/xml,application/xml,application/xhtml+xml,text/html;q=0.9,text/
plain;q=0.8, video/x-mng, image/png, image/jpeg, image/gif; q=0.2,
*/*; q=0.1
```

Note that Mozilla is making full use of the original conception of the Web in which the server and the client would negotiate to provide the user with the best possible file in response to a request for an abstract URL. The order of the MIME types in the Accept header is irrelevant. The browser indicates its preference with *quality values*, for example in the value `text/html;q=0.9`, Mozilla is indicating that plain vanilla HTML is less preferred than the three preceding XML types, which default to a quality of 1.0. To learn more about this system, see the section on "Quality Values" in the HTTP 1.1 specification, at http://www.w3.org/Protocols/rfc2616/rfc2616.html

---

A second method for distinguishing between desktop and microbrowsers is examining the `User-Agent` HTTP header. Consider the following two shell sessions, in which the user-typed input is highlighted in bold:

```
No Extra Headers                        Claiming to be a Palm

% telnet www.google.com 80              % telnet www.google.com 80
Trying 216.239.57.99...                 Trying 216.239.57.99...
Connected to www.google.com.            Connected to www.google.com.
Escape character is '^]'.               Escape character is '^]'.
GET / HTTP/1.1                          GET / HTTP/1.1
                                        User-Agent: UPG1 UP/4.0 (compatible; Blazer 1.0)
HTTP/1.1 200 OK
Date: Tue, 22 Apr 2003 01:20:53 GMT     HTTP/1.1 302 Found
Cache-control: private                  Date: Tue, 22 Apr 2003 01:37:18 GMT
Content-Type: text/html                 Location: http://www.google.com/palm
Server: GWS/2.0                         Content-Type: text/html
Content-length: 2691                    Server: GWS/2.0
                                        Content-length: 156
<html><head>
<meta http-equiv="content-type"         <HTML><HEAD><TITLE>302 Moved</TITLE></HEAD>
  content="text/html; charset=ISO-8859-1">  <BODY>
<title>Google</title><style>...</style>...  <H1>302 Moved</H1>
</head><body>...</body></html>          The document has moved
                                        <A HREF="http://www.google.com/palm">here</A>.
Connection closed by foreign host.      </BODY></HTML>

                                        Connection closed by foreign host.
```

Though neither request indicates a preferred media type, Google's server recognizes the "Blazer" browser that ships with Handspring palm-top devices and redirects the browser, via the response lines HTTP/1.1 302 Found and Location: http://www.google.com/palm. Sadly, there is no centrally maintained registry of user agents, and therefore success with this method is largely a matter of programmer diligence.

Exercise 3

Summary   Paste the XHTML-MP example document above, starting with the <?xml...> declaration and running through the closing </html> tag, into a file called ex1.html on your Web server and load the example into different kinds of browsers. We recommend that you place this file in a /mbl/ subdirectory underneath your Web server's page root.

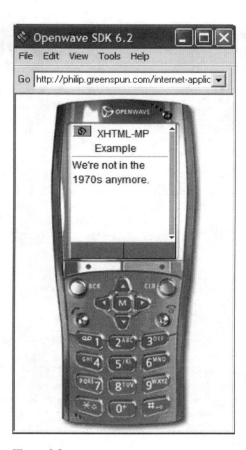

Figure 9.2

Step 1—mobile browser   Load the page into a mobile browser and admire your handiwork. If you do not have access to a Web-enabled phone, install or locate emulator software, either a PC microbrowser emulator or Web-based tool. See the links at the end of this chapter for suggestions. Suppose for a moment that you had placed the document at `/mbl/software-engineering-for-internet-applications/examples/example1.html`. Would that affect the amount of time required to complete this exercise?

Step 2—desktop browser   Now load the page into your favorite desktop browser program. Marvel at the cross-browser compatibility of your document. Compare your subjective experience of the content in the two cases, then answer the following question: In a world where desktop browsers and mobile browsers can parse the same markup syntax, do we need to distinguish between the two, or can we serve the same document to every type of user?

Keypad Hyperlinks

Let's look at a page with hyperlinks:

```
<?xml version="1.0" encoding="UTF-8"?>
<!DOCTYPE html PUBLIC "-//WAPFORUM//DTD XHTML Mobile 1.0//EN"
    "http://www.wapforum.org/DTD/xhtml-mobile10.dtd">

<html xmlns="http://www.w3.org/1999/xhtml" xml:lang="en">

  <head>
    <title>
     Student Life
    </title>
  </head>
  <body>
    <ol>
      <li><a href="calendar" accesskey="1">Calendar</a></li>
      <li><a href="/academics/grades" accesskey="2">Grades</a></li>
      <li><a href="urgent-messages" accesskey="3">Urgent Messages</a></li>
      <li><a href="events/frat-parties" accesskey="4">Fraternity Parties</a></li>
      <li><a href="http://news.google.com/" accesskey="5">News</a></li>
    </ol>
  </body>

</html>
```

A numbered series of choices is presented in a list, with each choice hyperlinked to the appropriate target. We take advantage of the anchor tag's `accesskey` attribute to improve usability by letting the user link to any of the choices with a single keypress.

Exercise 4

Forms and server-side processing work the same way for mobile browsers as they do for desktop browsers. Write an XHTML-MP document that prompts for an email address (or screen name, if you've decided to ignore the sociolo-

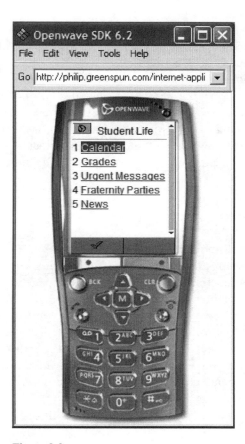

Figure 9.3

gists' advice about anonymity) and password, then POSTs these to a target on your server. The server's response should print back the email address entered and the first character of the password, followed by one period for each subsequent password character. We recommend that you place your code so that it is accessible via URIs starting with "/mbl/."

Exercise 5: Authentication via Cookies

The phones and gateways in the U.S. that we've tried have supported HTTP cookies, including persistent cookies, in the same manner as standard Web browsers, with one exception: a comma in a cookie value breaks everything. (Note that commas are illegal in the strict HTTP specification, but desktop browsers have typically been permissive.)

For authentication via cookies, you need to go back to the form built for Exercise 4 and back it up with a script that generates a `Set-Cookie` header with an authentication token. We recommend that you make this cookie persistent since typing a full email address is pretty painful on a numeric keypad. Note that on an organization's intranet site you can autocomplete the "@foobar .com" or "@yow.org" portion of the email address for most users.

Exercise 6: Linking to a Phone Number

Check http://www.wapforum.org/what/technical.htm and http://developer .openwave.com (requires free registration) for information about the Wireless Telephony Application Interface (WTAI). Write a page entitled "mom.html" that serves a link anchored by the text "Here is a dime; Go call your mother and tell her there are serious doubts as to whether you will become a lawyer." When this link is followed, the telephone should dial your mother's phone number. We apologize for the inappropriate length of this hyperlink anchor, but just in case you end up in an organization where self-esteem is valued more than achievement, we thought it would be good to remind everyone what life is like at Harvard Law School.

Background: *The Paper Chase* (1973, dir. James Bridges).

Exercise 7: Build a Pulse Page

You're walking around and someone expresses skepticism that your online learning community is worthwhile. You whip out your phone and go to the "pulse" page on your server. This returns, in XHTML-MP, the following information:

- the number of new users registered in the last 24 hours and 7 days
- the number of new discussion forum messages in the last 24 hours and 7 days
- any other statistics that you, as the site owner, find interesting

Exercise 8: Design and Build the Mobile Interface to your Community

Now that you've mastered the fundamentals, design and build the mobile interface to your community. Keep in mind that

- Phones and emulators may behave differently.
- Microbrowsers are not nearly as forgiving as desktop browsers such as Internet Explorer; 100 percent correct syntax is required.
- Real phones may be unable to load pages from servers running on nonstandard ports.

The mobile interface should be accessible to the mobile user who types only the hostname of your site, that is, the user should not have to type in the "/mbl/" subdirectory. This is typically accomplished by an IF statement in the top-level script of your Web server's page root.

This is a good opportunity to be creative. Browsing from a phone can be slow, expensive, and painful. Every line of information has to be critically important to the user. Here are a few ideas to get you started:

- someone who has asked a question in an online community will be very interested in new answers to that question
- in a small community, a simple list of users and their phone numbers that can be dialed with one keypress from a mobile browser might be very useful

Exercise 9: Client Signoff

Mobile interfaces are a little too outré for many clients, and thus you can't ask them for ideas without first showing them something that works and that is relevant to their users. Show your mobile interface to the client, ideally in a face-to-face meeting where you use a real phone. If you can't arrange that, have a face-to-face meeting where you use an emulator. If that isn't practical, try to work through the interface in a conference call, during which the client uses either a phone or an emulator.

Write down the client's answers to the following questions:

- How useful do you think the mobile interface that you just saw will be?

- What extra information should we make available to mobile users?

- What are the most crucial tasks that users would like to be able to accomplish from their phones?

Watch for Opportunities to Push

Thus far we've considered the synchronous request/response model, brought over to mobile devices from the world of desktop Web surfing. In another common form of communication, the user receives asynchronously from a server robot or a fellow community member. Desktop users will recognize email alerts and instant messaging as applications of this mode. Two key requirements for asynchronous, user-bound communication are (a) the user must be addressable, for example, by an email address or a screen name, and (b) the user must be running software that is listening on their behalf, for example, a mail server or an instant messaging client. These capabilities are known collectively as *push* to the wireless industry.

Depending on the user's wireless service provider, there may be opportunities to push text or multimedia messages out to your user as interesting events unfold within your community. Many mobile phones, for example, can receive short text messages through the email system. The phone's "email address" is formed by appending a provider-specific domain to the phone's voice number. So if John's Verizon Wireless phone number is 617-555-1212, we can alert him by sending email to 6175551212@vtext.com.

The Future

In most countries the mobile Internet has not lived up to expectations of wide success. The standout exception is the i-mode system, which has become the dominant means of Internet access in Japan. We think that two reasons explain i-mode's relative success: always-on connectivity and revenue opportunities for publishers.

Western mobile Internet systems typically involved a dialup and sign-on delay of as long as two minutes for the first page; with the always-on i-mode system, the user gets consistent performance and relatively quick results for initial requests. Early Western mobile systems charged per minute, which was painful for users who typed text slowly on numeric keypads and received pages at 9800 baud. Always-on systems such as i-mode tend to charge a per-byte or flat per-month rate for access, which greatly reduces the possibility of a huge end-of-month bill.

In most mobile Internet systems, the phone company decides what sites are going to be interesting to users and places them on a set of default bookmarks. The phone company often charges the site publisher to be promoted to its customers. The result? Every early system in the United States made it easy to connect to amazon.com and shop for books, which turned out not to be a popular activity. DoCoMo, the Japanese company that runs the i-mode service, took a different approach. DoCoMo decided that they weren't creative enough to figure out what consumers would want out of the mobile Internet. They therefore came up with a system in which content providers are more or less equally available. Content providers can earn revenue via banner advertisements or by charging for premium content. When a provider wants to charge, DoCoMo handles the payment, taking a 5–9 percent commission.

The combination of always on and non-starvation for content providers created an explosion of creativity on the part of publishers. The most popular services seem to be those that connect people with other people, rather than business-to-consumer amazon.com-style e-commerce.

Is there hope that the mobile Internet will eventually become as popular as i-mode is in Japan? The first ray of hope was provided by General Packet Radio Service (GPRS). GPRS takes advantage of lulls in voice traffic within a cell to deliver a theoretically maximum of 160Kbits/second via unused frequencies at any particular moment. GPRS requires new handsets that are equipped to listen simultaneously on both the dedicated circuit-switched connection in use for a voice call and also monitor GPRS frequencies for incoming packets. In practice, GPRS may provide only three or four times faster throughput than existing WAP systems. More important is the fact that GPRS can, in theory, deliver an "always-on" experience similar to that of i-mode or a hardwired desktop computer.

As noted above, with GPRS the wireless Internet will become a place that supports simultaneous voice and text interaction. For example, the following scenario can be realized:

- User dials an airline phone number
- *Airline:* "Please speak your departure city"
- *User:* "London"

- *Airline:*   "Please speak your destination city"
- *User:*   "Paris"
- *Airline:*   sends a WAP document via GPRS to the user's phone, listing alternative flights
- *User:*   scrolls through the WAP document, scanning with eyes the flight times and prices, and picks with the phone keypad the desired flight
- ...

Notice that voice prompting and recognition are convenient when a user is choosing from among hundreds of alternatives, for example, the world's airports. However, voice becomes agonizing if the user must listen to a long list of detailed choices—prompting with text may be much better when more than two or three choices are available, especially if each choice requires elaborate specification. Keep in mind "The Magical Number Seven, Plus or Minus Two: Some Limits on Our Capacity for Processing Information" by George A. Miller (*Psychological Review* 63 [1956]: 81–97, http://www.well.com/user/smalin/miller.html).

There is no evidence that the phone companies outside Japan will wise up to the power of revenue sharing. However, with the introduction of GPRS the wireless Internet will become something better than a novelty. For more on the subject of GPRS, see Peter Rysavy, "Emerging Technology: Clear Signals for General Packet Radio Service," *Network Magazine*, December 2000 (http://www.rysavy.com/Articles/GPRS2/gprs2.html).

More

Standards information:

- http://www.openmobilealliance.org—Open Mobile Alliance, the standards-making body for mobile computing
- http://www.wapforum.org/what/technical.htm—Legacy site for the WAP Forum, a predecessor of the Open Mobile Alliance. Much of the WAP technical documentation, including the XHTML-MP, WTAI, and WAP architecture specifications reside here.
- http://www.w3.org/TR/css-mobile—CSS Mobile Profile 1.0 specification, for controlling the display style of XHTML-MP documents

Software development kits ("SDKs") and WAP-enabled browsers are available from

- http://developer.openwave.com/—Openwave Developer Website (requires free registration)
- http://www.forum.nokia.com/main.html—Nokia Website, in the WAP Developer Forum area (requires free registration)
- http://www.ericsson.com/mobilityworld/sub/open/index.html—Ericcson Developer's Zone (requires free registration)
- http://www.gelon.net/—Gelon WAPalizer, can be run through your browser.

General Packet Radio Service (GPRS):

- http://www.rysavy.com/Articles/GPRS2/gprs2.html

The old WML standard:

- the previous version of this chapter at http://philip.greenspun.com/seia/mobile/index-old

Time and Motion

Each member of the team should work through the basics, Exercises 1–6, individually and expect to spend roughly five hours doing so.

The team should plan to spend one to two hours together designing the mobile interface, but may divide the work of prototyping and refining the mobile interface. A reasonable scope is eight to twelve programmer-hours.

The time required for client signoff will vary depending on the client's level of interest and familiarity with the mobile Web. Plan to spend at least thirty minutes on the signoff.

10   Voice (VoiceXML)

In every computing era, programmers have been responsible for writing the fundamental application logic. During the desktop application era (1980s), the attention given to this logic was generally dwarfed by that given to the user interface, event handling, and graphics code that a programming team needed to write to get a computer program into the hands of users. Result: very little innovation at the individual level; most widely used computer programs were written by large companies.

During the Web era (1990s), the user interface and graphics were rendered by the Web browser, for example, Netscape Navigator or Microsoft Internet Explorer. Programmers were able to deliver a complete system to end-users after writing only the application logic and some simple HTML specifying the user interface behavior. Result: a revolution in innovation, with most Web applications written in a few months by a handful of people.

Suppose that you'd observed that telephones are much more common and portable than personal computers and Web browsers. Furthermore, you'd noticed that telephones are able to be used by almost everyone, whereas many consumers have little patience for the complexities of the PC. Thus, you'd want to make your information system accessible to a user with only a telephone. How would you have done it? In the 1980s, you'd rent a telephone line, buy a big specialized box to recognize utterances, buy another specialized box to talk to the user, and park those boxes right next to the main server for your application. In the 1990s, you'd have had to rent a telephone line, buy specialized software, and park a standard computer running that software next to the server running your application. Result in both decades: very little innovation, with only the largest organizations offering voice/telephone interfaces to their information systems.

With the advent of today's *voice browsers,* the coming years promise to be a period of tremendous innovation in the development of telephone-accessible Internet applications. With a Web application, you operate the HTTP server and run the application code; someone else runs the browser. The idea of the voice browser is the same. You operate a server and the application. Someone else, perhaps the phone company, runs the telephone lines and voice browser.

Bottom line: voice browsers allow you to build telephone voice applications with nothing more than an HTTP server. From this, great innovation shall spring.

Illustration

Suppose Tracy, a vice president at a Boston-based firm, has just flown into Los Angeles. She wants to know the telephone number and address of her company's Los Angeles office, as well as the direct number for one of the employees. Since her company intranet is not telephone-accessible, she has to call up her assistant and ask him to open up a Web browser to look up the information in the intranet.

With VoiceXML, it can take as little as a few hours for a developer to take virtually any information available on the Web and make it available by telephone—not just to callers with high-tech cellphones, but to anyone with *any* kind of telephone. Tracy would be able to dial a number and say which office or employee she is looking for. After searching through some of the intranet's database tables, the VoiceXML application can read aloud the phone numbers and addresses she wants. And next time Tracy arrives confused in a foreign city, she won't have to rely on her assistant being at his desk.

What Is VoiceXML?

VoiceXML, or VXML, is a markup language like HTML. The difference: HTML is rendered by your Web browser to format content and user-input forms; VoiceXML is rendered by a voice browser. Your application can speak to the user via synthesized speech or by prerecorded audio files. Your software can receive input from the user via speech or by the tones from their telephone keypad. If you've ever built a Web application, you're ready to get started with your phone application.

How to Make Your Content Telephone-Accessible

As in the old days, you can still rent a telephone line and run commercial voice recognition software and text-to-speech (TTS) conversion software. However, the most interesting aspect of the VoiceXML revolution is that you need not actually do so. There are free VoiceXML gateways, such as BeVocal (http://www.bevocal.com), Voxeo (http://www.voxeo.com), and VoiceGenie (http://www.voicegenie.com). These take VoiceXML pages from your Web server and read them to your user. If your application needs input from the user, the gateway will interpret the incoming response and pass that response to your server in a way that your software can understand.

You use a Web form to configure the gateway with the URL of your application, and it will associate a telephone number with it. Users can just dial your assigned telephone number from a regular telephone to talk to your application.

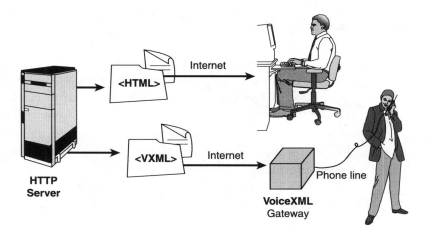

Figure 10.1   HTML: Publisher owns the HTTP server, which uses HTML to specify a user experience that is rendered on the reader's desktop computer. VoiceXML: Publishers owns the HTTP server, which uses VoiceXML to specify a user experience that is rendered on a third-party gateway system and delivered as audio to the user's telephone.

Exercise 1

Use Tellme (1-800-555-TELL) to

- get driving directions between two bastions of higher education: Caltech (1201 East California Boulevard, Pasadena, Calif.) and Pasadena City College (1570 East Colorado Boulevard, Pasadena, Calif.)
- find the latest price for a share of stock in Oracle Corporation
- listen to your horoscope
- listen to today's top news stories

Record the amount of time required to complete the first three tasks.

Exercise 2

Come up with a list of two or three services from your learning community that will be valuable to telephone users. You may find the following guidelines useful:

- It is difficult for users to log on. With voice applications, entering a username is even more tedious and error prone than with mobile applications. You may want to restrict your voice services to ones that can be accessed by the entire community and not just registered users. An alternative to the standard username/password authentication is to assign a numeric user_id and pin to each registered user, but that makes it more cumbersome to do Web/mobile/phone services all in one.
- It is easy to give information to the user, but it is hard for them to give information back to your service. It is typically practical for them to pick options from a menu, but impractical for them to provide any meaningful unstructured data.

A positive development in this area is that a number of voice gateways (e.g., Voice-Genie, www.voicegenie.com) are now partnering with providers of biometric voice authentication software such as VoiceTrust (www.voice-trust.com/) and Vocent (www.vocent.com).

VoiceXML Basics

The format of a VoiceXML document is simple. Here's how to say "Hello, World" to your visitors:

```
<?xml version="1.0"?>
<vxml version="2.0">
  <form>
    <block>
       <audio>Hello, World</audio>
    </block>
  </form>
</vxml>
```

The first tag, `<?xml version="1.0"?>`, specifies that the document to follow conforms to the XML 1.0 standard. All VoiceXML documents follow this standard.

As in any XML document, every opening tag (e.g., `<vxml>`) has to be closed, either with a closing tag like `</vxml>`, or with a slash (/) at the end of the tag, as in the `<else/>` tag in the next example. The other important rule to remember is that all attribute values must be enclosed in quotation marks, as in `version="2.0"`. XML is much stricter than HTML in these two regards.

The `<vxml version="2.0">` tag specifies that this is a VoiceXML 2.0 document. Within that is a `<form>`, which can either be an interactive element—requesting input from the user—or informational. You can have as many forms as you want within a VoiceXML document. A `<block>` is a container for your executables, meaning that all your tags that make your application *do* something, such as `<audio>`, `<goto>`, and a variety of others, can be clumped together inside of a block. `<audio>text</audio>` will read the text with a TTS converter, whereas `<audio src="wav_file_URL"/>` will play a prerecorded .wav audio file.

Exercise 3

Sign up for a developer account at one of the VoiceXML gateways (see the list at the end of this chapter). All of the gateways have free developer accounts and many useful services for developers. We prefer BeVocal for its extensive documentation and the plethora of tools it provides, including: a syntax checker; a Web-based emulator so that you can do some of your testing on your PC without using a telephone; an on-line debugger; a log of calls, including error messages, variable values, and even recordings of the actual user utterances; a library of grammars and code that you can use; and more. However, all of the gateways have their own strengths and weaknesses, so use the one you like the best; there is no wrong choice.

The gateway will assign you a telephone number or extension that you can point to your Web server. Point it to a file called hello-world.vxml that contains the VoiceXML example above. This example should work with most gateways, but each gateway employs slightly different VoiceXML syntax, so glance over the online documentation provided for the gateway you choose.

More VoiceXML

Here's an example that accepts user input and behaves differently depending on what the user says:

```
<?xml version="1.0"?>
<vxml version="2.0">
  <form id="animal_questionnaire">
    <field name="favorite_animal">
      <prompt>
        <audio>Which do you like better, dogs or cats?</audio>
      </prompt>
      <grammar>
      <![CDATA[
          [
            [dog dogs] {<option "dogs">}
            [cat cats] {<option "cats">}
          ]
        ]]>
      </grammar>
      <!-- if the user gave a valid response, the filled block
           is executed. -->
      <filled>
        <if cond="favorite_animal == 'dogs'">
          <!-- this would take the user to a form called
               popular_dog_facts within the same VoiceXML
               document -->
          <goto next="#popular_dog_facts"/>
```

```
            <else/>
                <!-- this expression is an EMCAScript (JavaScript)
                     expression, composed of a concatenated string
                     and variable; this will take the user to the
                     URI psychological_evaluation.cgi?affliction=cats
                -->
                <goto expr="'psychological_evaluation.cgi?affliction='
                     + favorite_animal"/>
            </if>
        </filled>
        <!-- if the user responded but it didn't match the
             grammar, the nomatch block is executed -->
        <nomatch>
            I'm sorry, I didn't understand what you said.
            <reprompt/>
        </nomatch>
        <!-- if there is no response for a few seconds, the
             noinput block is executed -->
        <noinput>
            I'm sorry, I didn't hear you.
            <reprompt/>
        </noinput>
    </field>
  </form>
  <!-- additional forms can go here -->
</vxml>
```

In this example, we:

- ask the caller whether they prefer dogs or cats
- listen for a response
- redirect the caller to another location based on the response

The structure of the VoiceXML code in this example is basically identical to that of the "Hello, World" example, with a few additional elements. The top two lines are present in every VoiceXML 2.0 document. Next, we have a form; this time the form is named, as we must do if we are to have more than one form in a document.

We created a variable called `favorite_animal` using the `<field>` tag. After we've prompted the user for a response, we have to specify what the user is allowed to answer by defining a grammar. You'll find that various gateways tend to use different grammar formats. The grammar in this example is in the

GSL (Nuance's Grammar Specification Language) format, which is used by Tellme and BeVocal, among others. The grammar above specifies that if the user says "dog" or "dogs," the value of `favorite_animal` becomes "dogs." If they respond "cat" or "cats," `favorite_animal` will be set to "cats."

Note on Grammars

In VoiceXML 1.0, the W3C did not specify the grammar format, allowing each Voice-XML platform to implement grammars as they chose. In VoiceXML 2.0, each platform is required to implement the XML format of the W3C's Speech Recognition Grammar Format (SRGF), the latest draft of which is available from http://www.w3.org/TR/grammar-spec/.

In one vendor's implementation, the following SRGF grammar can be used in place of the grammar in the example:

```
<grammar xml:lang="en-US"
type="application/srgs+xml" version="1.0">
  <rule id="animal" scope="public">
    <one-of>
      <item>
        <one-of tag="dogs">
          <item>dog</item>
          <item>dogs</item>
        </one-of>
      </item>
      <item>
        <one-of tag="cats">
          <item>cat</item>
          <item>cats</item>
        </one-of>
      </item>
    </one-of>
  </rule>
</grammar>
```

However, other vendors have implemented the SRGF slightly differently. As the SRGF specification graduates from a "candidate recommendation," vendors' implementations of SRGF should converge.

That's all there is to getting user input. Now we can use the value of their response in our program. In this example, if their answer is "dogs," they will be sent to a form named "popular_dog_facts" within the same Voice-XML document. If they answer "cats," they will be sent to a different URL, `psychological_evaluation.cgi?affliction=cats`. Note how we used a JavaScript expression in the goto tag in order to use the value of the `favorite_animal` variable.

Those two examples are enough to give you the gist of VoiceXML and hopefully an appreciation for the simplicity of voice application development using VoiceXML.

Excellent tutorial and reference material can be found on the developer sites at Tellme (http://studio.tellme.com/) and BeVocal (http://cafe.bevocal.com/).

Exercise 4: Grammar Accuracy

Create a simple page that asks the user to name a city in Canada. Start out with a small grammar, for example:

```
[vancouver toronto halifax] {<option "valid_city">}
```

Your application should respond to the user with something like "Yes, that is a Canadian city" or "I've never heard of that city."

Try out your application. Name some cities that are not on your list and see if it mistakenly thinks they are valid cities. Now add some more cities to your list (e.g., Calgary, Winnipeg, Victoria, Saskatoon). As you make your list longer and longer, you'll tend to start getting a few false positives.

Decide on a rule of thumb for how many elements it's reasonable to have in one grammar.

There are applications that have thousands of elements in a grammar. However, they've typically gone through a process of grammar tuning using representative probabilities for grammar matches. For this exercise, just extend the standard grammar above.

Exercise 5: What's New and Who's New

Add voice-accessible "what's new" and "who's new" features to your community. A user should be able to call up and hear the most recent five contributions by other community members and the names of the last five people who registered.

Consider that if you're authenticating users over the phone, the contributions that might be most interesting are any new responses to questions asked by that user.

Exercise 6: Content Approval/Rejection by Telephone

Many Web sites have user-created content that must be approved by an administrator or moderator before it becomes live on the site. Examples are the product reviews at amazon.com, article submissions at slashdot.org, and bulletin board postings in a moderated forum.

Typically you'd open your Web browser, log in, and go to an admin page from which you can approve, reject, or edit submissions.

But it sure would be nice to approve and reject submissions with your cellphone when you're out walking the dog. (Editing is harder to do by phone, but it's less common anyway, so it can wait until you're back at your desk.)

Create some simple voice-accessible admin pages. Since the typical username/password authentication is so tedious, you might want to make them accessible with just a numeric pin. Note that it isn't ideal in general to protect a set of pages with just one pin because that makes it harder to delegate/revoke admin privileges later, but it will do for this exercise.

Exercise 7: Implement Some Real Services

Depending on the complexity of the services you came up with in Exercise 2, implement one or two or three of them. If you implement more than one, you may wish to create a voice service menu as the entry point for all your voice users.

Exercise 8: Client Signoff

As with mobile browser interfaces, a voice interface is tough for most people to think about until they've actually used one. Try to sit down with your client face-to-face and observe them going through all the nooks and crannies of your VoiceXML interface. If that isn't practical, email your client explicit instructions and then follow up with a phone call.

Write down the client's answers to the following questions:

- How useful do you think the voice interface that you just tried will be?

- What extra information should we make available via voice?

- What are the most crucial tasks that users would like to be able to accomplish from a standard phone using only touch tones and voice?

Mobile versus Voice Applications

Mobile text browsers and VoiceXML each have strengths and weaknesses and are therefore appropriate for different applications—or for different parts of the same application (see fig. 10.2). One way to take advantage of the best of mobile and voice interfaces will be to develop multi-modal applications like the GPRS airline reservation system in the last chapter. A number of groups are actively developing specifications for multi-modal applications, including the Speech Application Language Tags (SALT) Forum (http://www.saltforum .org/).

Mobile Browser	VoiceXML
requires browser-enhanced telephones	can be used with any phone
user-input with uncomfortable keypads	speech or keypad input
works well in noisy environments	hard to use in noisy environments
you need to develop versions of your software for a variety of mobile gateways	you only need to develop one version of your software
works well for displaying long lists of information	works poorly for giving the user long lists of information
user can enter arbitrary information	user can only say predefined phrases

Figure 10.2

Beyond VoiceXML: Conversational Speech

Will all voice applications be VoiceXML applications? The current syntax of VoiceXML is geared to producing a user experience of navigating through hierarchical menus. State-of-the-art research is moving beyond this towards conversational systems in which any utterance makes sense at any time and where context is carried from exchange to exchange. For example, you can call the MIT Laboratory for Computer Science's server at 1-888-573-8255:

You   Will it rain tomorrow in Boston?

JUPITER   To my knowledge, the forecast calls for no rain tomorrow in Boston.

You   What about Detroit?

JUPITER   To my knowledge, the forecast calls for no rain tomorrow in Detroit.

You   Are there any floods in the United States?

JUPITER   Flood warnings have been issued for Louisiana and Mississippi.

You   Will it be sunny in Phoenix?

. . .

Notice how the system, more fully described at http://groups.csail.mit.edu/sls/applications/jupiter.shtml, assumed that you were still interested in rain when asking about Detroit, context carried over from the Boston question.

In the long run, as these more natural conversational technologies are perfected, the syntax of VoiceXML will have to grow to accommodate the full power of speech interpreters or be eclipsed by another standard.

More

VoiceXML gateways:

- Voxeo (http://www.voxeo.com/)
- BeVocal Cafe (http://cafe.bevocal.com/)
- Tellme (http://studio.tellme.com/)
- VoiceGenie (http://developer.voicegenie.com/)

- HeyAnita Freespeech (http://freespeech.heyanita.com/)

Related links:

- VoiceXML Forum (http://www.voicexml.org/)
- Voice articles at developer.com (http://www.developer.com/voice/)
- Specifications and news from the Web Consortium, http://www.w3.org/Voice/. Notably interesting specs at press time include
  - Voice Extensible Markup Language (VoiceXML) Specification Version 2.0 (http://www.w3.org/TR/voicexml20/)
  - Speech Recognition Grammar Specification Version 1.0 (http://www.w3.org/TR/grammar-spec/)
- source code and case studies from an earlier version of this article, "VoiceXML: Letting People Talk to Your HTTP Server through the Telephone", available at http://eveandersson.com/arsdigita/asj/vxml

Time and Motion

Each member of the team should work through the basics, Exercises 1–4, individually and expect to spend two to three hours.

The team should plan to spend one to two hours together designing the voice interface, but may divide the work of prototyping and refining the voice interface plus Exercises 5 and 6. A reasonable scope is eight to twelve programmer-hours.

The time required for client signoff will vary depending on the client's level of interest. Plan to spend at least thirty minutes on the signoff.

11   Scaling Gracefully

Let's look again at the passage from *A Pattern Language* (Christopher Alexander, Sara Ishikawa, and Murray Silverstein [Oxford Univ. Press, 1977]), quoted in the "Planning" chapter:

It is not hard to see why the government of a region becomes less and less manageable with size. In a population of N persons, there are of the order of N^2 person-to-person links needed to keep channels of communication open. Naturally, when N goes beyond a certain limit, the channels of communication needed for democracy and justice and information are simply too clogged, and too complex; bureaucracy overwhelms human process. . . .

    We believe the limits are reached when the population of a region reaches some 2 to 10 million. Beyond this size, people become remote from the large-scale processes of government. Our estimate may seem extraordinary in the light of modern history: the nation-states have grown mightily and their governments hold power over tens of millions, sometimes hundreds of millions, of people. But these huge powers cannot claim to have a natural size. They cannot claim to have struck the balance between the needs of towns and communities, and the needs of the world community as a whole. Indeed, their tendency has been to override local needs and repress local culture, and at the same time aggrandize themselves to the point where they are out of reach, their power barely conceivable to the average citizen.

Let's also remind ourselves of the empirical evidence that enormous online communities cannot satisfy every need. America Online has not subsumed all the smaller communities on the Internet. People unsubscribe from mailing lists when the traffic level becomes too high. Early adopters of USENET discussion groups (called "NetNews" or "Newsgroups" back in the 1970s and "Google Groups" to most people in 2005) stopped participating because they found the utility of the groups diminished when the community size grew beyond a certain point.

    So the good news is that, no matter how large one's competitors, there will always be room for a new online community. The bad news is that growth results in significant engineering challenges. Some of the challenges boil down to simple performance engineering: How can one divide the load of supporting an Internet application among multiple CPUs and disk drives? These can typically be solved with money, even in the absence of any cleverness. The deeper challenges cannot be solved with money and hardware. Consider, for example, the following questions:

- How can 100,000 people hold a conversation?
- How can an online learning community support 50,000 people with 50,000 different levels of passion for the topic and for participation?
- What is the electronic analog of keeping in touch with one's neighbors? With one's friends?

In this chapter we will first consider the straightforward hardware and software issues, then move on to the more subtle challenges that grow progressively more difficult as the user community expands.

Tasks in the Engine Room

Here are the fundamental tasks that are happening on the servers of virtually every interactive Internet application:

- transport-layer encryption (SSL, if the site has secure HTTPS pages)
- HTTP service
- presentation layer (page composition; script execution)
- abstraction provision (sometimes called "business logic"; any layer of code on top of the raw database where each procedure is used by more than one page)
- persistence

At a modestly visited site, it would be possible to have one CPU performing all of these tasks. In fact, for ease of maintenance and reliability it is best to have as few and as simple servers as possible. Consider your desktop PC, for example. How long has it been since the hardware failed? If you look into a room with 50 simple PCs or single-board workstations, how often do you see one that is unavailable due to hardware failure? Suppose, however, that you combine computers to support your application. If one machine is 99 percent reliable, a site that depends on 10 such machines will be only 0.99^{10} reliable or 90 percent. The probability analysis here is the same as flipping coins, but with a heavy 0.99 bias towards heads. You need to get 10 heads in a row in order to have a working service. What if you needed 100 machines to be up and running? That's only going to happen 0.99^{100}th of the time, or roughly 37 percent.

It isn't challenging to throw hardware at a performance problem. What is challenging is setting up that hardware so that the service is working if *any* of the components are operational rather than only if *all* of the components are operational.

We'll examine each layer individually.

Persistence Layer

For most interactive Web applications, the persistence layer is a relational database management system (RDBMS). The RDBMS server program is parsing SQL queries, writing transactions to the disk, rooting around on the disk(s) for seldom-used data, gluing together data in RAM, and returning it to the RDBMS client program. The average engineer's top-of-the-head viewpoint is that RDBMS performance is limited by the speed of the disk(s). The programmers at Oracle disagree: "A properly configured Oracle server will run CPU-bound."

Suppose that we have a popular application and need 16 CPUs to support all the database queries. And let's further suppose that we've decided that the RDBMS will run all by itself on one or more physical computers. Should we buy 16 small computers, each with one CPU, or one big computer with 16 CPUs inside? The local computer shop sells 1-CPU PCs for about $500, implying a total cost of $8,000 for 16 CPUs. If we visit the Web site for Sun Microsystems (www.sun.com) we find that the price of a 16-CPU Sunfire 6800 is too high even to list, but if the past is any guide we won't get away for less than $200,000. We will pay 25 times as much to get 16 CPUs of the same power, but all inside one physical computer.

Why would anyone do this?

Let's consider the peculiarities of the RDBMS application. The RDBMS server talks to multiple clients simultaneously. If Client A updates a record in the database and, a split-second later, Client B requests that record, the RDBMS is required to deliver the updated information to Client B. If we were to spread the RDBMS server program across multiple physical computers, it is possible that Client A would be served from Computer I and Client B would be served from Computer II. A database transaction cannot be committed unless it has been written out to the hard disk drive. Thus all that these computers need do is check the disk for updates before returning any results to Client B. Disk drives are 100,000 times slower than RAM. A single computer running an RDBMS keeps an up-to-date version of the commonly used portions of the database in RAM. So our multi-computer RDBMS server that ensures database coherency across processors via reference to the hard disk will start out 100,000 times slower than a single-computer RDBMS server.

Typical commercial RDBMS products, such as Oracle Parallel Server, work via each computer keeping copies of the database in RAM and informing each other of updates via high-speed communications networks. The machine-to-machine communication can be as simple as a high-speed Ethernet link or as complex as specialized circuit boards and cables that achieve memory bus speeds.

Don't we have the same problem of inter-CPU synchronization with a multi-CPU single box server? Absolutely. CPU I is serving Client A. CPU II is serving Client B. The two CPUs need to apprise each other of database updates. They do this by writing into the multiprocessor machine's shared RAM. It turns out that the CPU-CPU bandwidth available on typical high-end servers circa 2002 is 100 Gbits/second, which is 100 times faster than the fastest available Gigabit Ethernet, FireWire, and other inexpensive machine-to-machine interconnection technologies.

Bottom line: if you need more than one CPU to run the RDBMS, it usually makes most sense to buy all the CPUs in one physical box.

Abstraction Layer

Suppose that you have a complex calculation that must be performed in several different places within a computer program. Most likely you'd encapsulate that calculation into a procedure and then call that procedure from every part of the program where the calculation was required. The benefits of *procedural abstraction* are that you only have to write and debug the calculation code once and that, if the rules change, you can be sure that by updating the single procedure you've updated your entire application.

The abstraction layer is sometimes referred to as "business logic." Something that is complex and fundamental to the business ought to be separated out so that it can be used in multiple places consistently and updated in one place if necessary. Below is an example from an e-commerce system that Eve Andersson wrote. This system offered substantially all of the features of amazon.com circa 1999. Eve expected that a lot of ham-fisted programmers who adopted her open-source creation would be updating the page scripts in order to give their site a unique look and feel. Eve expected that laws and accounting procedures regarding sales tax would change. So she encapsulated the looking up of sales tax by state, the figuring out if that state charges tax on shipping, and the multiplication of tax rate by price into an Oracle PL/SQL function:

```
create or replace function ec_tax
  (v_price IN number, v_shipping IN number, v_order_id IN integer)
return number
IS
        taxes                    ec_sales_tax_by_state%ROWTYPE;
        tax_exempt_p             ec_orders.tax_exempt_p%TYPE;
BEGIN
        SELECT tax_exempt_p INTO tax_exempt_p
        FROM ec_orders
        WHERE order_id = v_order_id;

        IF tax_exempt_p = 't' THEN
                return 0;
        END IF;

        SELECT t.* into taxes
        FROM ec_orders o, ec_addresses a, ec_sales_tax_by_state t
        WHERE o.shipping_address=a.address_id
        AND a.usps_abbrev=t.usps_abbrev(+)
        AND o.order_id=v_order_id;

        IF nvl(taxes.shipping_p,'f') = 'f' THEN
                return nvl(taxes.tax_rate,0) * v_price;
        ELSE
                return nvl(taxes.tax_rate,0) * (v_price + v_shipping);
        END IF;
END;
```

The Web script or other PL/SQL procedure that calls this function need only know the proposed cost of an item, the proposed shipping cost, and the order ID to which this item might be added (these are the three arguments to ec_tax). That sales taxes for each state are stored in the ec_sales_tax_by_state table, for example, is hidden from the rest of the application. If an organization that adopted this software decided to switch to using third-party software for calculating tax, that organization would need to change only this one function rather than wading through hundreds of Web scripts looking for tax-related code.

Should the abstraction layer run on its own physical computer? For most applications, the answer is "no." These procedures are not sufficiently CPU-intensive to make splitting them off onto a separate computer worthwhile in terms of system administration effort and increased vulnerability to hardware failure. What's more, these procedures often do not even warrant a new execution environment. Most procedures in the abstraction layer of an Internet service require intimate access to relational database tables. That access is fastest when the procedures are running inside the RDBMS itself. All modern RDBMSs provide for the execution of standard procedural languages within the database server. This trend was pioneered by Oracle with PL/SQL and then Java. With the latest Microsoft SQL Server, one can supposedly run any .NET-supported computer language inside the database.

When should you consider a separate environment ("application server" process) for the abstraction layer? Suppose that a big bank, the result of several mergers, has an IBM mainframe to manage checking accounts, an Oracle RDBMS for managing credit accounts, and a SQL Server-based customer support system. If Jane Customer phones up the bank and asks to pay her credit card bill from her checking account, a computer program needs to perform a transaction on the mainframe (debit checking), a transaction on the Oracle system (credit Visa card), and a transaction on the SQL Server database (payment handled during a phone call with Agent 451). It is technically possible for, say, a Java program running inside the Oracle RDBMS to connect to these other database management systems, but traditionally this kind of problem has been attacked by a stand-alone "application server," usually a custom-authored C program. The term "application server" has subsequently become used to describe the physical computers on which such a program might run and, in the late 1990s, execution environments for Java or C programs that served some function on a Web site other than page presentation or persistence.

Another example of where a separate physical application server might be desirable is where substantial computation must be performed. On most photo sharing sites, every time a photo is uploaded, the server must create scaled versions in standard sizes. The performance challenge at the orbitz.com travel site is even more serious. Every user request results in the execution of a Lisp program written by MIT Artificial Intelligence Lab alumni at itasoftware.com.

This Lisp program searches through a database of two billion flights and fares. The database machines that are performing transactions such as ticket bookings would collapse if they had to support these searches as well.

If separate physical CPUs are to be employed in the abstraction layer, should they all come in the same box or will it work just as well to rack and stack cheap 1-CPU machines? That rather depends on where state is kept. Remember that HTTP is a stateless protocol. Somewhere the server needs to remember things such as "Registered User 137 wants to see pages in the French language," "Unregistered user who started Session 6781205 has placed the hardcover edition of *The Cichlid Fishes* in his or her shopping cart." In a multi-process multi-computer server farm, it is impossible to guarantee that a particular user will always be returned to the same running computer program, if for no other reason than you want the user experience to be robust to failure of an individual physical computer. If session state is being kept anywhere other than in a cookie or the persistence layer (RDBMS), your application server programs will need to communicate with each other constantly to make sure that their ad hoc database is coherent. In that case, it might make sense to get an expensive multi-CPU machine to support the application server. However, if all the layers are stateless except for the persistence layer, the application server layer can be handled by multiple cheap one-CPU machines. At orbitz.com, for example, racks of cheap computers are loaded with identical local copies of the fare and schedule database. Each time a user clicks to see the options for traveling from New York to London, one of those application server machines is randomly selected for action.

Presentation Layer

Computer programs in the presentation layer pull information from the persistence layer (RDBMS) and merge those results with a template appropriate to the user's preferences and client software. In a Web application these computer programs are doing an SQL query and merging the results with an HTML template for delivery to the user's Web browser. Such a program is so simple that it is often referred to as a "script." You can think of the presentation layer as "where the scripts execute."

The most common place for script execution is within the operating system process occupied by the Web server. In other words, the script language interpreter is built into the Web server. Examples of this architecture are Microsoft

Internet Information Server (IIS) and Active Server Pages, AOLserver and its built-in Tcl interpreter, Apache and the mod_perl add-in. If you've chosen to use one of these popular styles of Web development, you've chosen to merge the presentation layer with the HTTP service layer, and spreading the load among multiple CPUs for one layer will automatically spread it for the other.

The multi-CPU box versus multiple-separate-box decision here should again be based on whether or not the presentation layer holds state. If no session state is held by the running presentation scripts, it is more economical to add CPUs inside separate physical computers.

HTTP Service

HTTP service per se is so simple that it hardly warrants its own layer, unless you're delivering audio and video files to a mass audience. A high performance pure HTTP server program such as Zeus Web Server (see www.zeus.com) can handle more than 6,000 requests per second and saturate a 100 Mbps network link on a single 500 MHz Intel Celeron processor (that 100 Mbps link would cost about $50,000 annually as of February 2005, by the way). Why then would anyone ever need to deploy multiple CPUs to support HTTP service of basic HTML pages with embedded images?

The main reason that people run out of capacity on a single front-end Web server is that HTTP server programs are usually packaged with software to support computationally more expensive layers. For example, the Oracle RDBMS server, capable of supporting the persistence layer and the abstraction layer, also includes the necessary software for interpreting Java Server Pages and performing HTTP service. If you were running a popular service directly from Oracle you'd probably need more than one CPU. More common examples are Web servers such as IIS and AOLserver that are capable of handling the presentation and HTTP service layers from the same operating system process. If your scripts involve a lot of template parsing, it is easy to overload a single CPU with the demands of the Web server/script interpreter.

If no state is being stored in the HTTP Service layer it is cheapest to add CPUs in separate physical boxes. HTTP is stateless and user interaction is entirely mediated by the RDBMS. Therefore there is no reason for a CPU serving a page to User A to want to communicate with a CPU serving a page to User B.

Transport-Layer Encryption

Whenever a Web page is served, two application programs on separate computers have communicated with each other. As discussed in the "Basics" chapter, the client opens a Transmission Control Protocol (TCP) connection to the server, specifies the page desired, and receives the data back over that connection. TCP is one layer up from the basic unreliable Internet Protocol (IP). What TCP adds is reliability: if a packet of data is not acknowledged, it will be retransmitted. Neither TCP nor the IP of the 1990s, IPv4, provides any encryption of the data being transmitted. Thus anyone able to monitor the packets on the local-area network of the server or client or on the backbone routers may be able to learn, for example, the particular pages requested by a particular user. If you were running an online community about a degenerative disease, this might cause one of your users to lose his or her job.

There are two ways to protect your users' privacy from packet sniffers. The first is by using a newer version of Internet Protocol, IPv6, which provides native data security as well as authentication. In the glorious IPv6 world, we can be sure of the origin of a packet, whether it is from a legitimate user or a denial-of-service attacker. In the glorious IPv6 world, we can be sure that it will be impractical to sniff credit card numbers or other user-sensitive data from Web traffic. As of spring 2005, however, it isn't possible to sign up for a home IPv6 connection. Thus we are forced to fall back on the 1990s-style approach of adding a layer between HTTP and TCP. This was pioneered by Netscape Communications as Secure Sockets Layer (SSL) and is now being standardized as TLS 1.0 (see http://www.ietf.org/html.charters/tls-charter.html).

However it is performed, encryption is processor-intensive. On the client side, that's not a big deal. The client machine probably has a 2 GHz processor that is 98 percent idle. However on the server end, performing encryption can tie up a whole CPU per user for the duration of a request.

If you've run out of processing power the only thing to do is ... add processing power. The question is what kind and where. Adding general-purpose processors to a multi-CPU computer is very expensive as mentioned earlier. Adding additional single-CPU front-end servers to a two-tier server farm might not be a bad strategy, especially because, if you're already running a two-tier server farm, it requires no new thinking or system administration skills. It is possible, however, that special-purpose hardware will be more cost-effective or easier to administer. In particular it is possible to do encryption in the router for IPv6. SSL encryption for HTTP connections can be done with plug-in boards, an example of which is the Compaq AXL300 PCI card, available in 2005 for $1,400 and capable (it is claimed) of handling 330 SSL connections per second. Finally it is possible to interpose a hardware encryption machine between the Web server, which communicates via ordinary HTTP, and the client, which makes requests via HTTPS. This feature is, for example, an option on load-balancing routers from F5 Networks (www.f5.com).

Do You Have Enough CPUs?

After reading the preceding sections, you've gone out and gotten some computer hardware. How do you know whether or not it will be adequate to support the expected volume of requests? A good rule of thumb is that you can't handle more than 10 requests for dynamic pages per second per CPU. A "dynamic" page is one that involves the execution of any computer program on the server side other than simple HTTP service, that is, anything other than sending a JPEG or HTML file. The 10-per-second figure assumes either that the pages are not encrypted or that the encryption is done by additional hardware in front of the HTTP server. For example, if you have a 4-CPU RDBMS server handling persistence and abstraction and 4 1-CPU front-end machines handling presentation and HTTP service, you shouldn't expect to deliver more than 80 dynamic pages per second.

You might ask what CPU speed is this 10 hits per second per CPU number based upon? The number is independent of CPU speed! In the mid-1990s, we had 200 MHz CPUs. Web scripts queried the database and merged the results with strings embedded in the script. Everything ran on one physical computer so there was no overhead from copying data around. Only the final credit card processing pages were encrypted. We struggled to handle 10 hits per second. In the late 1990s, we had 400 MHz CPUs. Web scripts queried the database and merged the results with templates that had to be parsed. Data were networked from the RDBMS server to the Web server before heading to the user. We secured more pages in response to privacy concerns. We struggled to handle 10 hits per second. In 2000 we had 1 GHz CPUs. Web scripts queried the referer header to find out if the request came from a customer of one of our co-brand partners. The script then selected the appropriate template. We'd freighted down the server with Java Server Pages and Enterprise Java Beans.

We struggled to handle 10 hits per second. In 2002 we had 2 GHz CPUs. The programmers had decided to follow the XML/XSLT fashion. We struggled to handle 10 hits per second . . .

It seems reasonable to expect that hardware engineers will continue to deliver substantial performance improvements and that fashions in software development and business complexity will continue to rob users of any enjoyment of those improvements. So stick to 10 requests per second per CPU until you've got your own application-specific benchmarks that demonstrate otherwise.

Load Balancing

As noted earlier in this chapter, an Internet service with 100 CPUs spread among fifteen physical computers isn't going to be very reliable if all 100 CPUs must be working for the overall service to function. We need to develop a strategy for load balancing so that (1) user requests are divided more or less evenly among the available CPUs, (2) when a piece of hardware fails, it doesn't result in too many errors returned to users, and (3) we can reconfigure hardware and network without breaking users' bookmarks and links from other sites.

We will start by positing a two-tier server farm with a single multi-CPU machine running the RDBMS and multiple single-CPU front-end machines, each of which runs the Web server program, interprets page scripts, performs SSL encryption, and generally does any computation not being performed within the RDBMS. This is shown in figure 11.1.

Load Balancing in the Persistence Layer

Our persistence layer is the multi-CPU computer running the RDBMS. The RDBMS itself is typically a multi-process or multi-threaded application. For each database client, the RDBMS spawns a separate process or thread. In this case, each front-end machine presents itself to the RDBMS as one or more database clients. If we assume that the load of user requests are spread among the front-end machines, the load of database work will be spread among the multiple CPUs of the RDBMS server by the operating system process or thread scheduler.

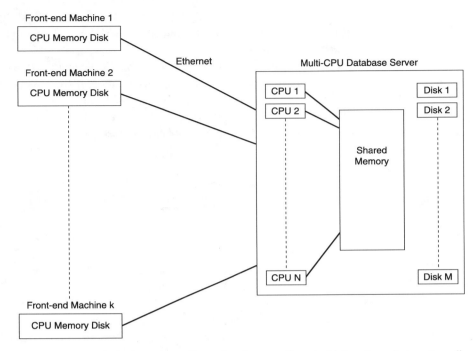

Figure 11.1   A typical server configuration for a medium-to-high volume Internet application. A powerful multi-CPU server supports the relational database management system. Multiple small 1-CPU machines run the HTTP server program.

Load Balancing among the Front-End Machines

Circa 1995 a popular strategy for high-volume Web sites was *round-robin DNS*. Each front-end machine was assigned a unique publicly routable IP address. The Domain Name System (DNS) server for the Web site was programmed to give different answers when asked for a translation of the Web server's hostname. For example, www.cnn.com was using round-robin DNS. They had a central NFS file server containing the content of the site and a rack of small front-end machines, each of which was a Web server and an NFS client. This architecture enabled CNN to update their site consistently by touching only one machine, that is, the central NFS server.

How was the CNN system experienced by users? When a student at MIT requested http://www.cnn.com/TECH/, his or her desktop machine would ask the local name server for a translation of the hostname www.cnn.com into a 32-bit IP address. (Remember that all Internet communication is machine-to-machine and requires numeric IP addresses; alphanumeric hostnames such as "www.amazon.com" or "web.mit.edu" are used only for user interface.) The MIT name server would contact the InterNIC registry to learn the IP addresses of the name servers for the cnn.com domain. The MIT name server would then contact CNN's name servers and learn that "www.cnn.com" was available at the IP address 207.25.71.5. Subsequent users within the same subnetwork at MIT would, for a period of time designated by CNN, get the same answer of 207.25.71.5 without the MIT name server going back to the CNN name servers.

Where is the load balancing in this system? Suppose that a Biology major at Harvard University requested http://www.cnn.com/HEALTH/. Harvard's name server would also contact CNN's name servers to learn the translation of "www.cnn.com." This time, however, the CNN server would provide a different answer: 207.25.71.20, leading that user, and subsequent users within Harvard's network, to a different front-end server than the machine providing pages to users at MIT.

Round-robin DNS is not a very popular load balancing method today. For one thing, it is not very balanced. Suppose that the CNN name server tells America Online's name server that www.cnn.com is reachable at 207.25.71.29. AOL is perfectly free to provide that translation to all of its more than 20 million customers. Another problem with round-robin DNS is the impact on users when a front-end machine dies. If the box at 207.25.71.29 were to fail, none of AOL's customers would be able to reach www.cnn.com until the expiration time on the translation had elapsed—the site would be up and running and providing pages to hundreds of thousands of users worldwide, but not to those users who'd received an unlucky DNS translation to the dead machine. For a typical domain, this period of time might be anywhere from 6 hours to 1 week. CNN, aware of this problem, could shorten the expiration and "minimum time-to-live" on cnn.com, but if these were cut down to, say, 30 seconds, the load on CNN's name servers might start approaching the intensity of the load on its Web servers. Nearly every user page request would be preceded by a request for a DNS translation. (In fact, CNN set their minimum time-to-live to 15 minutes.)

A final problem with round-robin DNS is that it does not provide abstraction. Suppose that CNN, whose primary servers were all Unix machines, wished to run some discussion forum software that was only available for

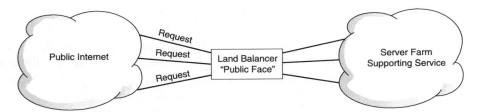

Figure 11.2 To preserve the freedom of rearranging components within the server farm, typically users on the public Internet only talk to a load balancing router, which is the "public face" of the service and whose IP address is what www.popularservice .com translates to.

Windows. The IP addresses of all of its servers are publicly exposed. The only way to direct users to a different machine for a particular part of the service would be to link them to a different hostname, which could therefore be translated into a distinct IP address. For example, CNN would link users to "http:// forums.cnn.com." Users who enjoyed these forums would bookmark the URL, and other sites on the Internet would insert hyperlinks to this URL. After a year, suppose that the Windows servers were dying and the people who knew how to maintain them had moved on to other jobs. Meanwhile, the discussion forum software has become available for Unix as well. CNN would like to pull the discussion service back onto its main server farm, at a URL of http:// www.cnn.com/discuss/. Why should users be aware of this reshuffling of hardware (see fig. 11.2)?

The modern approach to load balancing is the load balancing router. This machine, typically built out of standard PC hardware running a free Unix operating system and a thin layer of custom software, is the only machine that is visible from the public Internet. All of the server hardware is behind the load balancer and has IP addresses that aren't routable from the rest of the Internet. If a user requests www.photo.net, for example, this is translated to 216.127.244.133, which is the IP address of photo.net's load balancer. The load balancer accepts the TCP connection on port 80 and waits for the Web client to provide a request line, for example, "GET/HTTP/1.0." Only after that request has been received does the load balancer attempt to contact a Web server on the private network behind it.

Notice first that this sort of router provides some inherent security. The Web servers and RDBMS server cannot be directly contacted by crackers on the public Internet. The only ways in are via a successful attack on the load balancer, an attack on the Web server program (Microsoft Internet Information Server suffered from many buffer overrun vulnerabilities), or an attack on publisher-authored page scripts. The router also provides some protection against denial-of-service attacks. If a Web server is configured to spawn a maximum of 100 simultaneous threads, a malicious user can effectively shut down the site simply by opening 100 TCP connections to the server and then never sending a request line. The load balancers are smart about reaping such idle connections and in any case have very long queues.

The load balancer can execute arbitrarily complex algorithms in deciding how to route a user request. It can forward the request to a set of front-end servers in a round-robin fashion, taking a server out of the rotation if it fails to respond. The load balancer can periodically pull load and health information from the front-end servers and send each incoming request to the least busy server. The load balancer can inspect the URI requested and route to a particular server, for example, sending any request that starts with "/discuss/" to the Windows machine that is running the discussion forum software. The load balancer can keep a table of where previous requests were routed and try to route successive requests from a particular user to the same front-end machine (useful in cases where state is built up in a layer other than the RDBMS).

Whatever algorithm the load balancer is using, a hardware failure in one of the front-end machines will generally result in the failure of only a handful of user requests, that is, those in-process on the machine that actually fails.

How are load balancers actually built? It seems that we need a computer program that waits for a Web request, takes some action, then returns a result to the user. Isn't this what Web server programs do? So why not add some code to a standard Web server program, run the combination on its own computer, and call that our load balancer? That's precisely the approach taken by the Zeus Load Balancer (http://www.zeus.com/products/zlb/) and mod_backhand (http://www.backhand.org/mod_backhand/), a load balancer module for the Apache Web server. An alternative is exemplified by F5 Networks, a company that sells out-of-the-box load balancers built on PC hardware, the NetBSD Unix operating system, and unspecified magic software.

Failover

Remember our strategic goals: (1) user requests are divided more or less evenly among the available CPUs; (2) when a piece of hardware fails it doesn't result in too many errors returned to users; (3) we can reconfigure hardware and network without breaking users' bookmarks and links from other sites.

It seems as though the load-balancing router out front and the load-balancing operating system on the RDBMS server in back have allowed us to achieve goals 1 and 3. And if the hardware failure occurs in a front-end single-CPU machine, we've achieved goal 2 as well. But what if the multi-CPU RDBMS server fails? Or what if the load balancer itself fails?

Failover from a broken load balancer to a working one is essentially a network configuration challenge, beyond the scope of this textbook. Basically what is required are two identical load balancers and cooperation with the next routing link in the chain that connects your server farm to the public Internet. Those upstream routers must know how to route requests for the same IP address to one or the other load balancer depending upon which is up and running. What keeps this from becoming an endless spiral of load balancing is that the upstream routers aren't actually looking into the TCP packets to find the GET request. They're doing the much simpler job of IP routing.

Ensuring failover from a broken RDBMS server is a more difficult challenge and one where a large variety of ideas has been tried and found wanting. The first idea is to make sure that the RDBMS server never fails. The machine will have three power supplies, only two of which are required. Each disk drive will be mirrored. If a CPU board fails, the operating system will gracefully fail back to running on the remaining CPUs. There will be several network cards. There will be two paths to each disk drive. Considering the number of moving parts inside, the big complex servers are remarkably reliable, but they aren't 100 percent reliable.

Given that a single big server isn't reliable enough, we can buy a whole bunch of them and plug them all into the same disk subsystem, then run something like Oracle Parallel Server. Database clients connect to whichever physical server machine is available. If they can't get a response from a particular server, the client retries after a few seconds to another physical server. Thus an RDBMS server machine that fails causes the return of errors to any in-process user requests being handled by that machine and perhaps a few seconds of interrupted or slow service for users who've been directed to the clients of that down machine, but it causes no longer term site unavailability.

As discussed in the "Persistence Layer" section of this chapter, this approach entails a lot of wasted CPU time and bandwidth as the physical machines keep each other apprised of database updates. A compromise approach introduced by Oracle in 2000 was to configure a two-node parallel server. The first machine would process online transactions. The second machine would be allowed to lag as much as, say, ten minutes behind the first in terms of updates. If you wanted a CPU-intensive report querying last month's user activity, you'd talk to the backup machine. If Machine 1 failed, however, Machine 2 would notice almost immediately and start rolling its own state forward from the transaction log on the hard disk. Once Machine 2 was up to date with the last committed transaction, it would begin offering service as the primary database server. Oracle proudly stated that, for customers willing to spend twice as much for RDBMS server hardware, the two-node failover configuration was "only a little bit slower" than a single machine.

Hardware Scaling Exercises

Exercise 1: Web Server-based Load Balancer

How can a product like the Zeus Load Balancer work? We were worried about our Web server program becoming overwhelmed so we added nine extra machines running nine extra copies of the program. Can it be a good idea to add the bottleneck of requiring all of our users to go through a Web server program running on one machine, which was probably how we had it set up in the first place?

Exercise 2: New York Times

Consider the basic New York Times Web site. Ignore any bag-on-the-side community features such as chat or discussion forums. Concentrate on the problem of delivering the core articles and advertising. Every user will see the same articles, but with potentially different advertisements. Design a server hardware and software infrastructure that will (1) let the New York Times staff update the site using Web forms with the user experience lagging those updates by no more than one minute, and (2) result in minimum cost of computer hardware and system administration.

Be explicit about the number of computers employed, the number of CPUs within each computer, and the connections among the computers.

Your answer to this exercise should be no longer than half a page of text.

Exercise 3: eBay

Visit www.ebay.com and familiarize yourself with their basic services of auction bidding and user ratings. Assume that you need to support 100 million registered users, 800 million page views per day, 10 million bids per day, 10 million searches per day, and 0.5 million new user ratings per day. Design a server hardware and software infrastructure that will represent a reasonable compromise among reliability (including graceful degradation), initial cost, and cost of administration.

Be explicit about the number of computers employed, the number of CPUs within each computer, and the connections among the computers. If you're curious about the real numbers, remember that eBay is a public corporation and publishes annual reports, which are available at http://investor.ebay.com/.

Your answer to this exercise should be no longer than one page.

Exercise 4: eBay Proxy Bidding

eBay offers a service called "proxy bidding" or "automatic bidding" in which you specify a maximum amount that you're willing to pay and the server itself will submit bids for you in increments that depend on the current high bid. How would you implement proxy bidding on the infrastructure that you designed for the preceding exercises? Rough out any SQL statements or triggers that you would need. Be explicit about where the code for proxy bidding would execute: on which server? in which execution environment?

Exercise 5: Uber-eBay

Suppose that eBay went up to one billion bids per day. How would that change your design, if at all?

Exercise 6: Hotmail

Suppose that Hotmail were an RDBMS-backed Internet service with 200 million active users. What would be the minimum cost hardware configuration that still provided reasonable reliability and maintainability? What is the fundamental difference between Hotmail and eBay?

Note: http://philip.greenspun.com/ancient-history/webmail/ describes an Oracle-backed Web mail system built by Jin S. Choi.

Exercise 7: Scorecard

Justifying your decisions, provide a one-paragraph design for the server infra-structure behind www.scorecard.org.

Moving on to the Hard Stuff

We can build a big server. We can support a lot of users. As the community grows in size, though, can those users continue to interact in the *purposeful* manner necessary for our service to be an online learning community? How can we prevent the discussion and the learning from devolving into chaos and chat?

Perhaps we can take some ideas from the traditional face-to-face world. Let's look at some of the things that make for good offline communities and how we can translate them to the online world.

Translating the Elements of Good Communities from the Offline to the Online World

A face-to-face community is almost always one in which people are identified, authenticated, and accountable. Suppose that you're a 50-year-old, 6-foot tall, 250 lb. guy, known to everyone in town as "Fred Jones." Can you walk up to the 12-year-old daughter of one of your neighbors and introduce yourself as a 13-year-old girl? Probably not very successfully. Suppose that you fly a Nazi flag out in front of your house. Can you express an opinion at the next town meeting without people remembering that you were "the Nazi flag guy"? Seems unlikely.

How do we translate the features of identifiability, authentication, and accountability into the online world? In private communities, such as corporate knowledge management systems or university coordination services, it is easy. We don't let anyone use the system unless they are an employee or a registered student and, in the online environment, we identify users by their full names. Such heavyweight authentication is at odds with the practicalities of running a public online community. For example, would it be practical to schedule face-to-face meetings with each potential registrant of photo.net, where the new user would show an ID? On the other hand, as discussed in the "User Registration and Management" chapter, we can take a stab at authentication in a public online community by requiring email verification and by requiring alternative authentication for people with Hotmail-style email accounts. In both public and private communities, we can enhance accountability simply by making each user's name a hyperlink to the complete record of their contributions to the site.

In the face-to-face world, a speaker gets a chance to gauge audience reaction as he or she is speaking. Suppose that you're a politician speaking to a women's organization, the WAGC ("Women Against Gun Control," www.wagc.com). Your schedule is so heavy that you can't recall what your aides told you about this organization, so you plan to trot out your standard speech about how you've always worked to ensure higher taxes, more government intervention in individuals' lives, and, above all, to make it more difficult for Americans to own guns. Long before you took credit for your contribution to the assault rifle ban, you'd probably have noticed that the audience did not seem very receptive to your brand of paternalism and modified your planned speech. Typical computer-mediated communication systems make it easy to broadcast your ideas to everyone else in the service, but without an opportunity to get useful feedback on how your message is being received. You can send the long email to the big mailing list. You'll get your first inkling as to whether people liked it or not after the first 500 have it in their inbox. You can post your reply to an emotionally charged issue in a discussion forum, but you won't get any help from other community members, at least not through the same software, before you finalize that reply.

Perhaps you can craft your software so that a user can expose a response to a test audience of 1 percent of the ultimate audience, get a reaction back from those sample recipients, and refine the message before authorizing it for delivery to the whole group.

When groups too large for effective discussion assemble in the offline world, there is often a provision for breaking out into smaller groups and then reassembling. For example, academic conferences usually are about half "one to very many" lectures and half breaks and meals during which numerous "handful to handful" discussions are held. Suppose that an archived discussion forum is used by 10,000 people. You're pretty sure that you know the answer to a question, but not sure that your idea is sufficiently polished for exposure to 10,000 people and permanent enshrinement in the database. Wouldn't it be nice to shout out the proposed response to those users who happen to be logged in at this moment and try the idea out with them first? The electronic equivalent of shouting to a roomful of people is typing into a chat room. We experimented at photo.net by comparing an HTML- and JavaScript-based chatroom run on our own server to a simple hyperlink to a designated chatroom on the AOL Instant Messenger infrastructure:

```
<a href="aim:gochat?RoomName=photonet">photo.net chatroom</a>
```

This causes a properly configured browser to launch the AIM client (try it). Although the AIM-based chat offered superior interactivity, it was not as successful due to (1) some users not having the AIM software on their computers, (2) some users being behind firewalls that prevented them from using AIM, but mostly because (3) photo.net users knew each other by real names and could not recognize their friends by their AIM screen names. It seems that providing a breakout and reassemble chat room is useful, but that it needs to be tightly integrated with the rest of the online community and that, in particular, user identity must be preserved across all services within a community.

People like computers and the Internet because they are fast. If you want an answer to a question, you turn to the search engine that responds quickest and with the most relevant results. In the offline world, people generally desire speed. A Big Mac delivered in thirty seconds is better than a Big Mac delivered in ten minutes. However, when emotions and stakes are high, we as a society often choose delay. We could elect a president in two weeks, but instead we choose presidential campaigns that last nearly two years. We could have tried and sentenced Thomas Junta immediately after July 5, 2000, when he beat Michael Costin, father of another ten-year-old hockey player, to death in a Boston-area ice rink. After all, the crime was witnessed by dozens of people and there was little doubt as to Junta's guilt. But it was not until January 2002 that Junta was brought to trial, convicted, and sentenced to six to ten years in prison. Instant messaging, chat rooms, and Web-based discussion forums don't always lend themselves to thoughtful discourse, particularly when the topic is emotional. For some communities, it may be appropriate to consider adding an artificial delay in posting. Suppose that you respond to Joe Ranter's message by comparing Ranter to Adolf Hitler. Twenty-four hours later you get an email message from the server: "Does the message below truly represent your best thinking? Choose an option by clicking on one of the URLs below: confirm | edit | discard." You've had some time to cool down and think. Is Joe Ranter really similar to Adolf Hitler in relevant and significant ways? Upon reflection, you find that the comparison to Hitler was inapt, and so you choose to edit the message before it becomes public.

As an online discussion grows longer, the probability of a comparison involving Nazis or Hitler approaches 1.

—(Mike) Godwin's Law

How difficult is it in the offline world to find people interested in the issues that are important to us? If you believe that charity begins at home and all politics is local, finding people who share your concerns is as simple as walking around your neighborhood. One way to translate that to the online world would be to build separate communities for each geographical region. If you wanted to find out about the environment in your state, you'd go to massachusetts.envrionmentaldefense.org. But what if your interests were a bit broader? If you were interested in the environment throughout New England, should you have to visit five or six separate servers in order to find the hot topics? Or suppose that your interests were narrower. Should you have to wade through a lot of threads regarding the heavily populated eastern portion of Massachusetts if you live right up against the New York State border and are worried about a particular chemical plant?

The *geospatialized discussion forum*, developed by Bill Pease and Jin S. Choi for the scorecard.org service, is an interesting solution to this problem. Try out the following pages:

- discussions about problems in a bunch of Western states: http://www .scorecard.org/bboard/usgeospatial-2.tcl?topic=Pollution%20in%20Your%20 Community&epa_region=9

- the same forum, but narrowed to threads about California: http://www .scorecard.org/bboard/usgeospatial-one-state.tcl?topic=Pollution%20in%20 Your%20Community&usps_abbrev=CA

- the same forum, but narrowed to threads about Santa Clara County: http:// www.scorecard.org/bboard/usgeospatial-one-county.tcl?topic=Pollution%20 in%20Your%20Community&fips_county_code=06085

- the same forum, but narrowed to threads about one factory: http://www .scorecard.org/bboard/usgeospatial-one-facility.tcl?topic=Pollution%20in% 20Your%20Community&tri_id=95050WNSCR960CE

A user could bookmark any of these pages and enter the site periodically to participate in as wide a discussion as interest dictated.

Another way to look at geospatialization is of the users themselves. Consider, for example, an online learning community centered around the breeding of African Cichlids. Most of the articles and discussion would be of interest to all users worldwide. However it would be nice to help members who were geographically proximate find each other. Geographical clumps of members can share information about the best aquarium shops and can arrange to get together on weekends to swap young fish. To facilitate geospatialization of users, your software should solicit country of residence and postal code from each new user during registration. It is almost always possible to find a database of latitude and longitude centroids for each postal code in a country. In the United States, for example, you should look for the "Gazetteer files" on www.census .gov, in particular those for ZIP Code Tabulation Areas (ZCTAs).

Despite applying the preceding tricks, it is always possible for growth in a community to outstrip an old user's ability to cope with all the new users and their contributions. Every Internet collaboration system going back to the early 1970s has drawn complaints of the form "I used to like this [mailing list|newsgroup|MUD|Web community] when it was smaller, but now it is big and full of flaming losers; the interesting thoughtful material is buried under a heavy layer of dross." The earliest technological fix for this complaint was the *bozo filter*. If you didn't like what someone had to say, you added them to your bozo list and the software would hide their contributions from your view of the community.

In mid-2001 we added an "inverse bozo filter" facility to the photo.net community. If you find a work of great creativity in the photo sharing system or a thoughtful response in a discussion forum you can mark the author as "interesting." On subsequent logins you will find a "Your Friends" section in your personal workspace on the site. The people that you've marked as interesting are listed in order of their most recent contribution to the site. Six months after the feature was added, 5,000 users had established 25,000 "I think that other user is interesting" relationships.

Human Scaling Exercises

Exercise 8: A Newspaper's Online Community

Pick a discussion forum server operated by an online newspaper with a national or international audience, for example, www.nytimes.com, and so on. Select a discussion area that is of interest to you. How effectively does this function as an online learning community? What are the features that are helpful? What features would you add if this were your service?

What is it about a newspaper that makes it particularly tough for that organization to act as the publisher of an online community?

Exercise 9: Amazon.com

List the features of amazon.com that would seem to lead to more graceful scaling of their online community. Explain how each feature helps.

Exercise 10: Scaling Plan for Your Community

Create a document at the abstract URL `/doc/planning/YYYYMMDD-scaling` on your server and start writing a scaling plan for your community. This plan should list those features that you expect to modify or add as the site grows. The features should be grouped by phases.

Add a link to your new plan from `/doc/` or a planning subindex page.

Exercise 11: Implement Phase 1

Implement Phase 1 of your scaling plan. This could be as simple as ensuring that every time a user's name or e-mail address appears on your service, the text is an anchor to a page showing all of that person's contributions to the community (accountability). Or it could be as complex as complete geospatialization. It really depends on how large a community your client expects to serve in the coming months.

Spam-Proofing Public Online Communities

A public online community is one in which registration is accepted from any IP address on the public Internet and one that serves content back to the public Internet. In a private online community, for example, a corporate knowledge-sharing system that is behind a company firewall and that only accepts members who are employees, you don't have to worry too much about spam, where *spam* in this case is defined as "Any content that is off-topic, violates the terms of use, is posted multiple times in multiple places, or is otherwise unhelpful to other community members trying to learn."

Let's look at some concrete scenarios. Let's assume that we have a public community in which user-contributed content goes live immediately, without having to be approved by a moderator. The problem of spam is greatly reduced in any community where content must be pre-approved before appearing to other members, but such communities require a larger staff of moderators if discussion is to flow freely.

Scenario 1: Sarah Moneylover has registered as User 7812 and posted 50 article comments and discussion forum messages with links to her "natural Viagra" sales site. Sarah clicked around by hand and pasted in a text string from a word processor open on her desktop, investing about 20 minutes in her spamming activity. The appropriate tool for dealing with Sarah is a set of efficient administration pages. Here's how the clickstream would proceed:

1. site administrator visits a "all content posted within the last 30 days" link, resulting in page after page of stuff

2. site administrator clicks a control up at the top to limit the display to only content from newly registered users, who are traditionally the most problematic, and that results in a manageable 5-screen listing

3. site administrator reviews the content items, each presented with a summary headline at the top and the first 200 words of the body with a "more" hyperlink to view the complete item and a hyperlinked author's name at the end

4. site administrator clicks on the name "Sarah Moneylover" underneath a posting that is clearly off-topic and commercial spam; this brings up a page summarizing Sarah's registration on the server and all of her contributed content

5. site administrator clicks the "nuke this user" link from Sarah Moneylover and is presented with a "Do you really want to delete Sarah Moneylover, User 7812, and all of her contributed content?"

6. site administrator confirms the nuking and a big SQL transaction is executed in which all rows related to Sarah Moneylover are deleted from the RDBMS. Note that this is different from a moderator marking content as "unapproved" and having that content remain in the database, but not displayed on pages. The assumption is that commercial spam has no value and that Sarah is not going to be converted into a productive member of the community. In fact the row in the users table associated with User 7812 ought to be deleted as well.

The site administrator, assuming he or she was already reviewing all new content on the site, spent less than 30 seconds removing content that took the spammer 20 minutes to post, a ratio of 40:1. As long as it is much easier to remove spam than to post it, the community is relatively spam-proof. Note that Sarah would not have been able to deface the community if a policy of pre-approval for content contributed by newly registered users was established.

Scenario 2: Ira Angrywicz, User 3571, has developed a grudge against Herschel Mellowman, User 4189. In every discussion forum thread where Herschel has posted, Ira has posted a personal attack on Herschel right underneath. The procedure followed to deal with Sarah Moneylover is not appropriate here because Ira, prior to getting angry with Herschel, posted 600 useful discussion forum replies that we would be loathe to delete. The right tool to deal with this problem is an administration page showing all content contributed by User 3571 sorted by date. Underneath each content item's headline are the first 200 words of the body so that the administrator can evaluate without clicking down whether or not the message is anti-Herschel spam. Adjacent to each content item is a checkbox and at the bottom of all the content is a button marked "Disapprove all checked items." For every angry reply that Ira had to type, the administrator had to click the mouse only once on a checkbox, perhaps a 100:1 ratio between spammer effort and admin effort.

Scenario 3: A professional programmer hired to boost a company's search engine rank writes scripts to insert content all around the Internet with hyperlinks to his client's Web site. The programs are sophisticated enough to work through the new user registration pages in your community, registering 100 new accounts each with a unique name and email address. The programmer has also set up robots to respond to email address verification messages sent by your software. Now you've got 100 new (fake) users each of whom has posted two messages. If the programmer has been a bit sloppy, it is conceivable that all of the user registrations and content were posted from the same IP address in which case you could defend against this kind of attack by adding an `originating_ip_address` column to your content management tables and building an admin page letting you view and potentially delete all content from a particular IP address. Discovering this problem after the fact, you might deal with it by writing an admin page that would summarize the new user registrations and contributions with a checkbox bulk-nuke capability to remove those users and all of their content. After cleaning out the spam you'd probably add a "verify that you're a human" step in the user registration process in which, for example, a hard-to-read word was obscured inside a patterned bitmap image and the would-be registrant had to recognize the word amidst the noise and type it in. This would prevent a robot from establishing 100 fake accounts.

No matter how carefully and intelligently programmed a public online community is to begin with, it will eventually fall prey to a new clever form of spam. Planning otherwise is like being an American circa 1950 when antibiotics, vaccines, and DDT were eliminating one dreaded disease after another. The optimistic new suburbanites never imagined that viruses would turn out to be smarter than human beings. Budget at least a few programmer days every six months to write new admin pages or other protections against new ideas in the world of spam.

More

- "Face-to-Face and Computer-Mediated Communities, a Comparative Analysis" by Amitai Etzioni and Oren Etzioni, from *The Information Society* 15, no. 4 (October–December 1999): 241–248 or http://www.gwu.edu/~ccps/etzioni/E31.html.
- The Linux Virtual Server, a very simple load balancer based purely on packet rewriting; www.linuxvirtualserver.org

Time and Motion

The hardware scaling exercises should take one half to one hour each. Students not familiar with eBay should plan to spend an extra half hour familiarizing themselves with it. The human scaling exercises might take one to two hours. The time required for Phase I will depend on its particulars.

12   Search

Recall from the "Planning" chapter our principles of sustainable online community:

1. magnet content authored by experts
2. means of collaboration
3. *powerful facilities for browsing and searching both magnet content and contributed content*
4. means of delegation of moderation
5. means of identifying members who are imposing an undue burden on the community and ways of changing their behavior and/or excluding them from the community without them realizing it
6. means of software extension by community members themselves

A sustainable online community is one that can accommodate new users. If Joe Novice, via browsing and searching, cannot find existing content relevant to his needs, he will ask questions that will annoy other community members: "Didn't you search the archives?" "Haven't you read the FAQ?" Long-term community members, instead of being stimulated by discussion of new and interesting topics, find their membership a tiresome burden of directing new users to pages that they "should" have been able to find on their own.

A community's first line of defense is high quality information architecture and navigation, as discussed at the end of the "Content Management" chapter. Users are better at browsing than formulating search queries. A community's second line of defense, however, is a superb full-text search facility. The search database must include both publisher-authored and user-contributed content. Here are some example query categories:

- question answering: e.g., planning a trip to Sanibel Island (Florida) to take pictures of birds and wanting to know which long telephoto lens to rent, the user types "best lens Sanibel"

- navigation: the user knows that a document exists on the server, but can't remember where it is, e.g., remembering that a tutorial exists on how to take pictures in gardens, the user types "garden photography"

- task accomplishment: the user wants to find the photo upload page, not find discussions of photo sharing when he or she types "photo sharing"

- housekeeping: the user wants to find the site's privacy policy, not a discussion about privacy policies, after typing "privacy policy"

On a large site a user might wish to restrict the search in some way. If the search form is at the top of a document that is a chapter of an online book, it might make sense to offer "whole site" and "within the chapters of this book" options. If the publisher or the other users have gone to the trouble of rating content, the default search might limit results to those documents that have been rated of high quality. If there are multiple discussion forums on the site, each of which is essentially a self-contained subcommunity, the search boxes on those pages might offer a "restrict searching to postings in this forum" option. If a user hasn't visited the site for a month and wants to see if there is anything new and relevant, the site should perhaps offer a "restrict searching to content added within the last 30 days" option.

What's Wrong with SQL (Search Quality)

The relational database management system (RDBMS) sounds like the perfect tool for this job. We have a lot of data and we want to provide a lot of flexibility in querying. Suppose a person comes to a site for athletes and types "running" into the search form. The site sends the following SQL query to the database:

```
select *
from content
where body like '%' || :user_query || '%'
```

which, by the time the bind variable :user_query is substituted, turns into

```
select *
from content
where body like '%running%'
```

In Oracle this won't pick up a row whose message contains the same word, but with a different capitalization. Instead we do

```
select *
from content
where upper(body) like upper('%running%')
```

What if the user typed multiple words? The query

```
select *
from content
where upper(body) like upper('%running shoes%')
```

would not pick up a message that contained the phrase "shoes for running." Instead we'll need multiple where clauses:

```
select *
from content
where upper(body) like upper('%running%')
and upper(body) like upper('%shoes%')
```

This AND clause isn't quite right. If there are lots of documents that contain both "running" and "shoes," these are the ones that we'd like to see. However, if there aren't any rows with all query terms, we should probably offer the user rows that contain some of the query terms. We might need to use OR, a scoring function, and an ORDER BY so that the rows containing both query terms are returned first. If we insist on the AND clause, we've created a situation in which the more the user tells us about her interests the fewer documents we'll return in response to a search, eventually returning "0 results found" if she keeps adding words. (Note that public search engines circa 2005, such as Google, Yahoo, A9, and MSN, *do* implicitly use AND and *do* return 0 results if a user keeps adding words to a query and there aren't any documents in the database that contain each and every one of those words.)

There are some deeper problems with the Caveperson SQL Programmer approach to full-text search. Suppose that a message contains the phrase "My brother-in-law Billy Bob *ran* 20 miles yesterday" but not the word "running." Or a message contains the phrase "My cousin Gertrude *runs* 15 miles every day." These should be returned as relevant to the query "running," but the LIKE clause won't do the job. What is needed is a system for *stemming* both the query terms and the indexed terms: "running," "runs," and "ran" would all be bashed down to the stem word "run" for indexing and retrieval.

What about a message saying "I attended the 100th anniversary Boston Marathon"? The LIKE query won't pick that up. What is needed is a system for expanding queries through a thesaurus powerful enough to make the connection between "running" and "marathon."

What's Wrong with SQL (Performance)

Let's return to the simplest possible LIKE query:

```
select *
from content
where body like '%running%'
```

The RDBMS must examine every row in the `content` table to answer this query, that is, it must perform a sequential table scan (O[N] time, where N is the number of rows in the table). Suppose that a standard RDBMS index is defined on the `body` column. The values of `body` will be used as keys for a B-tree and we could perform

```
select *
from content
where body = 'running'
```

and maybe, depending on the implementation,

```
select *
from content
where body like 'running%'
```

in O[log N] time. But the user's interest isn't restricted to documents whose only word is "running" or documents that begin with the word "running." The user wants documents in which the word "running" may be buried. A single B-tree index is not going to help.

Abandoning the RDBMS

We can solve both the performance and search quality problems by dumping all of our data into a *full-text search system*. As the name implies, these systems index every word in a document, not just the first words as with the standard

RDBMS B-tree. A full-text index can answer the question "Find me the documents containing the word 'running'" in time that approaches O[1], that is, an amount of time that does not vary with the size of the *corpus* indexed. If there are 10 million documents in the corpus, a search through those 10 million documents will not take much longer than a search through a corpus of 1,000 documents. (Getting close to constant time in this situation would require that the 10-million-document collection did not use a larger vocabulary than the 1,000-document collection and that it was not the case that, say, 90 percent of the documents contained the word "running.")

How does it work? Like every other indexing strategy: extra work at insertion time is traded for less work at query time. Consider constructing a big table of every word in the English language next to the database keys of those documents that contain the word:

Word	Document IDs
absquatulate	612
bedizen	36, 9211
cryptogenic	9
dactylioglyph	7214
exheredate	57, 812, 4010
feuilleton	87, 349, 1203
genetotrophic	5000
hartebeest	710
inspissate	549, 21, 3987
. . .	
samoyed	17, 91, 1000, 3492
sesquipedalian	723
the	1, 2, 3, 4, 5, 6, 7, 8, 9, 10, 11, 12, 13, 14, 15, 16, . . .
uberous	6, 800
velutinous	45, 2307
widdershins	7300
xenial	3611
ypsiliform	5607
zibeline	4782

If we build this as a hash table, we have O[1] access to a row in the table. If we merely keep the rows in sorted order, we have O[log W] access to any row in the table, where W is the number of words in our vocabulary. Performance does not vary with the number of documents in the collection ... or does it? Just about every English document will contain the word "the" and therefore simply returning the value of the `document_ids` column for the word "the" will take O[N] time, where N is the number of documents in the corpus. This row isn't useful anyway because it isn't selective, that is, we could get the same information almost as fast with a sequential scan of the documents table, collecting all the document IDs. While indexing a document, a full-text search system will refer to a list of *stopwords*, words that are too common to be worth indexing. For standard English, the stopword list includes such words as "a," "and," "as," "at," "for," "or," "the," and so forth.

Inserting a new document into the collection will be slow. We'll have to go through the document, word by word, and update as many rows in the index as there are distinct words in the document. But that extra work at insertion time pays off in a reduction in query time from O[N] to O[1].

Given a data structure of the preceding form, we can quickly find all documents containing the word "running." We can also quickly find all documents containing the word "shoes." We can intersect these result sets quickly, giving us the documents that contain both "running" and "shoes." With some fancier indexing data structures, we can restrict our search to documents that contain the contiguous phrase "running shoes" as opposed to documents where those words appear separately. But suppose that there are 1,000 documents in the collection containing these two words. Which are the most relevant to the user's query of "running shoes"?

We need a new data structure: the *word-frequency histogram*. This will tell us which words occur in a document and how frequently they occur in a way that is easily adjusted for the total length of a document.

Here's a word-frequency histogram for the first sentence of Tolstoy's *Anna Karenina*:

Word	Count	Frequency
all	1	1/16
another	1	1/16
but	1	1/16
each	1	1/16

families	1	1/16
family	1	1/16
happy	1	1/16
in	1	1/16
is	1	1/16
its	1	1/16
one	1	1/16
own	1	1/16
resemble	1	1/16
unhappy	2	2/16
way	1	1/16

One might argue that this sentence makes better literature as "All happy families resemble one another, but each unhappy family is unhappy in its own way," but the full-text search software finds it more useful in this form.

After the crude histogram is made, it is typically adjusted for the prevalence of words in standard English. So, for example, the appearance of "resemble" is more interesting than "happy" because "resemble" occurs less frequently in standard English. Stopwords such as "is" are thrown away altogether. *Stemming* is another useful refinement. In the index and in queries, we convert all words to their stems. The stem word for "families," for example, is "family." With stemming, a query for "families" would match a document containing "family" and vice versa.

Given a body of histograms it is possible to answer queries such as "Show me documents that are similar to this one" or "Show me documents whose histogram is closest to a user-entered string." The inter-document similarity query can be handled by comparing histograms already stored in the text database. The search string "platinum mines in New Zealand" might be processed first by throwing away the stopwords "in" and "new." By using histogram comparison, the software would deliver articles that have the most occurrences of "platinum," "mines," and "Zealand." Suppose that "Zealand" is a rarer word than "platinum." Then a document with one occurrence of "Zealand" is favored over one with one occurrence of "platinum." A document with one occurrence of each word is preferred to an article where only one of those words shows up. A document that contains *only* the words "platinum mines Zealand" is a better match than a document that contains 100,000 words, three of which happen to match the query terms.

The power of this kind of system is enticing and raises the question "Can we run our entire Web application from a specialized full-text search database system?" Indeed, why not chuck the RDBMS altogether?

We don't chuck the RDBMS because we put it in to handle the problem of concurrency: two users trying to update the same item simultaneously. A better query tool is nice, but we can't adopt it as our primary database management system unless it handles the concurrency problem as well as the RDBMS.

A pragmatic approach would seem to start by keeping all the documents in the RDBMS: articles, user comments, discussion forum postings, and so on. Either once per night or every time a new document was added, update a full-text search system's collection. Pages that are part of the standard user experience and workflow operate from the RDBMS. The search box at the upper right corner of every page, however, queries against the full-text search system. Let's call this a *split-system* design, shown in figure 12.1.

One argument against the split-system approach is that two copies of the document collection are being kept. In an age of $200 disk drives of absurdly high capacity, this isn't a powerful argument. It is nearly impossible to fill a modern disk drive with words typed by humans. One can fill up a disk drive with video or audio streams, but not text. And in any case some full-text search systems can build an index to a document collection without themselves keeping the original document around, that is, you would in fact have only one copy of the document in the RDBMS.

A second argument against using RDBMS and full-text search systems simultaneously is that the collections will get out of sync. If the Web server crashes in the middle of an RDBMS transaction, all work is rolled back. If the Web server was simultaneously inserting a document into a full-text search system, it is possible that the full-text database will contain a document that is not in fact available on the main pages of the site—the site being generated from the RDBMS. Alternatively, the RDBMS insert might succeed while the full-text insert fails, leading to a document that is available on the site, but not searchable. This argument, too, ultimately lacks power. It is true that the RDBMS is a convenient and nearly foolproof means of managing transactions and concurrency. However, it is not the only way. If one were to hire sufficiently careful programmers and sufficiently dedicated system and database administrators, it would be possible to keep two databases in sync.

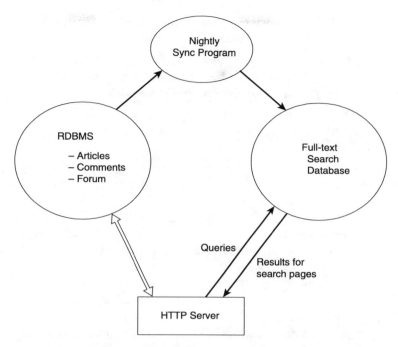

Figure 12.1 A *split-system* approach to providing full-text search. The application's content is stored in a relational database management system. Scripts periodically maintain a second copy in a specialized text database. The Web server program performs queries, inserts, and updates to the RDBMS. When a user requests a full-text search, however, the query is sent to the text database.

A third argument against the split system is the disparity of interfaces. Suppose that our RDBMS is Oracle. The Web developers know how to talk to Oracle through Active Server Pages. The desktop programmers know how to talk to Oracle through the C API. The marketing people know how to talk to Oracle through various reporting tools. Some individual users have figured out to talk to Oracle from standard desktop programs such as Microsoft Excel and Microsoft Access. The cost of bringing in a new programmer grows if you have to teach that person not only about an RDBMS, but also about specialized tools, each with its own library of interfaces.

However, the best argument against using both an RDBMS and a "bag-on-the-side" full-text search system is that the split system does not naturally support the kinds of queries that are necessary:

- show me documents matching "best restaurants" written by users whose recorded street address is within 10 miles of zip code 02138

- show me documents matching "studio photography" written by users whose contributions have been rated above average by other users (said content item ratings being stored in RDBMS tables)

- show me documents matching "best advertising tricks" written by users whose recent classified ads have attracted more than 5 bids each

Augmenting the RDBMS

Consider a full-text indexing system. It needs a way of writing stuff down (the index data structures) and typically chooses the operating system file system. It needs a way of performing computation in a procedural computer language, typically C circa 2005.

Consider a modern relational database management system. It offers a way of writing stuff down: CREATE TABLE and INSERT. It offers a way of executing software written in a procedural language: C, Java, or PL/SQL in the case of Oracle; any .NET-supported computer language in the case of Microsoft SQL Server.

Why couldn't one build a full-text search indexer inside the RDBMS? That's exactly what some of the commercial RDBMS vendors have done. Oracle was a pioneer in this area and the relevant Oracle product is called "Oracle Text."

```
create table content (
        content_id          integer primary key,
        refers_to           references content_raw,
        -- who contributed this and when
        creation_user       not null references users,
        creation_date       not null date,
        modified_date       not null date,
        mime_type           varchar(100) not null,
        one_line_summary    varchar(200) not null,
        body                clob,
        editorial_status    varchar(30)
           check (editorial_status in ('submitted','rejected','approved','expired'))
);

-- create an Oracle Text index (the product used to be called
-- Oracle Context, hence the CTX prefixes on many procedures)
```

```
create index content_text
on content(body)
indextype is ctxsys.context;

-- let's look at opinions on running shoes from
-- users who registered in the last 30 days, sorting
-- results in order of decreasing relevance

select
  score(1),
  content.content_id,
  content.one_line_summary,
  users.first_names,
  users.last_name
from content, users
where contains(body, 'running shoes', 1) > 0
and users.registration_date > current_timestamp - interval '30' day
and content.creation_user = users.user_id
order by score(1) desc;
```

In the preceding example, Oracle Text builds its own index on the `body` column of the `content` table. When a Text index is defined on a table, it becomes possible to use the `contains` operator in a WHERE clause. The Oracle RDBMS SQL query processor is smart enough to know how to use the Text index to answer this query without doing a sequential table scan. It is possible to have more than one call to `contains` in the same query. Thus the last argument of `contains` is an integer identifying the query, in this case "1." It is possible to get a relevance score out in the select list or in an ORDER BY clause with the function `score` and an argument identifying from which `contains` call the score should be pulled.

Oracle Text is one of the more difficult and complex Oracle RDBMS products to use. For example, if you want to be able to search for a phrase that occurs in either the `one_line_summary` or `body` and combine the relevance score, you need to build a multi-column index:

```
ctx_ddl.create_preference('content_multi','MULTI_COLUMN_DATASTORE');

ctx_ddl.set_attribute('content_multi', 'COLUMNS', 'one_line_summary, body');

create index content_text
on content(modified_date)
indextype is ctxsys.context
parameters('datastore content_multi');
```

Notice that the index itself is built on the column `modified_date`, which is not itself indexed. The call to `ctx_ddl.set_attribute` in which the COLUMNS attribute is set is what determines which columns get indexed.

For an example of a system that tackles the challenge of indexing text from disparate Oracle tables, see http://philip.greenspun.com/seia/examples-search/site-wide-search.

Oracle Text also has the property that its default search mode is exact phrase matching. A user who types "zippy pinhead" into a search engine will expect to find documents that contain the phrase "Zippy the Pinhead." This won't happen if your script passes the raw user query right through to the `Contains` operator. More problematic is what happens when a user types a query string that contains characters that Oracle Text treats specially. This can result in an error being raised by the SQL query and a "Server Error 500" returned to the user if you don't catch the error in your procedural script. It would be nice if Oracle Text had a built-in procedure called "ProcessRawQueryFromWebForm" or something. But it doesn't, at least we couldn't find one in the documentation for Oracle version 10g. The next best thing is a procedure called `pavtranslate`, available from http://technet.oracle.com/sample_code/products/text/htdocs/query_syntax_translators/query_syntax_translators.html.

Oracle Text, via the "INSO filters" option, has the capability to index a remarkable variety of documents in a BLOB column. For example, the software can recognize a Microsoft Excel spreadsheet, pull the text out, and add it to the index. At the same time it is smart enough to know when to ignore a document entirely, for example, if the BLOB column were filled with a JPEG photograph.

Exercise 1: Expected Queries

Ask your client what kinds of queries he or she expects to be most common in your community. For example, in a site for academics, it might be very important to type in a person's name and get all of the publications authored by that person. In a site for shoppers, it might be essential to query for a brand name and get back product reviews. Only your client can say authoritatively.

Exercise 2: Document Your Design

Place a document at /doc/search in which you describe your team's plan for providing full-text search over the content on your site. If your content management system has left you with a mixed bag of stuff in the file system and stuff in the RDBMS, explain how you're going to synchronize and unify these documents in one full-text index. If nightly maintenance scripts are required, document them here.

Include your client's answers to Exercise 1 in this document.

Exercise 3: Build the Basic Search Module

Build a basic search module that provides the following functions:

- user query from the URI /search/, targeting /search/results
- administrator ability to view statistics on the size and structure of the corpus (how many documents of each type, total size of collection)
- administrator ability to drop and rebuild the full-text index. Sadly, this is necessary periodically with most tools and you don't want the publisher to be forced into obscure shell commands. An ideal solution will be completely maintainable from a Web browser.

Exercise 4: Big Brother

Generally users prefer to browse rather than search. If users are resorting to searches in order to get standard answers or perform common tasks, there may be something wrong with a site's navigation or information architecture. If users are performing searches and getting zero results back from your full-text search facility, either your index or the site's content needs augmentation.

Record user search strings in an RDBMS table and let admins see what the popular search terms are (by the day, week, or month). Make sure to highlight any searches that resulted in the user seeing a page "No documents matched your query." Ask yourself whether it would be ethical to implement a facility whereby the site administrators could view a report of search strings and the users who typed them in.

Update your /doc/search file to reflect the addition of this facility.

Exercise 5: Linkage

Find logical places among your community's pages to link to the search facility. For example, on many sites it will make sense to have a quick search box in the upper-right corner of every page served. On most sites, it makes sense to link back to search from the search results page with a "search again" box filled in by default with the original query.

Make sure that your main documentation page links to the docs for this new module.

Working with the Public Search Engines

If your online community is on the public Internet you probably would like to see your content indexed by public search engines such as Google (www .google.com). First, Google has to know about your server. This happens either when someone already in the Google index links to your site or when you manually add your URL from a form off the google.com home page. Second, Google has to be able to read the text on your server. At least as of 2005 none of the public search engines implemented optical character recognition (OCR). This means that text embedded in a GIF, Flash animation, or a Java applet won't be indexed. It might be readable by a human user with perfect eyesight, but it won't be readable by the computer programs that crawl the Web to build databases for public search engines. Third, Google has to be able to get into all the pages on your server. If you've been requiring registration to view discussions, for example, those discussions won't be indexed by Google unless your software is smart enough to recognize that it is Google behind the request and make an exception. How to recognize Google? Here's a one-line snippet from the philip.greenspun.com access log (newlines inserted for readability):

```
66.249.71.53 - - [10/Feb/2005:02:13:15 -0500]
"GET /sql/triggers.html HTTP/1.0" 200 0 ""
"Googlebot/2.1 (+http://www.google.com/bot.html)"
```

Notice the user-agent header at the end: Googlebot/2.1, with its included suggestion that Web publishers check http://www.google.com/bot.html for more information. Because some search engines archive what they index, you would not want to provide registration-free access to content that is truly private to members. In theory a `<META NAME="ROBOTS" CONTENT="NOARCHIVE">` placed in the HEAD of your HTML documents would prevent search engines from archiving the page, but robots are not guaranteed to follow such directives.

Some search engines allow you to provide indexing hints and hints for presentation once a user is looking at a search results page. For example, in the online table of contents page for this book, we have the following META tags in the HEAD:

```
<meta name="keywords" content="web development
online communities MIT 6.171 textbook">

<meta name="description" content="This is the textbook for the MIT
course Software Engineering for Internet Applications">
```

The "keywords" tag adds some words that are relevant to the document, but not present in the visible text. This would help someone who decided to search for "MIT 6.171 textbook," for example. The "description" tag can be used by a search engine when summarizing a page. If it isn't present, a search engine may show the first 20 words on the page or follow some heuristics to build a reasonable summary. These tags have been routinely abused. A publisher might add popular search terms such as "sex" to a site that is unrelated to those terms, in hopes of capturing more readers. A company might add the names of its competitors as keywords. Users wouldn't see these dirty tricks unless they went to the trouble of using the View Source command in their browser. Because of this history of abuse, many public search engines ignore these tags.

See http://searchenginewatch.com/resources/metasuits.html for accounts of various lawsuits that have been fought over the contents of meta tags.

A particularly destructive practice is "cloaking," in which a Web server is programmed to send entirely different pages to the search engines and human users (identified by having "Mozilla" or "MSIE" in their user-agent headers). An unscrupulous publisher would find out what are the current most popular search terms on public search engines (http://searchenginewatch.com/facts/searches.html offers a list of windows into various search services), string those terms together, and serve a mishmash of those to search engines. Meanwhile, when a regular user came to the site the page presented would be a banal product pitch. Google threatens to ban from their index any site that engages in this practice.

The /robots.txt File

Suppose that you don't want the public search engines indexing anything underneath the /staging/ directory on your server. This content isn't exactly secret, but neither do you want it released before its time. Nor do you want two copies of the same content in the Google index, one copy in the staging area and one copy in its final position on the site.

You need to read the Standard for Web Exclusion, a protocol for communication between Web publishers and Web crawlers, available from http://www.robotstxt.org/wc/norobots.html. You the publisher put a file on your site, accessible at /robots.txt, with instructions for robots. Here's an example that excludes the staging directory:

```
User-agent: *
# let's keep the robots away from our half-baked stuff
Disallow: /staging
```

The User-agent line specifies for which robots the injunctions are intended. Each Disallow asks a robot not to look in a particular directory. Nothing requires a robot to observe these injunctions, but the standard seems to have been adopted by all the major indices nonetheless.

Visit http://www.ibm.com/robots.txt to get a bit of insight into how a site may evolve over time.

Exercise 6: robots.txt

Place a file on your server at /robots.txt that excludes robots from appropriate portions of your server. Put some comments at the top of the file explaining who created this, when it was created, and the rationale behind the exclusions.

If you're doing a 100 percent database-backed content management system, you are free to put the content of the robots.txt file in the RDBMS, just so long as it is served when the URI `/robots.txt` is requested.

Exercise 7: Client Signoff

Review the search facility, both user and admin pages, with your client. Write down your client's reaction to this new module, paying particular attention to any new ideas that the client might have for what will be typical queries on the site.

The Future

As an online community grows older and larger, it becomes ever more likely that a user will be overwhelmed with "100,000 documents matched your query." When a community is new and small, it is possible to search for an answer merely by reading the titles of everything on the site, that is, by browsing. As a community grows, therefore, the greater the importance of information retrieval tools. The exercises in this chapter focus on answering a user's query by presenting links to relevant documents. Suppose that we build a search facility that always returns the very most relevant document in the corpus. Is that an optimal solution? Only if you believe that users like to read.

Suppose that Joe User visits photo.net and types "At what shutter speeds is a tripod required?" into the search box. Is it reasonable to assume that Joe wants to read a 10,000-word document that contains the answer to this question? Or would Joe rather get ... the answer to his question? The answer "at shutter speeds slower than 1/lens-focal-length" is a lot smaller and quicker to read than a document containing this information.

To get a feel for how a question-answering system can be built on top of a full-text indexer, read "Scaling Question Answering to the Web" (Cody

Kwok, Oren Etzioni, Dan Weld, WWW10 conference, May 2001, http://www
.www10.org/cdrom/papers/pdf/p120.pdf), which describes a system built at the
University of Washington. This system includes all of the expected linguistic
gymnastics plus code to sort out the Internet-specific problem of *noise*. Traditional information retrieval systems are designed to work with authoritative
documents, for example, the *Encyclopedia Britannica*, a binder of corporate
policies, or the design notes for a jetliner. The documents in the corpus are presumed to be authoritative. There won't be four different answers, three of them
flat wrong, to questions such as "In what year was Gioacchino Rossini born?"
"How many signatures are required for a purchase of $57,300?" or "How wide
is the wingspan of the airplane?" With user-authored content in an online community, however, it seems safe to assume that while the average answer is likely
to be correct, for every 100 correct answers there will be at least three or four
incorrect ones. Even when the data require no interpretation, there will be
typos. For example, a Google search for "rossini 1792-1868" returned 50,900
documents in February 2005; a search for "rossini 1792-**1869**" returned 43
documents. A question-answering system built on top of lightly moderated
user-authored content will have to exercise the same sort of judgment as do
humans: How many documents contain Answer A versus Answer B? What is
the relative authority of conflicting documents? Which of two conflicting documents is more recent?

Mobile Internet devices put an even greater stress on information retrieval. Connection speeds are slower. Screens are smaller. It isn't practical for
a user to drill down into 20 documents returned by a search engine as possibly
relevant to a query, especially if the user is driving a car and using a voice
browser.

If you want to emerge as a hero from the dust of the next Internet collapse,
work on information retrieval.

More

- http://www.oracle.com/technology/products/text/, technical overviews for
  Oracle Text
- http://trec.nist.gov/, for the proceedings of the Text REtrieval Conferences
  (TREC)

Time and Motion

The two client interviews, at the beginning of the exercises and again at the end, should each take under an hour.

The search design and documentation should be a team effort, and take one to two hours.

The luckiest teams will be able to get their search systems up and running in an hour. Unlucky teams using difficult-to-install search systems may require the better part of a day. Teams with a single content table and no static html pages should be able to build the basic page scripts in one to two hours. Additional time will be required for designs that manage content across multiple tables and the filesystem.

The remaining exercises should be doable in 2 to 4 programmer-hours.

13 Planning Redux

A lot has changed since the the "Planning" chapter. You have a better understanding of the challenge, which may have sparked new service ideas in your mind. Your clients have had a chance to see a prototype of the ultimate service, which may have sparked new ideas in their minds. Your clients should have an increased respect for your abilities and therefore an increased willingness to devote thought and attention to this project. Consider that most computer programmers suffer from profound deficits in the following areas:

- thinking critically about what a computer application should do
- writing down a design
- writing down an implementation plan
- documenting important features or design decisions
- clean modular design
- exercising good judgment (e.g., don't try to build something complete and complex when you only have a week or two)
- communicating project status

To the extent that you've demonstrated that you're a cut above software developers with whom your clients have worked in the past, you'll find that their confidence in you has increased since the beginning of the class.

Why You Are Talking to the Client

Recall how much you learned in conducting the usability test in the "Discussion" chapter. Computer science textbooks and RDBMS manuals can teach you how to handle concurrency, but only observations of and interactions with users can teach you how to build a better user experience. Your client holds the keys to the kingdom: (1) content to attract people; (2) authority to launch the service; (3) editorial power over existing Web sites that can link to the new service; (4) email addresses and phone numbers of people who would be likely to find the new service useful.

If you can launch your online learning community before the end of the course, you'll have an opportunity to learn from the first users and, by making minor changes, end up with a vastly improved application by the last day of the class.

Clean Up the Code

Before beginning the planning process for the rest of the course, it is worth going through what you've done already in order to (a) clean it up a bit, and (b) familiarize yourself with things that will need significant rewrites. Work through every page script, data model file, and documentation page and ask yourselves the following questions:

- Is every script signed and dated? Does the header explain what the script does? Is that description still accurate?
- Are all of the SQL queries within scripts readable and properly indented? (see http://philip.greenspun.com/sql/style for some tips)
- Do the data model files contain appropriate comments?
- Are the file and variable names consistent?
- Is the structure consistent with the standards that you set forth in the "Software Modularity" chapter exercises?
- If you're using some sort of templating or code-behind system, are you using it on every page?
- Is the documentation all signed, dated, and appropriately linked?
- Is the documentation consistent with the standards that you set forth in the "Software Modularity" chapter exercises?

Fix the small discrepancies and record the large ones for inclusion in your rest-of-course implementation plan (see below).

Clean Up the User Experience

With multiple programmers working on a system, it is easy for small inconsistencies to creep into the designs of various pages. Come up with a set of representative tasks that are important for users to accomplish within your application and document these tasks at `/doc/testing/representative-tasks`. Work through the tasks as a team to see if indeed there are small things that should be cleaned up in terms of what the user sees.

At the same time look for larger problems. Ask yourself how consistent task accomplishment within the application you've built is with the page design and flow at popular public Internet applications, such as Amazon, eBay, and Google. Remember that it is unique *content* that should distinguish one Web site from another, not unique interface.

Are you bubbling information up to the highest possible level? For example, on a page that shows categories of things from a database table does your application display a count next to each category of how many items are within that category? Or must the user click down one more level to find out how many items are in a category (then back up and click down to another, then back up and click down to another . . .)?

Are you letting the information be the interface? For example, in the preceding example of the list of categories, does the user navigate down by clicking on the name of the category ("the information") or must she click on a "click here for more info" text string or icon?

How much of the screen space is taken up by site bureaucracy versus how much is available for displaying information? Site bureaucracy includes such things as identifying logos, navigation links and icons, mini search forms, and copyright and policy notes. Could some of that bureaucracy be eliminated or, at the very least, be pushed to the bottom of the page?

Exercise 1: Usability Test Lite

Between the discussion forum user test and the clean-up items in this chapter, you've cleaned up the obvious problems with your user interface. This is a good time to do another usability test, this time a bit less structured than the last one.

Find someone who has never seen your project before and ask them to work through the tasks in `/doc/testing/representative-tasks` with your entire team observing. Write down a brief report of how it went at `/doc/testing/planning-redux-usability`.

Exercise 2: Feature Grid

By telephone or in a face-to-face meeting, work with your client to determine what work must be done before your online learning community can be launched. The launch can be private (limited to invitees), soft (public, but not advertised), or public. The important thing is that the application is treated as complete and presented to at least a few dozen users.

Be careful of the layperson's tendency to try to pack in as many features as he or she can conceive. When a site is young, it should be simple and have few collaboration areas. If there are 30 separate discussion forums and comment areas, how are the first 15 users going to find each other? Remind your client that www.slashdot.org, "news for nerds," has operated since 1997 as a single uncategorized forum and in 2005 was serving approximately 250 million pages per month to 10 million readers.

Does a competitive site have lots of bells and whistles? That's not a reason to delay launch until an equivalently complex user interface has been built. Are users of the competitive site actually using all of those features? Or are most of them congregating in a couple of places?

People new to the world of online communities tend to see Launch Day as the most important day in the life of an Internet application. In fact, far more users will come to a site in its 36th month of existence compared to its first month. The only risk is launching something so terrible that a test user will be alienated and never return. In a world of 6 billion people, this might not seem like a serious problem, but if the potential users are, for example, corporate employees invited to try a new intranet, it may be essential to make a good first impression. Here are some minimum requirements for making a good first impression:

- high quality content, unavailable elsewhere on the Internet and relevant to users' current tasks
- easy and fast user interface (no 30-second Flash downloads or confusing blind alleys)

If a client proposes a feature that is unnecessary for meeting these requirements, ask the question "Why does this keep us from launching?" Every day the service isn't launched is a day that you're not learning from users. Every day the service isn't launched is a day that the client's organization isn't learning how to operate the service.

In collaboration with your client, develop a feature grid dividing the desired features into the following categories:

1. Minimum Launchable Feature Set, i.e., things that are required for the launch

2. Version 1.0 (try to finish by the end of this course)

3. Version 2.0 (write down so that a planned follow-on implementation can be accomplished)

Most admin pages can be excluded from the Minimum Launchable Feature Set. Until there are users, there won't be any user activity and therefore little need for statistics or moderation and organization of content. Things that are valuable to the users and client and reasonably easy to implement should be in Version 1.0. Anything that requires serious programming effort or that cannot be completely specified right now should be pushed out to Version 2.0.

Place your feature grid at `/doc/planning/YYYYMMDD-feature-grid`.

Exercise 3: Implementation Plan

Now that you've figured out what you're going to do, it is time to write down how you're going to do it. Write an implementation plan that covers all activity by team members and the client through the last day of this course. The implementation plan should include dates for code freezes, acceptance testing, launch, and any relaunches. The implementation plan should be explicit and specific about which team member is going to do what and, more important, *what the client's responsibilities are.* "Joe Client will deliver additional site content by early May" is too vague. Better: "Joe Client will deliver copy for the /about-us, /privacy, /copyright, and /contact pages by May 2."

Keep in mind that your goal is to launch the service as soon as possible so that everyone can learn from interaction with real live users.

How can you estimate the number of hours that will be required to execute the tasks in the plan? After all, you've never done the things in the implementation plan before or they wouldn't be in the "to-be-implemented plan." The best tool for estimating a new project is a record of how long it took to do a bunch of old projects. To what is the new project most similar? Suppose that it took you three days to build a discussion forum system, for example, and you're asked to build a classified ad system. Both systems need a comparable number of database tables. Both systems accept content from users and require some sort of administrator approval. If built on the same server that is currently running the discussion forum, the classified ad system doesn't require any new software, subsystems, or other tools that you haven't already installed and used. Thus it would probably be safe to estimate the classified ad system as a three-day project.

When it's ready, place your completed plan at `/doc/planning/YYYYMMDD-implementation` and email your client(s) and instructors notifying them that the plan is available for final review.

Is This Necessary?

Suppose that your team is only two people and your client is one team member's mother, owner of a local scuba diving shop. Is it necessary to engage in such a formal process? Wouldn't it be possible to obtain a successful result by sitting down in one room and hacking out code, periodically calling Mom over to look at what's been done?

Absolutely.

Why the emphasis on process then when the teams are so small? It is a good habit for every software developer to get into, especially as modern software projects tend to stretch across corporate and international borders.

Consider a software project from a Jane Decision-Maker's perspective. Jane doesn't know enough to distinguish between good code and bad code. Nor can she look at a mostly finished project and figure out how much more coding is required to make it work. Jane Decision-Maker is not going to be comforted by a team of programmers with a track record of pulling everything together with a last-minute miracle. How does she know that the miracle will happen again on her project?

What Jane will be comforted by is process and programmers who appear to operate in a manner that is predictable to them and their client. The more detailed the plain-language plans, the more comforted Jane will be, especially if the work has been contracted out to a separate corporation.

In summary, larger teams require more process, longer projects require more process, and work that is spread across enterprises and/or international borders requires more process. Your project for this class is being done by a small team on a condensed schedule and, ideally, within the same city as the client. What benefit is there to you from using a process that isn't absolutely necessary?

One benefit from using a more thorough process is that you'll tend to impress people a lot more in presentations of your work. People who conduct programmer job interviews have seen plenty of code monkeys, but they won't have seen too many who show up with printouts of their clear plans and schedules and then can talk about how they met those plans and schedules.

A deeper benefit is that you'll get good at the process and it will become less of an effort on succeeding projects.

The deepest benefit is that working with a written plan will become an unconscious habit. Pilots are trained to follow checklists and procedures extremely carefully and consistently. The plane won't fall out of the sky if things aren't done in the same order or same way on every flight, and a lot of the stuff doesn't matter if you're flying on a sunny day in a well-maintained airplane. Unless the checklists and procedures have become a habit, however, the pilot who encounters bad weather or mechanical problems has a good chance of dying. People tell themselves "I'm being sloppy today because this is an unchallenging flight, but I'll be careful when I need to be," but in fact the skills of carefulness aren't very useful unless they are habitual.

Exercise 4 (For the Instructor)

Call up each student team's clients and ask how strongly they agree with the following statements:

1. I consider the work that my student team has done to be comparable in quality to the services that I visit every day on the public Internet.

2. The service that my student team has built is a complete solution to the challenges we outlined at the beginning of the semester.

3. The service that my student team has built is well organized and easy to use.

4. I am impressed with the information and utility available to me on the administration pages.

5. I understand what work has been done, what is going to be done by the end of the course, and what is left for a Version 2.0.

6. My student team has made it easy for me to check on their progress myself.

7. My student team has kept me well informed of their progress.

8. My student team has involved me appropriately in design and feature decisions.

9. I was impressed by the thoroughness of the user testing done by my student team.

10. I am impressed by the clarity and thoroughness of the documentation.

11. I think it would be easy for a new programmer to take this project over in the event that my student team disappeared.

12. I am impressed by the mobile phone interface to my service.

13. I am impressed by the VoiceXML interface to my service.

14. My student team is the best group of engineers that I have ever worked with.

15. My student team consists of people that I would very much like to work with again.

Score this exercise by adding scores from each question: 0 for "disagree" or wishy-washy agreement (clients won't want to say bad things about young volunteers), 1 for "agree," 2 for "strongly agree."

Time and Motion

The whole team working together ought to be able to do the code and user experience clean-ups in one working day or six to eight hours. The usability test should require no more than one hour. For a team that has kept its planning documents, schedule, and client meetings up-to-date, the feature grid and implementation plan should take less than one hour because this information is already written down and on their server. For a team that has let planning and documentation slip, it could be five hours to restore currency.

14   Distributed Computing with HTTP, XML, SOAP, and WSDL

I think there is a world market for maybe five computers.
—Thomas Watson, chairman of IBM, 1943

Perhaps Watson was off by four.

In the early 1990s, few people had heard of Tim Berners-Lee's World Wide Web, and, of those that had, many fewer appreciated its significance. After all, computers had been connected to the Internet since the 1970s, and transferring data among computers was commonplace. Yet the Web brought something really new: the perspective of viewing the whole Internet as a single information space, where users accessing data could move seamlessly and transparently from machine to machine by following links.

A similar shift in perspective is currently underway, this time with application programs. Although distributed computing has been around for as long as there have been computer networks, it's only recently that applications that draw upon many interconnected machines as one vast computing medium are being deployed on a large scale. What's making this possible are new protocols for distributed computing built upon HTTP and that are designed for *programs interacting with programs*, rather than for *people surfing with browsers*.

There are several kinds of protocols:

1. **Data exchange**   Something better than scraping text from Web pages intended for humans to read. As you saw in the "Basics" chapter, you can use XML here.

2. **Program invocation**   Some way to do *remote method invocation*, that is, for programs to call programs running on other machines and to reply to such invocations. The emerging standard here, submitted to the Web Consortium in May 2000, is called SOAP (Simple Object Access Protocol).

3. **Self-description**   A machine-readable way for programs to describe how they are supposed to be called, e.g., with Web Services Description Language (WSDL).

4. **Discovery**   A way for programs to automatically learn about other programs, e.g., with Universal Description Discovery and Integration (UDDI), standardized by www.uddi.org.

We're currently moving from an environment where applications are deployed on individual machines and Web servers, to a world where applications are composed of pieces—called *services* in the current jargon—that are spread across many different machines, and where the services interact seam-

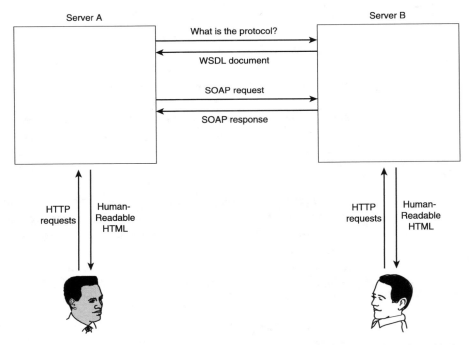

Figure 14.1   A Web services interaction. Human users talk to servers A and B via the HTTP protocol receiving results in HTML pages. When Server A needs to invoke a procedure on Server B it first tries to figure out what the names of the functions are and their arguments. This information comes back in a Web Services Description Language (WSDL) document. Using the information in that WSDL document, Server A is able to formulate a legal Simple Object Access Protocol (SOAP) request and process the results.

lessly and transparently to produce an overall effect. While the consequences of this change could be minor, it's also possible that they could be as profound as the introduction of the Web. In any case, companies are introducing new *Web service* frameworks that exploit the new infrastructure. Microsoft's *.NET* is one such framework.

In this chapter, you'll build applications that consume Web services to combine data from your online learning community with remote data in Google and Amazon. You'll be building SOAP clients to these public services. In the final exercises, you'll be creating your own service that provides information about recent content appearing in your community. You'll make this service available both in the *de jure* standard of SOAP and the *de facto* standard of RSS, a breakout from the world of weblogs.

SOAP on the Wire

Depending on what tools you're using, you might never need to know what SOAP requests and replies actually look like. Nonetheless, let's start with a behind-the-scenes look at *SOAP messages*, which are typically sent across the network embedded in HTTP POSTs.

Here's a raw SOAP request/response pair for a hypothetical "who's online" service that returns information about users who have been active in the last N seconds:

Request (plus white space for readability)

```
POST /services/WhosOnline.asmx HTTP/1.1
Host: somehost
Content-Type: text/xml; charset=utf-8
Content-Length: length
SOAPAction: "http://jpfo.org/WhosOnline"

<?xml version="1.0" encoding="utf-8"?>
<soap:Envelope
    xmlns:xsi="http://www.w3.org/2001/XMLSchema-instance"
    xmlns:xsd="http://www.w3.org/2001/XMLSchema"
    xmlns:soap="http://schemas.xmlsoap.org/soap/envelope/">
```

```
  <soap:Body>
    <WhosOnline xmlns="http://jpfo.org/">
      <n_seconds>600</n_seconds>
    </WhosOnline>
  </soap:Body>
</soap:Envelope>
```

Response (plus white space for readability)

```
HTTP/1.1 200 OK
Content-Type: text/xml; charset=utf-8
Content-Length: length

<?xml version="1.0" encoding="utf-8"?>
<soap:Envelope
    xmlns:xsi="http://www.w3.org/2001/XMLSchema-instance"
    xmlns:xsd="http://www.w3.org/2001/XMLSchema"
    xmlns:soap="http://schemas.xmlsoap.org/soap/envelope/">
  <soap:Body>
    <WhosOnlineResponse xmlns="http://jpfo.org/">
      <WhosOnlineResult>
        <user>
          <first_names>Eve</first_names>
          <last_name>Andersson</last_name>
          <email>eve@eveandersson.com</email>
        </user>
        <user>
          <first_names>Philip</first_names>
          <last_name>Greenspun</last_name>
          <email>philg@mit.edu</email>
        </user>
        <user>
          <first_names>Andrew</first_names>
          <last_name>Grumet</last_name>
          <email>aegrumet@alum.mit.edu</email>
        </user>
      </WhosOnlineResult>
    </WhosOnlineResponse>
  </soap:Body>
</soap:Envelope>
```

Exercise 1: Community Reading List, Data Model, and Amazon API

Your goal in this exercise is to provide a facility for your community members to develop a shared reading list, a set of books that new or novice members might find useful. You'll use the SOAP interface that is part of Amazon Web Services (http://www.amazon.com/webservices/) to retrieve product information directly from the Amazon servers that will then be displayed within your server's HTML pages.

Start by writing a design document that lays out your SQL data model and how you're going to use the Amazon API (which functions to call? which values to process?). Your `recommended_books` table probably should be keyed by the International Standard Book Number (ISBN). For most of your career as a data modeler, it is best to use generated keys. However, in this case there is an entire infrastructure to ensure the uniqueness of the ISBN (see www.isbn .org) and therefore it is safe for use as a primary key.

For each book, your data model ought to be able to record at least the following:

- title
- authors (either mushed together in one column, a horrifying violation of First Normal Form, or broken out if you have the energy)
- description
- URL for a photo of the cover and the width and height in pixels of that image, if you can get them easily
- when this book was recommended
- who recommended the book
- a comment by the person who recommended the book as to why it is particularly relevant to this community

You may wish to start your exploration of the Amazon SOAP API by locating the Web Services Description Language (WSDL) file for the service. The WSDL file is a formal description of the callable functions, argument names and types, and return value type. Most Internet application development environments provide a SOAP toolset that transforms the WSDL file into a set of proxy classes or function libraries that can be called as if the service were implemented in the local runtime. In Microsoft Visual Studio .NET, this operation is referred to as "Adding a Web Reference." If you're not a Microsoft

Achiever, you might find the "SOAP Implementations" links at the end of the chapter useful.

Exercise 2: Community Reading List, Building the Pages

We suggest creating a subdirectory at `/reading-list/` for the page scripts that will make up your new module. We suggest implementing the following URLs:

- an index page, listing the books on the reading list by title, author, and with cover art displayed, and perhaps the first 100 words of the description

- a `/reading-list/one-book` page, which will show the full description, who recommended the book and why

- a `/reading-list/search` page, the target of a text entry box on the index page, which returns a list of books from the Amazon API that match a query string; books that are already in the reading list should be displayed, but grayed out and somehow marked as already on the list (and there shouldn't be a button to add them again!). Books that aren't on the list should be hyperlinks to an "add-book" URL. (You can make the title of the book be the hyperlink anchor; remember always to *let the information be the interface*.)

- a `/reading-list/add-book` page, which solicits a comment from the suggesting user as to why this particular book is good for other community members

---

A good rule of thumb is that every table you add to your data model implies roughly 5 user-accessible URLs and 5 administrative URLs. So far we're up to 4 user pages, and if you were to launch this feature, you'd need to build some admin pages.

Exercise 3: Encouraging Searching before Asking and the Google APIs

A major challenge threatening online communities is the clutter of recurring questions and the effort of pointing those who ask them to the FAQ or the search engine. An existing content item on your server or elsewhere on the Internet might not provide a complete answer to Joe Newbie's question, but reading it would perhaps cause him to focus his query in a different direction.

In this exercise, you'll create an alternative post confirmation process that will entail writing two new Web scripts, the search capabilities that you developed in the "Search" chapter, and the Google Web APIs service (http://www.google.com/apis/). The goal is to put some internal and external links in front of Joe Newbie and encourage him to look at them before finalizing his question for presentation to the entire community.

Your new post confirmation process should be invoked only for questions that start a discussion thread, not for answers to a question. Our experience with online communities is that it is more important to moderate the questions that determine what will be discussed rather than individual answers.

If your current post confirmation page is at `/forum/confirm`, we suggest adding a `-query` suffix for your new script, for example, `/forum/confirm-query`. This page should have the following form:

1. at the top, the user's question as it will appear in the forum, with "Confirm" and "Edit" buttons underneath

2. the top 5–10 matches among the site's articles and existing discussion forum postings that match the user's question in a full-text search (feed the one-line summary or perhaps the entire question to your local search engine)

3. the top 5–10 matches in the Google database for the user's question, again using the user's question as the Google query string

At this point you have something of a challenge. Suppose that you want the user to browse down into some of the internal and external links before posting. Let's assume that, in fact, the question is a new one. You don't want to force Joe Newbie to back up to find the confirm page (and you really don't want the browser to say "Page Expired" and force Joe to resubmit). Ideally, Joe can go forward into the links and yet still have those Confirm and Edit buttons in front of him at all times.

There are a few ways to achieve this. One is to make all of the links target a separate window using the HTML `target=` syntax for the anchor (`<a`) tag. Novice users might become confused, however, as the extra window pops up on their screen and they might not know how to use their browser or operating system to get back to the Confirm/Edit page. A JavaScript pop-up in a small size might reduce the scale of this problem. Another option is to use the dreaded Frames feature of HTML, putting the Confirm/Edit page in one frame and the other stuff in another frame. When Joe finally decides to Confirm/Edit, the Frames syntax provides a mechanism for the server to tell the browser "go back to only one window now." A third option is to do a "server-side frame"

in which you build pages of the form `/forum/confirm-follow-link` in which the full posting with Confirm/Edit buttons is carried through and the content of the external or internal link is presented inside a single page.

For the purpose of this exercise, you're free to choose any of these methods or one that we haven't thought of. Note that this exercise should not require modifying any of your database tables or existing scripts except for one link from the "ask a new question" page.

Exercise 4: Related Books to a Thread (Amazon Again)

In this exercise you'll put a list of related books somewhere alongside the presentation of a discussion forum thread. This is useful for the following reasons: (a) a reader might find it very useful to learn that there is a relevant book on the topic being discussed, and (b) the Amazon Associates program provides Web publishers with a referral fee ("kickback") every time a community member follows an encoded link over to Amazon and buys something.

How can the server tell which books are related to a question-and-answer exchange? Start by building a procedure that will go through the question and all replies to build a list of frequently occurring words. Your procedure should exclude those words that are in a stopwords list of exceedingly common English words such as "the," "and," "or," and so forth. Whatever full-text search tool that you used in the "Search" chapter probably contains such a list somewhere in a file system file or a database table. You can use the top few words in this list to query Amazon for a list of matching titles.

For the purpose of this exercise, you can fetch your Amazon data on every page load. In practice, on a production site this would be bad for your users due to the extra latency and bad for your relationship with Amazon because you might be performing the same query against their services several times per second. You'd probably decide to store the related books in your local database, along with a "last message" stamp and rebuild periodically if there were new replies to a thread.

Each related book should have a link to the product page on Amazon.com, optionally keyed with an Amazon Associates ID. Here's an example reference:

```
<a href="http://www.amazon.com/exec/obidos/ASIN/0240804058/
pgreenspun-20"><cite>Basic Photographic Materials and
Processes</cite></a>
```

The ISBN goes after the "ASIN," and the Associates ID in this example is "pgreenspun-20."

Exercise 5: What's New Page

If you don't already have one, build an HTML page that lists the ten most recently added content items in your community. For each content item, display the following:

- title or one-line summary
- A text summary of the content or, if appropriate, the content itself
- The name of the person that created the item, hyperlinked to that person's user profile page
- The time the item was created (RFC 822 format, precise to the second, e.g. `Wed, 29 Oct 2005 00:09:19 GMT`)

Make this page available at `new-content` in a directory of your choice. Note that it should be easy to build this page using a function drawing on the inter-module API that you defined as part of your work on the "Software Modularity" chapter exercises.

Exercise 6: What's New Web Service

Expose your procedure to the wider world so that other applications can take advantage via remote method invocation. Install a SOAP handler that accomplishes the following:

- handles HTTP requests to `/services/new-content` and checks for correct SOAP syntax
- pulls the `n_items` parameter out of the request, if present
- executes the procedure call and fetches the results
- delivers the results as a valid SOAP response containing zero or more "item" records, with the fields listed in Exercise 5 for each item

Your development platform may provide tools that, once you've mapped the external Web service to the internal procedure call, handle the HTTP and

SOAP mechanics transparently. If not, you will need to skim the examples in the SOAP specification and read the introductory articles linked below.

Exercise 7: Self-Description

Write a WSDL contract that describes the inputs and outputs for your new-content service. Note that if you are using Microsoft .NET, these WSDL contracts will be automatically generated in most cases. You need only expose them.

Your WSDL should be available either by adding a ?WSDL to the URL of the service itself (convenient for Microsoft .NET users) or available by adding a .wsdl extension to the URL of the service itself.

Validate your WSDL contract and SOAP methods by inviting another team to test your service. Do the same for them. Alternatively, look for and employ validation tools out on the Web.

The March of Progress

The initial Web standards, circa 1990, were simple. HTTP is simple enough that any competent programmer can write a basic server in a day or two. HTML is simple enough that programmers were able to build their first page within thirty minutes and non-programmers weren't far behind. In fact, the initial Web standards were so simple that academic computer scientists predicted that the system wouldn't work.

Within a decade, however, the Web Consortium was focussing its efforts on the "Semantic Web" and Resource Description Framework (see http://www.w3.org/RDF). Where standards committee members once talked about whether or not to facilitate adding a caption to a photograph, you now hear words like "ontology" thrown around. Web development has thus become as challenging as cracking the Artificial Intelligence problem.

Where do SOAP and WSDL sit on this continuum from the simplicity of HTML to the AI-complete problem of a semantic Web? Apparently they are closer to RDF than to HTML because it is taking many years for SOAP and WSDL to catch on as opposed to the wildfire-like spread of the human-readable Web.

The dynamic world of weblogs has settled on a standard that has spread very quickly indeed and enabled the construction of quite a few computer programs that aggregate information from multiple weblogs. This standard, pushed forward primarily by Userland's Dave Winer, is known as *Really Simple Syndication* or *RSS* and is documented at http://blogs.law.harvard.edu/tech/rss.

Exercise 8: What's New Syndication Feed

As a kindness to the thousands of people who run desktop weblog aggregators, create an RSS feed for your content at `/services/new-content-rss.xml`. The feed should contain just the title, description, and a globally unique identifier (GUID) for each item. You are encouraged to use the fully qualified URL for the item as its GUID, if it has one.

Validate your feed using an RSS reader or the validator at http://rss .scripting.com.

Template

```xml
<?xml version="1.0"?>
<rss version="2.0">
      <channel>
              <title>{site name}</title>
              <link>{site url}</link>
              <description>{site description}</description>
              <language>en-us</language>
              <copyright>Copyright {dates}</copyright>
              <lastBuildDate>{rfc822 date}</lastBuildDate>
              <managingEditor>{your email addr}</managingEditor>
              <pubDate>{rfc822 date}</pubDate>
              <item>
                      <title>{item1 title}</title>
                      <description>{description for item1}</description>
                      <guid>{guid for item1}</guid>
                      <pubDate>{rfc822 date for when item1 went live}</pubDate>
                      </item>

              <item>
                      <title>{item2 title}</title>
                      <description>{description for item2}</description>
                      <guid>{guid for item2}</guid>
                      <pubDate>{rfc822 date for when item2 went live}</pubDate>
                      </item>
              </channel>
      </rss>
```

Remember to escape any markup in your titles and descriptions, so that, for example, `<em>Whoa!</em>` becomes `&lt;em&gt;Whoa!&lt;/em&gt;`.

More

- http://www.soapware.org/bdg—A Busy Developer's Guide to SOAP
- http://www-106.ibm.com/developerworks/library/ws-soap/?dwzone=components#2—Using WSDL in SOAP Applications (An Introduction to WSDL for SOAP Programmers)
- http://www.w3.org/TR/SOAP—Simple Object Access Protocol (SOAP)
- http://www.w3.org/TR/wsdl.html—Web Service Description Language (WSDL)
- http://www.sun.com/software/sunone/wp-arch/—Sun Open Net Environment (Sun One) White Papers
- http://www.xmlrpc.com—XML-RPC
- http://dmoz.org/Computers/Programming/Internet/Web_Services/SOAP/Implementations—A directory of SOAP implementations
- http://www.jabber.org—an instant messaging client plus open platform for XML messaging and presence information that interoperates with AOL Instant Messenger, MSN Messenger, Yahoo messenger, ICQ and IRC
- http://www.ietf.org/rfc/rfc0822.txt?number=822—RFC822 standard for the format of Internet text messages
- http://blogs.law.harvard.edu/tech/directory/5/aggregators—a directory of RSS readers
- http://rss.scripting.com—RSS validator

Time and Motion

Teams using a SOAP toolkit ought to be able to complete the three major API-consuming sections (Amazon, Google, Amazon again) in two to four hours each. If working in divide-and-conquer mode, it might make sense to have the same team members do both Amazon sections. The remaining exercises (5 through 8) should each take an hour or less.

15   Metadata (and Automatic Code Generation)

In this section you'll build a machine-readable representation of the requirements of an application and then build a computer program to generate the computer programs that implement that application. We'll treat this material in the context of building a knowledge management system, one of the most common types of online communities, and try to introduce you to terminology used by business people in this area.

Organizations have complex requirements for their information systems. A period of rapid economic growth can result in insane schedules and demands that a new information system be ready within weeks. Finally, organizations are fickle and have no compunction about changing the requirements midstream.

Technical people have traditionally met these challenges . . . by arguing over programming tools. The data model can't represent the information that the users need, the application doesn't do what what the users need it to do, and instead of writing code, the "engineers" are arguing about Java versus Lisp versus ML versus C# versus Perl versus VB. If you want to know why computer programmers get paid less than medical doctors, consider the situation of two trauma surgeons arriving at an accident scene. The patient is bleeding profusely. If surgeons were like programmers, they'd leave the patient to bleed out in order to have a really satisfying argument over the merits of two different kinds of tourniquet.

If you're programming one Web page at a time, you can switch to the language du jour in search of higher productivity. But you won't achieve significant gains unless you quit writing code for one page at a time. Think about ways to write down a machine-readable description of the application and user experience, then let the computer generate the application automatically.

War Story

The authors were asked to help Siemens and Boston Consulting Group (BCG) realize a knowledge sharing system for 17,000 telephone switch salespeople spread among 84 countries. This was back in the 1990s when (a) telephone companies were expanding capacity, and (b) corporations invested in information systems as a way of beating competitors.

Siemens had spent 6 months working with a Web development contractor that was expert in building HTML pages but had trouble programming SQL. They'd promised to launch the elaborately specified system 6 weeks from our first meeting. We concluded that many of the features that they wanted could be adapted from the source code behind the photo.net online community but that adding the "knowledge repository" would require 4 programmers working full-time for 6 weeks. What's worse, in looking at the specs we decided that the realized system would be unusably complex, especially for busy salespeople.

Instead of blindly cranking out the code, we assigned only one programmer to the project, our friend Tracy Adams. She turned the human-readable design notebooks into machine-readable database metadata tables. Tracy proceeded to build a program-to-write-the-program with no visible results. Siemens and BCG were nervous until Week 4 when the completed system was available for testing.

"How do you like it?" we asked. "This is the worst information system that we've ever used," they replied. "How do you compare it to your specs?" we asked. "Hmmm ... maybe we should simplify the specification," they replied.

After two more iterations the system, dubbed "ICN Sharenet" was launched on time and was adopted quickly, credited by Siemens with $122 million in additional sales during its first year of operation.

One thing that we hope you've learned during this course is the value of testing with users and iterative improvement of an application. If an application is machine-generated, you can test it with users, edit the specification based on their feedback, and regenerate the application in a matter of minutes, ready for a new test.

We're going to explore *metadata* (data about the data model) and automatic code generation in the problem domain of *knowledge management*.

What Is "Knowledge Management"?

A *knowledge management* or *knowledge-sharing* system is a multi-user information system enabling users to share *knowledge* about a shared domain of expertise or inquiry. What is "knowledge"? One way to answer this question is to spend ten years in a university philosophy department's epistemology group. From the perspective of a relational database management system, however, it may be easier to define knowledge as "text, authored by a user of the community, to which the user may attach a document, photograph, or spreadsheet." Other users can comment on the knowledge, submitting text and optional attachments of their own. From this definition, it would seem that the discussion forum you built earlier would meet the users' needs. Indeed, it is true that an archived-and-indexed question-and-answer forum may serve many of the needs of a *community of practice*, a group of people trying to solve similar problems who can learn from each others' experiences. However, there are a few features beyond a discussion forum that an organization may request, for example the following:

- links among knowledge "objects" (this is the term used by MBAs in the field)
- more structured facilities for browsing and searching than provided by a raw discussion forum, possibly including a link to an existing structured data set (e.g., in Example 2 below, the list of all airports in the United States)
- tracking and rewarding of contributions and reuse

Why Do Organizations Want Knowledge Management?

In any enterprise, the skills and experience of a group of workers or students will have an approximately Gaussian distribution: a handful of people who know almost nothing (beginners, incompetents, lazy bones), a handful of wizards who know almost everything (old-timers, geniuses, grinds), and a big hump in the middle of people who are moderately knowledgeable. The managers of the enterprise ask themselves "How much more could we accomplish if all of the people in this enterprise were as knowledgeable as the wizards?" Typically, the initial assumption is that knowledge is finite and this results in the construction of a system to contain a mostly static body of knowledge, to be extracted from the brains of the experts and codified into a series of files or database rows. Users quickly discover, however, that the situations they are facing are not quite analogous to the situations described in the "knowledge base" and the "knowledge management system" comes to be seen rather as a "knowledge mortuary."

An organization's second attempt at an information system intended to help beginners and average performers with the expertise of the most capable

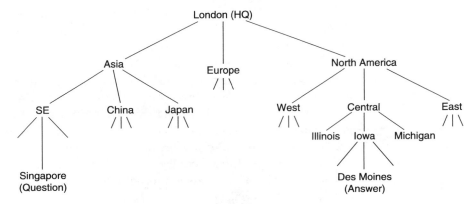

Figure 15.1 Multinational corporations are organized around a command-and-control hierarchy. This is good for assigning profit-and-loss responsibility, but creates information flow bottlenecks. Building a knowledge-sharing system is one way to facilitate information flow among the leaves of the tree.

is typically dubbed *knowledge sharing*. In a knowledge-sharing system, User A has the ability to put a question in front of the community so that Users B, C, and D can write new material and/or point A to previously authored articles.

If nothing else, a knowledge-sharing system provides a means for employees at the leaf nodes of a hierarchy to converse with each other. Consider the organization depicted in figure 15.1. Suppose that a worker in Singapore has a question that could be answered by a worker in Des Moines. The act of finding the coworker and getting assistance requires going all the way up the hierarchy to the chief executive in London and then back down a different path through the hierarchy to Des Moines. This bottleneck could be eliminated by eliminating the hierarchy. However, most organizations don't want to eliminate their hierarchies. It is the hierarchy that enables the corporation to reduce management complexity by establishing profit-and-loss responsibility at intermediate levels. Better to *supplement* the hierarchy with an informal mechanism by which the Singapore-based worker can ask for help and the Des Moines-based worker can offer it, that is, a knowledge-sharing system.

Exercise 1: Develop an Ontology

The American Heritage Dictionary defines *ontology* as "The branch of metaphysics that deals with the nature of being." Computer science researchers speak of "an ontology" as a structure for knowledge representation, that is, the ontology constrains the kinds of information that we can record (you will be forgiven if you confuse this advanced computer science concept with mere data modeling).

Your ontology will consist of class definitions and, because a relational database is the source of persistence behind your online community, your implementation of this ontology will consist of SQL table definitions, one table for each class. To assist you in developing a useful ontology for your community, here are a couple of examples.

Example Ontology 1: Computer Science

Corporations all have knowledge management systems even though generally they may not have any knowledge. Universities claim to have knowledge, and yet none have knowledge management systems. What would a knowledge management system for a university computer science department look like?

Let's assume that we'll have at least the following types in our ontology:

- person
- publication
- data structure
- system
- algorithm
- problem
- language

For each of these types, we will define a table and call a row in one of those tables an "object." To say that "John McCarthy developed the Lisp programming language," the author would create two objects: one of type `language` and one of type `person`. Why not link to the `users` table instead? John McCarthy might not be a registered user of the system. Some of the people you'll be referencing, for example, John von Neumann, are dead.

Each object comprises a set of elements. An element is stored in a column. For every object in the system, we want to record the following elements:

- name (a short description of the thing)
- overview (a longer description)

- who created this object
- when they created it
- who modified it last
- when they modified it
- who has the right to modify it
- who has the right to view it
- does it need approval?
- has it been approved?
- if so, by whom and when?
- if so, under what section?

In addition to these housekeeping elements, we will define type-specific elements:

for the person type   date_of_birth, title

for the language type   syntax_example, garbage_collection_p (whether the language has automatic storage allocation like Lisp or memory leaks like C), strongly_typed_p, type_inferencing_p, lexical_scoping_p, date_first_used

for the publication type   this is for storing references to books and journal articles so you want all the fields that you'd expect to see when referencing something; include also an abstract field

for the data structure type   complexity_for_insertion, complexity_for_retrieval (varchars containing "O(1)," "O(N)," etc.)

for the system type   examples of systems are "Multics," "Xerox Alto," "TCP/IP," "MIT Lisp Machine," "Apple Macintosh," "Unix," "World Wide Web." Includes fields for date_of_conception, date_of_birth, organization_name, open_source_p. No need to include fields for the names of developers because we can instead use links to objects of type person to represent prime developers or promoters.

for the problem type   examples of problems are "traveling salesman," "dining philosophers," "sort," "query for inclusion in sorted list." We'll want elements for storing initial conditions and solution criteria. In general, objects of type problem will be linked to objects of type algorithm (algorithms that solve the problem), publication (papers that set forth the problem), and person (people who were involved in stating or solving the problem)

for the `algorithm` type   examples include "Quicksort" and "binary search" elements for pseudo_code and high_level_explanation. In general, objects of type `algorithm` will be linked to objects of type `problem` (what need the algorithm addresses), `publication` (papers that describe the algorithm or implementations of it), and `person` (people who were involved in developing the algorithm)

For an example of what a completed system of this nature might look like, visit Paul Black's *Dictionary of Algorithms, Data Structures, and Problems* at http://www.nist.gov/dads/.

Example Ontology 2: Flying

We want a system that will enable pilots to assist each other by relating experience, for example, "The autopilot in N123 is not to be trusted," "Avoid the nachos at the airport cafe in Hopedale," with the comments anchored by official U.S. government information regarding airports, runways, and radio beacons for navigation.

Object types include:

- person
- publication
- airplane design
- airplane
- airport
- runway
- navigation aid ("navaid")
- restaurant
- hotel
- flight school
- flight instructor

In addition to the housekeeping elements defined in Example 1, we define type-specific elements:

for the `airplane design` type   For each kind of airplane flying, there is one entry in this table. An example might be "Cessna 172" or "Boeing 747." We need elements to specify performance such as stall_speed (how slow you can go before tumbling out of the sky), approach_speed (how fast you should go when coming near the runway to land), and cruise_speed. We want elements such as date_certified, manufacturer_name, and manufacturer_address to describe the design.

for the `airplane` type   An entry in this table is a specific airplane, very likely a rental machine belonging to a flight school. We want elements such as date_manufactured, ifr_capable_p (legal to fly in the clouds?), and optional_ equipment.

for the `airport` type   We want to know where the airport is: lat_long; elevation; relation_to_city (distance and direction from a named town). We want to know whether the airport is military only, private, or public. We want to know whether or not the airport has a rotating green/white beacon and runway lights. We want to store the frequencies for weather information, contacting other pilots (if non-towered) or the control tower (if towered), and air traffic control for instrument flight clearances. We need to record runway lengths and conditions. An airport may have several runways, however, thus giving rise to a many-to-one relation, which is why we model runways separately and link them to airports.

for the `runway` type   number (e.g., "09/27"), length, condition. Note that the runway number implies the magnetic orientation: 09 implies a heading of 090 or landing facing magnetic east; if the wind favors a landing on the same strip of asphalt in the opposite direction, you're on 27, which implies a heading of 270 or due west (36 faces north; 18 faces south).

for the `navigation aid` type   The U.S. Federal Aviation Administration maintains a nationwide network of Very High Frequency Omni Ranging beacons (VORs). These transmit two signals, one of which is constant in phase regardless of an airplane's bearing to the VOR. The second signal varies in phase as one circles a VOR. Thus a VOR receiver in the airplane can compare the phase of the two signals and determine that an airplane is, for example, on the 123-degree radial from the VOR. If you didn't have a Global Positioning System receiver in your airplane, you'd determine your position on the chart by plotting radials out from two VORs. For a navaid, we need to store its type (could be an old non-directional beacon, which simply puts out an AM radio-style broadcast), frequency, position, and Morse code ID (you want to listen to the dot-dash pattern to make sure that you're receiving the proper navaid).

for the `restaurant` type menu_excerpt, hours, distance_from_airport, phone_number, url, email, street_address

for the `hotel` type price, distance_from_airport, phone_number, url, email, street_address

For an example of a running system along these lines, visit http://www .airnav.com/airports/ and type in the name or code for your favorite airport.

Back to Your Ontology

Following the structure that you designed in the "Software Modularity" chapter, create a module called "km" (for "knowledge management") and start the high-level document for this module with (a) a statement of purpose for the subsystem, and (b) a list of object types, housekeeping elements shared among types, and type-specific elements.

For ease of evaluation and interaction with your classmates, we suggest placing the user pages at http://yourservername/km/.

Exercise 2: Design a Metadata Data Model

The document that you wrote in the preceding exercise is a good basis for discussion among your team members, the client, and teaching assistants. However, it is not machine readable. In theory, nothing would be wrong with developing a machine-readable metadata repository in a tab-separated file system file, to be edited with a text editor. In practice, however, systems are cleaner when there are fewer mechanisms underneath. Thus far your primary source of persistence has been the relational database management system, so you might as well use that for your metadata repository as well. At the very least, the database is where a programmer new to the project would expect to find the metadata.

Here's an example SQL data model for a metadata repository:

```
-- note that this is designed for the Oracle 8i/9i RDBMS

-- we'll have one row in this table for every object type
-- and thus for every new SQL table that gets defined; an
-- object type and its database table name are the same;
-- Oracle limits schema objects to 30 characters and thus
```

```
-- we limit a table_name to 21 characters so that we can
-- have some freedom to create schema objects whose names
-- are prefixed with an object type

-- a "pretty name" is a synonym used when presenting pages
-- to users; the prettiness could be as simple as replacing
-- underscores with spaces or spelling out abbreviations;
-- e.g., for an object type of "airplane_design", the pretty
-- form might be "airplane design", and pretty_plural
-- "airplane designs"

create table km_metadata_object_types (
        table_name              varchar(21) primary key,
        pretty_name             varchar(100) not null,
        pretty_plural           varchar(100)
);

-- here is the table for elements that are unique to an object type
-- (the housekeeping elements can be defined implicitly in the source
-- code for the application generator); there will be one row in
-- the metadata table per element

create table km_metadata_elements (
        metadata_id             integer primary key,
        table_name              not null references km_metadata_object_types,
        column_name             varchar(30) not null,
        pretty_name             varchar(100) not null,
        abstract_data_type      varchar(30) not null,     -- ie. "text" or "shorttext" "boolean" "user"
          -- this one is not null except when abstract_data_type is "user"
        oracle_data_type        varchar(30),    -- "varchar(4000)"
        -- e.g., "not null" or "check foobar in ('christof', 'patrick')"
        extra_sql               varchar(4000),
        -- values are 'text', 'textarea', 'select', 'radio',
          -- 'selectmultiple', 'checkbox', 'checkboxmultiple', 'selectsql'
        presentation_type       varchar(100) not null,
        -- e.g., for textarea, this would be "rows=6 cols=60", for select, Tcl list,
        -- for selectsql, an SQL query that returns N district values
        -- for email addresses mailto:
        presentation_options    varchar(4000),
        -- pretty_name is going to be the short prompt,
          -- e.g., for an update page, but we also need something
          -- longer if we have to walk the user through a long form
        entry_explanation       varchar(4000),
          -- if they click for yet more help
        help_text               varchar(4000),
        -- note that this does NOT translate into a "not null" constraint in Oracle
```

```
-- if we did this, it would preclude an interface in which users create rows incrementally
mandatory_p               char(1) check (mandatory_p in ('t','f')),
-- ordering in Oracle table creation, 0 would be on top, 1 underneath, etc.
sort_key                  integer,
-- ordering within a form, lower number = higher on page
form_sort_key             integer,
-- if there are N forms, starting with 0, to define this object,
  -- on which does this go? (relevant for very complex objects where
  -- you need more than one page to submit)
form_number               integer,
-- for full text index
include_in_ctx_index_p    char(1) check (include_in_ctx_index_p in ('t','f')),
-- add forms should be prefilled with the default value
default_value             varchar(200),
  check ((abstract_data_type not in ('user') and oracle_data_type is not null)
      or
      (abstract_data_type in ('user')))),
unique(table_name,column_name)
);
```

Exercise 3: Write a Program to Generate DDL Statements

Begin an admin interface to your km module, starting with a page whose URL ends in "ddl-generate." This should be a script that will generate CREATE TABLE (data definition language) statements from the metadata tables. You'll want to have a look at the SQL before feeding it to the RDBMS, and therefore you may wish to write your script so that it simply outputs the DDL statements to the Web browser with a MIME type of text/plain. You can save this to your local file system as km-generated.sql and feed it to your SQL client when you're satisfied.

In addition to the housekeeping elements that you've defined for your application, each object table should have an object_id column. The value of this column should be unique across all of the tables in the km module, which is easy to do in Oracle if you use a single sequence to generate all the keys. Given unique object IDs across types, if you were to add a km_object_registry table, you'd be able to publish cleaner URLs that pass around only object IDs rather than object IDs and types.

In addition to the metadata-driven object table definitions, your script should define a generalized mapping table to support links between knowledge objects. Here's an Oracle-syntax example:

```
create table km_object_object_map (
        object_id_a             integer not null,
        object_id_b             integer not null,
        -- the objects are uniquely identified above but let's save ourselves
        -- hassle by recording in which tables to find them
        table_name_a            not null references km_metadata_object_types,
        table_name_b            not null references km_metadata_object_types,
        -- User-entered reason for relating two objects, e.g.
        -- to distinguish between John McCarthy the developer of
        -- Lisp and Gerry Sussman and Guy Steele, who added lexical scoping
        -- in the Scheme dialect
        map_comment             varchar(4000),
        creation_user           not null references users,
        creation_date           date default sysdate not null,
        primary key (object_id_a, object_id_b)
);
```

Notice that this table allows the users to map an object to any other object in the system, regardless of type.

For simplicity, assume that associations are bidirectional. Suppose that a knowledge author associates the Huffman encoding algorithm (used in virtually every compression scheme, including JPEG) with the person David A. Huffman (1925–1999; an MIT graduate student at the time of his invention, which was submitted as a term paper). We should also interpret that to mean that the person David A. Huffman is associated with the algorithm for Huffman encoding. This is why the columns in km_object_object_map have names such as "object_id_a" instead of "from_object."

In an Oracle database, the primary key constraint above has the side effect of creating an index that makes it fast to ask the question "What objects are related to Object 17, where Object 17 happens to appear in the A slot?" For efficiency in querying "What objects are related to Object 17, where Object 17 happens to appear in the B slot?" create a concatenated index on the columns in the reverse order from that of the primary key constraint.

The "Trees" chapter of *SQL for Web Nerds*, at http://philip.greenspun.com/sql/trees, gives some examples of concatenated indices. If you're using Oracle, you may want to read the composite indices section of the *Performance Guide and Reference* manual (online and in the product documentation) and the *SQL Reference* manual's section on "Create Index."

Exercise 4: Write a Program to Generate a "Drop All Tables" Script

Write a script in the same admin directory as `ddl-generate`, called `drop-tables-generate`. This should generate DROP TABLE statements from the metadata tables. You probably won't get your data model right the first time, so you might as well be ready to clear out the RDBMS and start over.

Feed the database management system the results of your data model creation and clean-up scripts until you stop getting error messages.

Dimensional Controls

When displaying a long list of information on a page, consider adding *dimensional controls* to the top. Suppose for example that you wish to help an administrator browse among the registered users of a site. You have a feeling that the user community will grow too large for the complete list to be useful. You therefore add an intermediate page with the following options:

- show users who've registered in the last 30 days
- show users from the same geographical area as me (site administration tends to be divided up by region)
- show users who have contributed more than 5 items
- show users whose content has been rated below "C" (looking for people who add a lot of crud to the database)

A well-designed page of this form will have a number placed discreetly next to each option, showing the number of users who will be displayed if that option is selected. A poorly designed page will simply leave the administrator guessing as to how much information will be shown after an option is selected.

This traditional approach has some drawbacks. First, it adds a mouse click before the administrator can see any user names. Ideally, you want every page of an application to display information and/or potential actions rather than pure bureaucracy and navigation. Second, and more seriously, this approach doesn't scale very well. When an administrator says "I need to see users who've registered within the last 30 days, who've contributed more than 4 product reviews, and who've bought at least $100 of stuff so that I can spam them with a coupon," another option must be added to the list. Eventually the navigation page groans with choices.

Imagine instead that the very first mouse click takes the administrator to a page that shows all the users who've registered in the last 30 days, in one big long list. At the top are sliders. Each slider controls a dimension, each of which can restrict or expand the number of items in the list. Here are some example dimensions for a community e-commerce site such as amazon.com:

- recency of registration, from 1 day ago (restrictive) to the beginning of time (loose)
- geographical proximity, from same postal code (restrictive) to same city to same state to anywhere in the world (loose)
- total purchases, from at least $10,000 (restrictive) to at least $500 to $0 or more (loose)
- review activity, from Top 100 Reviewer (restrictive) to Top 1000 Reviewer to 0 or more reviews (loose)
- content quality, from average review rated 4.5 stars or better (restrictive) to any average

If the default page shows too many names, the administrator will adjust a slider or two to be more restrictive. If the administrator wants to see more names, he or she will adjust a slider towards the loose end of that dimension.

How to implement dimensional controls? Sadly, there is no HTML tag that will generate a little continuous slider. You can simulate a slider by offering, for each dimension, a set of discrete points along the dimension, each of which is a simple text hyperlink anchor. For example, for content quality you might offer "4 or better," "3 or better," "2 or better," "all."

Exercise 5: Build the Knowledge Capture Pages

Here is a list of URLs that we think you'll want to create, named with a "noun-verb" convention:

- index
- object-create
- object-display

- object-summarize
- object-edit-element
- link-add
- one-type-browse

Start by creating an index page in your `/km/` directory. At the very least, the index page should display an unordered list of object types and, next to each type, options to "browse" or "create." You don't have any information in the database, so you should build a script called `object-create` first. This page will query the metadata tables to build a data entry form to create a single object of a particular type.

When your object creation pipeline is done inserting the row into the database, it should redirect the author's browser to a page where the object is displayed (name the script `object-display` if you don't have a better idea). Presumably, the original author has authority to edit this object and therefore this page should display small hyperlinks to edit single fields. All of these links can target the URL `object-edit-element` with different arguments. The object display page should also summarize all the currently linked objects and have an "add link" hyperlink whose target is `link-add`.

The page returned by `link-add` will look virtually identical to the index page, that is, a list of object types. Each object type can be a hyperlink to a multi-purpose script at `one-type-browse`. When called with only a `table_name` argument, this page will display a table of object names with dimensional controls at the top. The dimensions should be "mine|everyone's" and "creation date." The user ought to be able to click on a table header and sort by that column.

When called with extra arguments, `one-type-browse` will pass those arguments through to `object-summarize`, a script very similar to `object-display`, but only showing enough information that the author can positively identify the object and with the additional ability to accept arguments for a potential link, for example, `table_name_a` and `object_id_a`.

Carrots and Sticks; Chicken and Egg

Most workers get rewarded for working; why would they want to take time out to author knowledge and answer questions in an online system? People take the time to ask questions in venues where they can expect answers. If nobody is answering, nobody will ask, thus leading to a chicken-and-egg problem.

It is important to create an incentive system that rewards users for exhibiting the desired behavior. At amazon.com, for example, the site owners want users to write a lot of reader reviews. At the same time, they apparently don't want to pay people to write reviews. The solution circa 2005 is to recognize contributors with a "reviewer rank." If a lot of other Amazon users have clicked to say that they found your reviews useful, you may rise above 1,000 and a "Top 1000 Reviewer" icon appears next to your name. From the home page of Amazon, navigate to "Friends and favorites" (under "Special Features"). Then, underneath "Explore," click on "Top Reviewers." Notice that some of the top 10 reviewers have written more than 5,000 reviews, all free of charge to Amazon!

What makes sense to reward in an online community? We could start with a couple of obvious activities: content authoring and question answering. Every night our system could query the content tables and update user ranks according to how many articles and answers they'd posted into the database. Is it really a good idea to reward users purely on the basis of volume? Shouldn't we give more weight to content that has actually helped people? For example, suppose that there are ten answers to a discussion forum question. It makes sense to give the maximum reward to the author of the answer that the person asking the question felt was most valuable. If a question can be marked "urgent" by the asker, it probably makes sense to give greater rewards to people who answer urgent questions than non-urgent ones. An article is nice, but an article that prompts another user to say "I reused this idea in my area of the organization" is much nicer and should be encouraged with a greater reward.

Exercise 6: Gather Statistics

Rather than do surgery on the discussion forum system right now, let's start by adding an accounting system to our new knowledge management data model. Start by creating a table to hold object views. Here's an example:

```
create sequence km_object_view_id;

create table km_object_views (
        object_view_id integer primary key,
        -- which user
```

```
            user_id          not null references users,
            -- two columns to specify which object
            object_id        integer not null,
            table_name       varchar(21) not null,
            view_time        timestamp(0) not null,
            reuse_p          char(1) default 'f' check(reuse_p in ('t','f'))
    );
```

Modify `object-view-one` so that it will insert a row into the `km_object_views` table if and only if there isn't already a log row for this user/object pair within twenty-four hours. You can do this with the following procedure:

1. open a transaction

2. lock the table

3. count the number of matching rows within the last 24 hours

4. compare the result to 0 and insert if necessary

5. close the transaction

This appears to be an awfully big hammer for a seemingly simple problem. Is it possible to do this in one statement?

Let's start with Oracle. Here's an example of an INSERT statement that only has an effect if there isn't already a row in the table:

```
insert into km_object_views (object_view_id, user_id, object_id, table_name, view_time)
select km_object_view_id.nextval, 227, 891, 'algorithm', current_timestamp(0)
from dual
where 0 = (select count(*)
            from km_object_views
            where user_id = 227
            and object_id = 891
            and view_time > current_timestamp - interval '1' day);
```

The structure of this statement is "insert into KM_OBJECT_VIEWS the result of querying the 1-row system table DUAL." We're not pulling any data from the DUAL table, only including constants in the SELECT list. Nor is the WHERE clause restricting results based on information in the DUAL table; it is querying KM_OBJECT_VIEWS. This is a seemingly perverse way to use SQL, but in fact is fairly conventional because there are no IF statements in standard SQL.

Suppose, however, that two copies of this INSERT start simultaneously. Recall that a transaction processing system provides the ACID guarantees:

Session A	**Session B**
Sends INSERT to Oracle at system change number ("SCN", a pseudo-time internal to Oracle) 30561.	Sends INSERT to Oracle at system change number 30562, a tick after Session A started its transaction but several ticks before Session A accomplished its insertion.
Oracle counts the rows in `km_object_views` and finds 0.	Oracle, busy with other users, doesn't start counting rows in `km_object_views` until SCN 30568, after the insert from Session A. The database, however, will return 0 blocks because it is presenting Session B with a view of the database as it was at SCN 30562, when the transaction started.
Oracle inserts a row into `km_object_views` at SCN 30567 (took a while for the COUNT(*) to complete; meanwhile other users have been inserting and updating rows in other tables).	
	Having found 0 rows in the count, the INSERT proceeds to insert one row, thus creating a duplicate log entry.

Figure 15.2

Atomicity, Consistency, *Isolation*, and Durability. Oracle's implementation of *isolation*, "the results of a transaction are invisible to other transactions until the transaction is complete," works by giving each user a virtual version of the database as it was when the transaction started.

More: See the "Data Concurrency and Consistency" chapter of *Oracle10g Database Concepts*, one of the books included in Oracle documentation.

Now consider the same query running in SQL Server:

```
insert into km_object_views (user_id, object_id, table_name, view_time)
select 227, 891, 'algorithm', current_timestamp
where 0 = (select count(*)
           from km_object_views
           where user_id = 227
           and object_id = 891
           and datediff(hour, view_time, current_timestamp) < 24)
```

There are minor syntactic differences from the Oracle statement above, but the structure is the same. A new row is inserted only if no matching rows are found within the last twenty-four hours.

SQL Server achieves the same isolation level as Oracle ("Read Committed"), but in a different way. Instead of creating virtual versions of the database, SQL Server holds exclusive locks during data-modification operations. In the example above, Session B's INSERT cannot begin until Session A's INSERT has completed. Once it is allowed to begin, Session B will see the result of Session A's insert, and will therefore not insert a duplicate row.

More: See the "Understanding Locking in SQL Server" chapter of *SQL Server Books Online*, the Microsoft SQL Server documentation.

Whenever you are performing logging, it is considerate to do it on the server's time, not the user's. In many Web development environments, you can do this by calling an API procedure that will close the TCP connection to the user, which stops the upper-right browser corner icon from spinning/waving. Meanwhile your thread (IIS, AOLserver, Apache 2) or process (Apache 1.x) is still alive on the server and can run whatever code is necessary to perform the logging. Many Web servers allow you to define filters that run after the delivery of a page to the user.

Help with date/time arithmetic: see the "Dates" chapter of *SQL for Web Nerds* at http://philip.greenspun.com/sql/dates.

Exercise 7: Gather More Statistics

Modify `object-view-one` to add a "I reused this knowledge" button. This should link to `object-mark-reused`, a page that updates the `reuse_p` flag of the most recent relevant row in `km_object_views`. The page should raise an error if it can't find a row to update.

Exercise 8: Explain the Concurrency Problem in Exercise 7

Given an implementation of `object-view-one` that does its logging on the server's time, explain the concurrency problem that arises in Exercise 7 and talk about ways to address it.

Write up your solutions to these non-coding exercises either in your km module overview document or in a file named `metadata-exercises` in the same directory.

Exercise 9: Do a Little Performance Tuning

Create an index on `km_object_views` that will make the code in Exercises 6 and 7 go fast.

Exercise 10: Display Statistics

Build a summary page, for example, at `/km/admin/statistics` to show, by day, the number of objects viewed and reused. This report should be broken down by object type and all the statistics should be links to "drill-down" pages where the underlying data are exposed, for example, which actual users viewed or reused knowledge and when.

Exercise 11: Think about Full-Text Indexing

Write up a strategy for adding the objects authored in this system to the site-wide full-text index.

Exercise 12: Think about Unifying with Your Content Tables

Write up a strategy for unifying your preexisting content tables with the system that you built in this chapter. Discuss the pros and cons of using new tables for the knowledge management module or extending old ones.

Feel Free to Hand-Edit

Suppose that an autogenerated application is more or less complete and functional, but you can see some room for improvement. Is it acceptable practice to pull some of the generated code into a text editor and change it by hand? Absolutely! The point of using metadata is to tackle extreme requirements and get a prototype in front of real users as quickly as possible. Don't feel like a failure because you haven't solved the fifty-year-old research problem of automating programming altogether.

Time and Motion

The team should work together with the client to develop the ontology. These discussions and the initial documentation should require two to three hours. Designing the metadata data model may be a simple copy/paste operation for teams building with Oracle, but in any case should require no more than an hour. Generating the DDL statements and drop tables script should take about two hours of work by one programmer. Building out the system pages, Exercises 5 through 10, should require eight to twelve programmer-hours. This part can be divided to an extent, but it's probably best to limit the programming to two individuals working together closely since the exercises build upon one another. Finally, the writeups at the end should take one to two hours total.

16   User Activity Analysis

This chapter looks at ways that you can monitor user activity within your community and how that information can be used to personalize a user's experience.

Step 1: Ask the Right Questions

Before considering what is technically feasible, it is best to start with a wishlist of the questions about user activity that have relevance for your client's application. Here are some starter questions:

- What are the URLs that are producing server errors? (answer leads to action: fix broken code)

- How many users requested nonexistent files, and where did they get the bad URLs? (answer leads to action: fix bad links)

- Are at least 50 percent of users visiting /foobar/, our newest and most important section? (answer leads to action: maybe add more pointers to the new section from other areas of the site)

- How popular are the voice and wireless interfaces to the application? (answer leads to action: invest more effort in popular interfaces)

- Which pages are causing users to get stuck and abandon their sessions? I.e., what are the typical last pages viewed before a user disappears for the day? (answer leads to action: clarify user interface or annotation on those pages)

- Suppose that we operate an e-commerce site and that we've purchased advertisements on Google and www.nytimes.com. How likely are visitors from those two sources to buy something? How do the dollar amounts compare?

(answer leads to action: buy more ads from the place that sends high-profit users)

Step 2: Look at What's Easily Available

Every HTTP server program can be configured to log its actions. Typically the server will write two logs: (1) the "access log," containing one line corresponding to every user request, and (2) the "error log," containing complete information about what went wrong during those requests that resulted in program errors. A "file not found" will result in an access log entry, but not a error log entry because the server did not have to catch a script bug. By contrast, a script sending an illegal SQL command to the database will result in both an access log and an error log entry.

Below is a snippet from the file http://philip.greenspun.com/seia/examples-user-activity-analysis/2003-03-06.log.gz, which records one day of activity on this server (philip.greenspun.com). Notice that the name of the log file, "2003-03-06," is arranged so that chronological success will result in lexicographical sorting succession and therefore, when viewing files in a directory listing, you'll see a continuous progression from oldest to newest. The file itself is in the "Common Logfile Format," a standard developed in 1995.

```
193.2.79.250 - - [06/Mar/2003:09:11:59 -0500] "GET /dogs/george
HTTP/1.1" 200 0 "http://www.photo.net/" "Mozilla/4.0 (compatible;
MSIE 5.0; Windows NT; DigExt)"
193.2.79.250 - - [06/Mar/2003:09:11:59 -0500] "GET /dogs/sky-and-
philip.jpg HTTP/1.1" 200 9596 "http://philip.greenspun.com/dogs/
george" "Mozilla/4.0 (compatible; MSIE 5.0; Windows NT; DigExt)"
193.2.79.250 - - [06/Mar/2003:09:11:59 -0500] "GET /dogs/george-
28.jpg HTTP/1.1" 200 10154 "http://philip.greenspun.com/dogs/george"
"Mozilla/4.0 (compatible; MSIE 5.0; Windows NT; DigExt)"
193.2.79.250 - - [06/Mar/2003:09:11:59 -0500] "GET /dogs/nika-36.jpg
HTTP/1.1" 200 8627 "http://philip.greenspun.com/dogs/george"
"Mozilla/4.0 (compatible; MSIE 5.0; Windows NT; DigExt)"
193.2.79.250 - - [06/Mar/2003:09:11:59 -0500] "GET /dogs/george-
nika-provoke.jpg HTTP/1.1" 200 11949 "http://philip.greenspun.com/
dogs/george" "Mozilla/4.0 (compatible; MSIE 5.0; Windows NT;
DigExt)"
152.31.2.221 - - [06/Mar/2003:09:11:59 -0500] "GET /comments/
attachment/36106/bmwz81.jpg HTTP/1.1" 200 38751 "http://
philip.greenspun.com/materialism/cars/nsx.html" "Mozilla/4.0
(compatible; MSIE 6.0; Windows NT 5.1)"
```

```
193.2.79.250 - - [06/Mar/2003:09:12:00 -0500] "GET /dogs/george-
nika-grapple.jpg HTTP/1.1" 200 7887 "http://philip.greenspun.com/
dogs/george" "Mozilla/4.0 (compatible; MSIE 5.0; Windows NT;
DigExt)"
193.2.79.250 - - [06/Mar/2003:09:12:00 -0500] "GET /dogs/george-
nika-bite.jpg HTTP/1.1" 200 10977 "http://philip.greenspun.com/dogs/
george" "Mozilla/4.0 (compatible; MSIE 5.0; Windows NT; DigExt)"
193.2.79.250 - - [06/Mar/2003:09:12:00 -0500] "GET /dogs/george-
29.jpg HTTP/1.1" 200 10763 "http://philip.greenspun.com/dogs/george"
"Mozilla/4.0 (compatible; MSIE 5.0; Windows NT; DigExt)"
193.2.79.250 - - [06/Mar/2003:09:12:00 -0500] "GET /dogs/philip-and-
george-sm.jpg HTTP/1.1" 200 9574 "http://philip.greenspun.com/dogs/
george" "Mozilla/4.0 (compatible; MSIE 5.0; Windows NT; DigExt)"
152.31.2.221 - - [06/Mar/2003:09:12:00 -0500] "GET /comments/
attachment/44949/FriendsProjectCar.jpg HTTP/1.1" 200 36340 "http://
philip.greenspun.com/materialism/cars/nsx.html" "Mozilla/4.0
(compatible; MSIE 6.0; Windows NT 5.1)"
193.2.79.250 - - [06/Mar/2003:09:12:00 -0500] "GET /comments/
attachment/35069/muffin.jpg HTTP/1.1" 200 15017 "http://
philip.greenspun.com/dogs/george" "Mozilla/4.0 (compatible; MSIE
5.0; Windows NT; DigExt)"
152.31.2.221 - - [06/Mar/2003:09:12:01 -0500] "GET /comments/
attachment/77819/z06.jpg HTTP/1.1" 200 46996 "http://
philip.greenspun.com/materialism/cars/nsx.html" "Mozilla/4.0
(compatible; MSIE 6.0; Windows NT 5.1)"
151.199.192.112 - - [06/Mar/2003:09:12:01 -0500] "GET /comments/
attachment/137758/GT%20NSX%202.jpg HTTP/1.1" 200 12656 "http://
philip.greenspun.com/materialism/cars/nsx" "Mozilla/4.0 (compatible;
MSIE 5.0; Mac_PowerPC)"
152.31.2.221 - - [06/Mar/2003:09:12:02 -0500] "GET /comments/
attachment/171519/photo_002.jpg HTTP/1.1" 200 45618
"http://philip.greenspun.com/materialism/cars/nsx.html" "Mozilla/4.0
(compatible; MSIE 6.0; Windows NT 5.1)"
151.199.192.112 - - [06/Mar/2003:09:12:27 -0500] "GET /comments/
attachment/143336/Veil%20Side%20Skyline%20GTR2.jpg HTTP/1.1" 200
40372 "http://philip.greenspun.com/materialism/cars/nsx" "Mozilla/
4.0 (compatible; MSIE 5.0; Mac_PowerPC)"
147.102.16.28 - - [06/Mar/2003:09:12:29 -0500] "GET /photo/pcd1253/
canal-street-43.1.jpg HTTP/1.1" 302 336 "http://
philip.greenspun.com/wtr/application-servers.html" "Mozilla/4.0
(compatible; MSIE 5.01; Windows NT)"
147.102.16.28 - - [06/Mar/2003:09:12:29 -0500] "GET /photo/pcd2388/
john-harvard-statue-7.1.jpg HTTP/1.1" 302 342 "http://
philip.greenspun.com/wtr/application-servers.html" "Mozilla/4.0
(compatible; MSIE 5.01; Windows NT)"
```

```
147.102.16.28 - - [06/Mar/2003:09:12:31 -0500] "GET /wtr/
application-servers.html HTTP/1.1" 200 0 "http://www.google.com/
search?q=application+servers&ie=ISO-8859-7&hl=el&lr=" "Mozilla/4.0
(compatible; MSIE 5.01; Windows NT)"
```

The first line can be decoded as follows:

A user on a computer at the IP address **193.2.79.250**, who is not telling us his login name on that computer nor supplying an HTTP authentication login name to the Web server (**- -**), on March 6, 2003 at 9 hours 11 minutes 59 seconds past midnight in a timezone 5 hours behind Greenwich Mean Time (**06/Mar/2003:09:11:59 -0500**), requested the file **/dogs/george** using the **GET** method of the **HTTP/1.1** protocol. The file was found by the server and returned normally (status code of **200**) but it was returned by an ill-behaved script that did not give the server information about how many bytes were written, hence the **0** after the status code. This user followed a link to this URL from **http://www.photo.net/** (the referer header) and is using a browser that first falsely identifies itself as Netscape 4.0 (**Mozilla 4.0**), but then explains that it is actually merely **compatible** with Netscape and is really Microsoft Internet Explorer 5.0 on Windows NT (**MSIE 5.0; Windows NT**). On a lightly used service we might have configured the server to use `nslookup` and log the hostname of `stargate.fs.uni-lj.si` rather than the IP address, in which case we'd have been able to glance at the log and see that it was someone at a university in Slovenia.

That's a lot of information in one line, but consider what is missing. If this user previously logged in and presented a `user_id` cookie, we can't tell and we don't have that user ID. On an e-commerce site we might be able to infer that the user purchased something by the presence of a line showing a successful request for a "complete-purchase" URL. However we won't see the dollar amount of that purchase, and surely a $1,000 purchase is much more interesting than a $10 purchase.

Step 3: Figure Out What Extra Information You Need to Record

If your client is unhappy with the kind of information available from the standard logs, there are three basic alternatives:

- configure the HTTP server program to add cookie header contents to the standard access log

- augment your software to log additional user activity into the RDBMS and construct ad hoc query pages in the site administrator area of the service
- construct a full dimensional data warehouse of user activity

If all that you need is the user ID for every request, it is often a simple matter to configure the HTTP server program, for example, Apache or Microsoft Internet Information Server, to append the contents of the entire cookie header or just one named cookie to each line in the access log.

When that isn't sufficient, you can start adding columns to database tables. In a sense you've already started this process. You probably have a `registration_date` column in your `users` table, for example. This information could be derived from the access logs, but if you need it to show a "member since 2001" annotation as part of their user profile, it makes more sense to keep it in the RDBMS. If you want to offer members a page of "new items since your last visit" you'll probably add `last_login` and `second_to_last_login` columns to the users table. Note that you need `second_to_last_login` because as soon as User 345 returns to the site your software will update `last_login`. When he or she clicks the "new since last visit" page, it might be only thirty seconds since the timestamp in the `last_login` column. What User 345 will more likely expect is new content since the preceding Monday, his or her previous session with the service.

Suppose the marketing department starts running ad campaigns on ten different sites with the goal of attracting new members. They'll want a report of how many people registered who came from each of those ten foreign sites. Each ad would be a hyperlink to an encoded URL on your server. This would set a session cookie saying "source=nytimes" ("I came from an ad on the New York Times Web site"). If that person eventually registered as a member, the token "nytimes" would be written into a `source` column in the `users` table. After a month you'll be asked to write an admin page querying the database and displaying a histogram of registration by day, by month, by source, and so forth.

The road of adding columns to transaction-processing tables and building ad hoc SQL queries to answer questions is a long and tortuous one. The traditional way back to a manageable information system with users getting the answers they need is the *dimensional data warehouse*, discussed at some length in the data warehousing chapter of *SQL for Web Nerds* at http://philip.greenspun.com/sql/data-warehousing. A data warehouse is a heavily denormalized copy of the information in the transaction-processing tables, arranged so as to facilitate queries rather than updates.

The exercises in this chapter will walk you through these three alternatives, each of which has its place.

Exercise 1: See How the Other Half Lives

Most Web publishers have limited budgets and therefore limited access to programmers. Consequently they rely on standard log analysis programs analyzing standard server access logs. In this exercise you'll see what they see. Pick a standard log analyzer, for example, the analog program referenced at the end of this chapter, and prepare a report of all recorded user activity for the last month.

An acceptable solution to this exercise will involve linking the most recent report from the site administration pages so that the publisher can view it. A better solution will involve placing a "prepare current report" link in the admin pages that will invoke the log analyzer on demand and display the report. An exhaustive (exhausting?) solution will consist of a scheduled process ("cron job" in Unix parlance, "at command" or "scheduled task" on Windows) that runs the log analyzer every day, updating cumulative reports and preparing a new daily report, all of which are accessible from the site admin pages.

Make sure that your report clearly shows "404 Not Found" requests (any standard log analyzer can be configured to display these) and that the referer header is displayed so that you can figure out where the bad link is likely to be.

Security Risks of Running Programs in Response to a Web Request

Running the log analyzer in response to an administrator's request sounds innocent, but any system in which an HTTP server program can start up a new process in response to a Web request presents a security risk. Many Web scripting languages have "exec" commands in which the Web server has all of the power of a logged-in user typing at a command line. This is a powerful and useful capability, but a malicious user might be able to, for example, run a program that will return the username/password file for the server.

In the Unix world the most effective solution to this challenge is `chroot`, short for *change root*. This command changes the file system root of the Web server, and any program started by the Web server, to some other place in the file system, for example, `/web/main-server/`. A program in the directory

`/usr/local/bin/` can't be executed by the chrooted Web server because the Web server can't even describe a file unless its path begins with `/web/main-server/`. The root directory, `/`, is now `/web/main-server/`. One downside of this approach is that if the Web server needs to run a program in the directory `/usr/local/bin/` it can't. The solution is to take all of the utilities, server log analyzers, and other required programs and move them underneath `/web/main-server/`, for example, to `/web/main-server/bin/`.

Sadly, there does not seem to be a Windows equivalent to `chroot`, though there are other ways to lock down a Web server in Windows so that its process can't execute programs.

Exercise 2: Comedy of Errors

The last thing that any publisher wants is for a user to be faced with a "Server Error" in response to a request. Unfortunately, chances are that if one user gets an error there will be plenty more to follow. The HTTP server program will log each event, but unless a site is newly launched chances are that no programmer is watching the error log at any given moment.

First make sure that your server is configured to log as much information as possible about each error. At the very least you need the server to log the URL where the error occurred and the error message from the procedure that raised the error. Better Web development environments will also log a stack backtrace.

Second, provide a hyperlink from the site-wide administration pages to a page that shows the most recent 500 lines of the error log, with an option to go back a further 500 lines, and so on.

Third, write a procedure that runs periodically, either as a separate process or as part of the HTTP server program itself, and scans the error log for new entries since the preceding run of the procedure. If any of those new entries are actual errors, the procedure emails them to the programmers maintaining the site. You might want to start with an interval of one hour.

Real-Time Error Notifications

The system that you built in Exercise 2 guarantees that a programmer will find out about an error within about one hour. On a high-profile site this might not be adequate. It might be worth building error notification into the software itself. Serious errors can be caught and the error handler can call a `notify_the_maintainers` procedure that sends email. This might be worth including, for example, in a centralized facility that allows page scripts to connect to the relational database management system (RDBMS). If the RDBMS is unavailable, the sysadmins, dbadmins, and programmers ought to be notified immediately so that they can figure out what went wrong and bring the system back up.

Suppose that an RDBMS failure were combined with a naive implementation of `notify_the_maintainers` on a site that gets 10 requests per second. Suppose further that all of the people on the email notification list have gone out for lunch together for one hour. Upon their return, they will find $60 \times 60 \times 10 = 36,000$ identical email messages in their inbox.

To avoid this kind of debacle, it is probably best to have `notify_the_maintainers` record a `last_notification_sent` timestamp in the HTTP server's memory or on disk and use it to ignore or accumulate requests for notification that come in, say, within 15 minutes of a previous request. A reasonable assumption is that a programmer, once alerted, will visit the server and start looking at the full error logs. Thus `notify_the_maintainers` need not actually send out information about every problem encountered.

Exercise 3: Talk to Your Client

Using the standardized Web server log reports that you obtained in an earlier exercise as a starting point, talk to your client about what kind of user activity analysis he or she would really like to see. You want to do this after you've got at least something to show so that the discussion is more concrete and because the client's thinking is likely to be spurred by looking over a log analyzer's reports and noticing what's missing.

Write down the questions that your client says are the most important.

Exercise 4: Design a Data Warehouse

Write a SQL data model for a dimensional data warehouse of user activity. Look at the retail examples in http://philip.greenspun.com/sql/data-warehousing for inspiration. The resulting data model should be able to answer the questions put forth by your client in Exercise 3.

The biggest design decision that you'll face during this exercise is the granularity of the fact table. If you're interested in how users get from page to page within a site, the granularity of the fact table must be "one request." On a site such as the national "don't call me" registry, www.donotcall.gov, launched in 2003, one would expect a person to visit only once. Therefore the user activity data warehouse might store just one row per registered user, summarizing their appearance at the site and completion of registration, a fact table granularity of "one user." For many services, an intermediate granularity of "one session" will be appropriate.

With a "one session" granularity and appropriate dimensions it is possible to ask questions such as "What percentage of the sessions were initiated in response to an ad at Google.com?" (source field added to the fact table) "Compare the likelihood that a purchase was made by users on their fourth versus fifth sessions with the service" (nth-session field added to the fact table), and "Compare the value of purchases made in sessions by foreign versus domestic customers" (purchase amount field added to the fact table plus a customer dimension).

More

- www.analog.cx—download the analog Web server log analyzer
- http://www.microsoft.com/technet/scriptcenter/tools/logparser/—Microsoft Log Parser
- www.cygwin.com—standard Unix tools for Windows

Time and Motion

Generating the first access log report might take anywhere from a few minutes to an hour depending on the quality of the log analysis tool. As a whole the first exercise shouldn't take more than two hours. Tracking errors should take two to four hours. Talking to the client will probably take about one hour. Designing the data warehouse should take about one to two hours, depending on the student's familiarity with data warehousing.

17   Writeup

If I am not for myself, who is for me?
When I am for myself, what am I?
If not now, when?
—Hillel (circa 70 BC–AD 10)

If I do not document my results, who will?
If the significance of my work is not communicated to others, what am I?
If not now, when?
—philg

Do you believe that the world owes you attention? If not, why do you think that anyone is going to spend thirty minutes surfing around the community that you've built in order to find the most interesting features? In any case, if much of your engineering success is embodied in administration pages, how would someone without admin privileges ever see them?

In code reviews at the beginning of this class, we often find students producing source code files without attribution ("I know who wrote it") and Web pages without email signatures ("nobody is actually going to use this"). Maimonides' commentary on Hillel's quote above is that a person acquires habits of doing right or wrong—virtues and vices—while young; youths should do good deeds now, and not wait until adulthood. That is, if you don't take steps to help other users and programmers now, as a university student, there is no reason to believe that you'll develop habits of virtue post-graduation. An alternative way of thinking about this is to ask yourself how you feel when you're stuck trying to use someone else's Web page and there is no clear way to send feedback or get help, or how much fun it is to be reading the source code for an application and not have any idea who wrote it, why, or where to ask questions. Continuing the Talmudic theme of the chapter, keep in mind Hillel's response to a gentile interested in Judaism: "That which is hateful to you, do not do to your neighbor. That is the whole Torah; the rest is commentary. Go and study it."

A comment header at the top of every source code file and an email address at the bottom of every page. That's a good start toward building a professional reputation. But it isn't enough. For every computer application that you build, you ought to prepare an *overview document*. This will be a single HTML page containing linear text that can be read simply by scrolling, that is, the reader need not follow any hyperlinks in order to understand your achievement. It is probably reasonable to expect that you can hold the average person's attention for four or five screens worth of text and illustrations. What to include in the overview illustrations? In-line images of Web or mobile browser screens that display the application's capabilities. If the application supports a complex workflow, perhaps a graphic showing all the states and transitions.

Here are some examples done by folks just like yourself:

- any of the reports in the 6.171 Project Galleries at http://philip.greenspun .com/seia/gallery/spring2002/ and http://philip.greenspun.com/seia/gallery/ fall2003/

From an earlier version of this course:

- http://philip.greenspun.com/seia/gallery/spring1999/arfdigita/
- http://philip.greenspun.com/seia/gallery/spring2000/poa/
- http://philip.greenspun.com/seia/gallery/fall2000/wap/ (a WAP-only application)
- http://philip.greenspun.com/seia/gallery/fall2000/eaa/

In case you're looking for inspiration, do remember that if Microsoft, Oracle, Red Hat, or Sun products either worked simply or simply worked, half of the people in the information technology industry would be out of jobs. Also keep in mind that for every person reading this chapter a poor villager in India is learning SQL and Java. A big salary can evaporate quickly. Between March 2001 and April 2004 roughly 400,000 American jobs in information technology were eliminated. Many of those who had coded Java in obscurity ended up as cab drivers or greeters at Wal-Mart. A personal professional reputation, by contrast, is a bit harder to build than the big salary, but is also harder to lose.

If you don't invest some time in writing (prose, not code), however, you'll never have any reputation outside your immediate circle of colleagues, who themselves may end up working at McDonald's and be unable to help you get an engineering job during a recession.

Exercise 1

Prepare an overview document for the application that you built this semester. Place the document at /doc/overview on your server.

Try to make sure that your audience can stop reading at any point and still get a complete picture. Thus the first paragraph or two should say what you've built and why it is important to this group of users. This introduction should say a little something about the community for whom the application has been built and why they can't simply get together in the same room at the same time.

It is probably worth concentrating on screen shots that illustrate your application's unique and surprising features. Things such as stand-alone discussion forums or full-text search pages can be described in a single bullet item or sentence and easily imagined by the reader.

If you find that your screen shots aren't very compelling and that it takes 5 or 6 screen shots to tell a story, consider redesigning some of your pages! If it makes sense to see all the site's most important features and information on one screen in your overview document, it probably makes sense for the every-day users of the site to see them on one screen as well.

You have two basic options for structure. If it is more or less obvious how people are going to use the service, you might be able to get away with the Laundry List Structure: list the features of the application, punctuated by screen shots. In general, however, the Day-in-the-Life Structure is probably more compelling and understandable. Here you walk through a scenario of how several users might come to the application and accomplish tasks. For example, on a photo critique site you might show the following:

1. Schlomo Mendelssohn uploads his latest photograph of his dog (screen shot of photo upload page)

2. Winston Wu views a page of the most recently submitted photos and picks Schlomo's

3. Winston uploads a comment on Schlomo's photo, attaching an edited version of the photo (screen shot of the "attach a file to your comment" page)

4. Schlomo checks in from his mobile phone's browser to see who has critiqued his photo

5. Winona Horowitz calls in from a friend's telephone and finds out from the VoiceXML interface that a lot of new content has been posted in the last 24 hours

6. Winona goes home to a Web browser and visits the administration page and deletes a duplicate posting and three off-topic posts (screen shot of the "all recently uploaded content")

7. . . .

You can work in all of the site's important features in such a scenario, while giving the reader an idea of how these features are relevant to user and administrator goals.

Note how the example above works in the mobile and VoiceXML interfaces of the site. All of your readers will have used Web sites before, but mobile and VoiceXML are relative novelties.

What Do We Mean by "Professional"?

What do we mean by "professional"? Does it even make sense in the context of software engineering? The standard professions (law and medicine) require a specific educational degree and certification by other professionals. By contrast, plenty of folks who never took a computer science course are coding up a storm in Java right now. Nor has their work in Java been evaluated and certified by other programmers. In theory, if your incompetence kills enough patients, your fellow physicians can prevent you from practicing medicine anymore. If you steal too much from your clients, your fellow lawyers are empowered by the state to prevent you from working.

Without a required educational program or state-imposed sanctions on entry to the field, what can it mean to be a "professional programmer"? Let's take a step back and look at degrees of professional achievement within medicine. Consider three doctors:

- Surgeon 1 does the same operation over and over in a Beverly Hills clinic and makes a lot of money.

- Surgeon 2 is competent in all the standard operations, but in addition has developed an innovative procedure and, because of the time devoted to innovation, makes less money than Surgeon 1.

- Surgeon 3 has developed an innovative procedure and practices it regularly, but also makes time for occasional travel to France, China, Japan, and Argentina to teach other doctors how to practice the innovation.

Most of their fellow physicians would agree that Surgeon 3 is the "most professional" doctor of the group. Surgeon 3 has practiced at the state of the art, improved the state of the art, and taught others how to improve their skills. Is there a way for a programmer to excel along these dimensions?

Professionalism in the Software Industry (circa 1985)

As the packaged software industry reached its middle age around 1985, it was difficult for an individual programmer to have an impact. Software had to be marketed via traditional media, burned onto a physical medium, put into a fancy package, and shipped to a retailer. Consequently, fifty or more people were involved in any piece of code reaching an end-user. It would have been tough for a software engineer to aspire to the same standards of professionalism that put Surgeon 3 over the top. How can the software engineer ensure that his or her innovation will ever reach an end-user if shipping it out the door requires fifty other people to be paid on an ongoing basis? How can the software engineer teach other programmers how to practice the innovation if the software is closed-source and his or her organization's employment agreements mandate secrecy?

The industrial programmer circa 1985 was a factory employee, pure and simple. He or she might aspire to achieve high standards of *craftsmanship*, but never *professionalism*.

What were a programmer's options, then, if in fact craftsmanship proved to be an unsatisfying career goal? The only escape from the strictures of closed-source and secrecy was the university. A programmer could join a computer science research lab at a university where, very likely, he or she would be permitted to teach others via publication, source code release, and face-to-face instruction of students. However, by going into a university, where the required team of fifty would never be assembled to deliver a software product to market, the programmer was giving up the opportunity to work at the state of the art as well as innovate and teach.

Professionalism in the Software Industry (circa 2000)

There is some evidence that standards are shifting. Richard Stallman and Linus Torvalds draw crowds of admirers worldwide. These pioneers in the open-source software movement are beginning to exhibit some of the elements of Surgeon 3 (above):

- they practice at the state of the art, writing computer programs that are used by millions of people worldwide (the GNU set of Unix tools and the Linux kernel)
- they have innovated; Stallman having developed the Emacs text editor (one of the first multi-window systems) and Torvalds having developed a new method for coordinating development worldwide
- they have taught others how to practice their innovation by releasing their work as open-source software and by writing documentation

The Internet makes it easier for an individual programmer to distribute work to a large audience, thus making it easier to practice at the state of the art. The open-source movement makes it easier for an individual programmer to find a job where it will be practical to release his or her creations to other programmers who might build on that work.

It is thus now within a programmer's power to improve his or her practice as a software engineering professional, where the definition of *professional* is similar to that used in medicine.

A Proposed New Definition

Suppose that we define software engineering professionalism with the following objectives:

1. *A professional programmer picks a worthwhile problem to attack*; we are engineers, not scientists, and therefore should attempt solutions that will solve real user problems.

2. *A professional programmer has a dedication to the end-user experience*; most computer applications built these days are Internet applications built by small teams and hence it is now possible for an individual programmer to ensure that end-users aren't confused or frustrated (in the case of a programmer working on a tool for other programmers, the goal is defined to be "dedication to ease of use by the recipient programmer").

3. *A professional programmer does high quality work*; we preserve the dedication to good system design, maintainability, and documentation, that constituted pride of craftsmanship.

4. *A professional programmer innovates*; information systems are not good enough, the users are entitled to better, and it is our job to build better systems.

5. *A professional programmer teaches by example*; open-source is the one true path for a professional software engineer.

6. *A professional programmer teaches by documentation*; writing is hard, but the best software documentation has always been written by programmers who were willing to make an extra effort.

7. *A professional programmer teaches face-to-face*; we've not found a substitute for face-to-face interaction, so a software engineering professional should teach fellow workers via code review, teach short overview lectures to large audiences, and help teach multi-week courses.

Could one create an organization where programmers can excel along these seven dimensions? In a previous life, the authors did just this! We created a free open-source toolkit for building Internet applications, that is, something to save customers the agony of doing what you've just spent all semester doing (building an application from scratch). Here's how we worked toward the previously stated objectives:

1. *Committing to attack the hardest problems for a wide range of computer users*; niche software products are easy and profitable to build but most of the programmers on such a product are putting in the 10,000th feature. Our company simultaneously attacked the problems of public online community, B2B e-commerce, B2C e-commerce, cooperative work inside an organization, cooperative work across organizations, running a university, accounting and personnel (HR) for a services company, and so forth. This gave our programmers plenty of room to grow.

2. *Staying lean on the sales, account management, user interface, and user experience specialists*; a programming team was in direct contact with the Internet service operator and oftentimes with end-users. Our programmers had a lot of control over and responsibility for the end-user experience.

3. *Hiring good people and paying them well*; it is only possible to build a high-quality system if one has high-quality colleagues. Despite a tough late 1990s recruiting market, we limited ourselves to hiring people who had demonstrated an ability to produce high-quality code on a trio of problem sets (originally developed for this course's predecessor at MIT).

4. *Giving little respect to our old code and not striving for compatibility with too many substrate systems*; we let our programmers build their professional reputation for innovation rather than become embroiled in worrying about whether a new thing will inconvenience legacy users (we had support contracts for them) or how to make sure that new code works on every brand of RDBMS.

5. *Having a strict open-source software policy*; reusable code was documented and open-sourced in the hope that it would aid other programmers worldwide.

6. *Dragging people out to writing retreats*; most programmers say that they can't write, but experience shows that peoples' writing skills improve dramatically if only they will practice writing. We had a beach house near our headquarters and dragged people out for long weekends to finish writing projects with help from other programmers who were completing their own writing projects.

7. *Establishing our own university, assistant teaching at existing universities, and mentoring within our offices*; a lot of Ph.D. computer scientists are reluctant to leave academia because they won't be able to teach. But we started our own one-year post-baccalaureate program teaching the normal undergraduate computer science curriculum, and we were happy to pay a developer to spend a month there teaching a course. We encouraged our developers to volunteer as teaching assistants or lecturers at universities near our offices. We insisted that senior developers review junior developers' code internally.

How did it work out? Adhering to these principles, we built a profitable business with $20 million in annual revenue. Being engineers rather than business people we thought we were being smart by turning the company over to professional managers and well-established venture capital firms. In search of higher profit, they abandoned our principles and, in less than two years, turned what had been monthly profits into losses, burning through $50 million in cash. The company, by now thoroughly conventional, tanked.

In short, despite the experiment having ended rather distressingly, it provided evidence that these seven principles can yield exceptionally high achievement and profits.

Exercise 2

Write down your own definition of software engineering professionalism. Explain how you would put it into practice and how you could build a sustainable organization to support that definition.

Final Presentation

In any course using this textbook, we suggest allocating 20 minutes of class time at the end of any course, per project, for a final presentation to a panel of outsiders. Each team then has an opportunity to polish its presentation skills to an audience of decision-makers, as distinct from the audience of technical peers that have listened to earlier in-class presentations.

Young engineers need practice in convincing people with money to write checks that will fund their work. Consequently, the best panelists are people who, in their daily lives, listen to proposals from technical people and decide whether or not to write checks. Examples of such people include executives at large companies and venture capitalists.

We suggest the following format for each presentation:

1. elevator pitch, a 30-second explanation of what problem has been solved and why the system is better than existing mechanisms available to people

2. demo of the completed system (see the "Content Management" chapter for some tips on making crisp demonstrations of multi-user applications) (5 minutes; make it clear whether or not the system has been publicly launched or not)

3. a slide showing system architecture and what components were used to build the system (1 minute)

4. discussion of the toughest technical challenges faced during the project and how they were addressed (2 minutes; possibly additional slides)

5. tour of documentation (2 minutes)—you want to convince the audience that there is enough for long-term maintenance

6. the future (1 minute)—what are the next milestones? Who is carrying on the work?

Total time: 12 minutes max.

Notice that the technical stuff is at the end. Nobody cares about technology until they've seen what problem has been solved.

Lessons from MIT

From observing interaction between our students and panelists at MIT, a few consistent themes have emerged.

Panelists love documentation. They've all seen code monkeys and they've all seen running programs. Very seldom in their lives have they seen clear and comprehensive documentation. We've seen senior executives from Microsoft Corporation get tears in their eyes looking at the documentation for a discussion forum module. The forum itself had attracted a "seen it before" yawn, but the executives perked up at the sight of a single document containing a three-paragraph overview, the SQL data model, a page flow diagram, a list of all the scripts, some sample SQL queries, and a list of all the helper functions.

Panelists need to have the rationale for the application clearly explained at the beginning. Otherwise the demo is boring. Practice your first few minutes in front of some people who've never seen your project, and ask them to explain back to you what problem you've solved and why.

Decision makers who are also good technologists like to have the scale of the challenge quantified. The chief information officer from a large enterprise wanted to know how many hours went into development of the application that he was seeing and how many tables were in the data model. He was beyond the point in his career when he was writing his own SQL code, but he knew that each extra table typically implies extra cost for development and maintenance.

You need to distinguish your application from packaged software and other systems that the panelists expect are easily available. Don't spend five minutes showing a discussion forum, for example. Every panelist will have seen that. Show one page of the forum, explain that there is a forum, that there are several levels of moderator and privacy, and then move on to what is unique about what you've built. After one presentation, a panelist said "Everything that you showed is built into Microsoft Sharepoint." A venture capitalist on the panel chimed in "If at any time during a pitch someone points out that there is a Microsoft product that solves the same problem, the meeting is over."

At the same time, unless you're being totally innovative, a good place to start is by framing your achievement in terms of something that the audience is already familiar with, for example, Yahoo! Groups or generic online community toolkits, and then talk about what is different. You don't want the decision-maker to think to herself "Hey, I think I've seen this before in Microsoft Sharepoint" and have that thought in her head unaddressed the whole time.

Decision-makers often bring senior engineers with them to attend presentations, and these folks can get stuck on personal leitmotifs. Suppose Joe Panelist chose to build his last project by generating XML from the database and then turning that into HTML via some expensive industry-leading middleware and XSLT, plus lots of Java and Enterprise Java Beans. This approach probably consumes 100 times more server resources than using Microsoft Visual Basic in Active Server Pages or a Perl script from 1993, but it is arguably cleaner and more modern. After a 12-minute presentation, no listener could have learned enough to say for sure that a project would have benefited from the XML/XSLT approach, but out he comes with the challenge. You could call him a pinhead because he doesn't know enough about your client and the original goals, for example, not having to buy a 100-CPU server farm to support a small community. You could demonstrate that he is a pinhead by pointing out large and successful applications that use a similar architecture to what you've chosen. But as a junior engineer these probably aren't the best ways to handle unfair or incorrect criticism from a senior engineer at a meeting, especially if that person has been brought along by the decision-maker. It is much better to flatter this person by asking them to schedule a 30-minute meeting where you can really discuss the issue. Use that 30-minute meeting to show why you designed the thing the way that you did initially. You might turn the senior engineer around to your way of thinking. At the very least, you won't be arguing in front of the decision-maker or appearing to be arrogant/overconfident.

To the Panelists

Imagine that each student team was hired by your predecessor. You're trying to figure out what they did, whether to fund the next version, and, if so, whether this is the right team to build and launch that next version.

As a presentation proceeds, write down numerical scores (1–10) for how well a team has done at the following:

- This team has communicated clearly what problem they've solved.
- The demo gave me a good feeling for how the system works.
- This team has done an impressive job tackling engineering challenges.
- This team has documented their system clearly and thoroughly.
- I'd really like to hire these people for my own organization.

Following a team's 12-minute presentation, tell them what they could have done better.

Don't be shy about interrupting with short questions during a team's presentation. If the presentation were from one of your subordinates or a startup company asking for funds and you'd interrupt them, then interrupt our students.

Parting Words

Work on something that excites you enough that you want to work 24/7 on it. Become an expert on data model and page flow. Build some great systems by yourself and link to their overview documents from your resume—be able to say "I built X" or "Susan and I built X" rather than "I built a piece of X as part of a huge team."

More

- 6.171 Project Gallery, Spring 2002 at http://philip.greenspun.com/seia/gallery/spring2002/
- 6.171 Project Gallery, Fall 2003 at http://philip.greenspun.com/seia/gallery/fall2003/

Time and Motion

The writeup should take four to six hours and may be split among team members. An effective division of labor might be: screen shot technician, writer, proofreader. Thinking about and writing down a definition of professionalism ought to take one to two hours. The presentation will go faster if the team has kept up with their documentation, but ought to take no more than a few hours to prepare plus an hour to practice a few times.

Reference Chapters

A   HTML

Hypertext Markup Language, or HTML, is the language used to specify how a browser should display a Web page. HTML is a *markup* language, as opposed to a programming language, meaning that it contains codes that say how a page should be formatted, but does not contain procedural code.

Let's take a look at a simple example:

Code Example

```
<p>
Don't look at your instruments
and adjust the flight controls
to, for example, keep the
altimeter steady. The
instruments have a tendency to
<b>lag behind reality</b> and
therefore you're overcorrecting
and oscillating.
</p>
```

Typical Rendering

Don't look at your instruments and adjust the flight controls to, for example, keep the altimeter steady. The instruments have a tendency to **lag behind reality** and therefore you're overcorrecting and oscillating.

HTML consists of tags, such as <p>, interspersed with plain text. The <p> tag begins a paragraph; </p> ends the paragraph. Similarly, <b> starts text emboldening and </b> ends it.

Basics

In HTML, almost every opening tag has a closing tag, as in the example above. There are a few exceptions, which we will encounter shortly, but the overwhelming majority of tags must be closed.

Some tags have *attributes*, such as the `face` attribute of the `<font>` tag. Example:

```
<font face=arial>
```

If an attribute value contains a space, it is necessary to enclose it in quotation marks:

```
<font face="arial narrow">
```

Logical Markup

HTML has two kinds of markup: logical markup and physical markup. Physical markup, such as the bold (`<b>`) tag specifies how the browser is supposed to render text. In contrast, logical markup, or *semantic tags*, specifies something about the *meaning* of what is being marked up; the browser is free to choose a rendering that is sensible for the user's hardware, for example, italics might be a good choice on a desktop PC, but reverse video might work better on a low-resolution mobile phone.

Here are a few examples of semantic tags:

Tag	Code Example	Typical Rendering
Emphasis `<em>`	`You can fly all day <em>in mid-air</em> without using the airplane's rudder.`	You can fly all day *in mid-air* without using the airplane's rudder.
Strong `<strong>`	`On short final, press relatively hard on <strong>both</strong> rudder pedals.`	On short final, press relatively hard on **both** rudder pedals.
Code `<code>`	`Alaska and Hawaii's airports are identified starting with a <code>PA</code> for "Pacific".`	Alaska and Hawaii's airports are identified starting with a PA for "Pacific".
Headline Level 1 `<h1>`	`<h1>Flight Plan</h1>`	# Flight Plan

Headline Level 2 `<h2>`	`<h2>Flight Plan</h2>`	# Flight Plan
Headline Level 3 `<h3>`	`<h3>Flight Plan</h3>`	## Flight Plan
Headline Level 4 `<h4>`	`<h4>Flight Plan</h4>`	**Flight Plan**
Headline Level 5 `<h5>`	`<h5>Flight Plan</h5>`	**Flight Plan**
Headline Level 6 `<h6>`	`<h6>Flight Plan</h6>`	**Flight Plan**

Physical Markup

Here are some common physical markup tags and attributes:

Tag	Code Example	Typical Rendering
Bold `<b>`	Use the flight controls to keep the nose of the airplane at `<b>a constant attitude</b>` relative to the horizon.	Use the flight controls to keep the nose of the airplane at **a constant attitude** relative to the horizon.
Italics `<i>`	Have you read `<i>Stick and Rudder</i>`?	Have you read *Stick and Rudder*?
Underline `<u>`	Flying in the clouds on a summer afternoon, you run the risk of entering an `<u>embedded thunderstorm</u>`.	Flying in the clouds on a summer afternoon, you run the risk of entering an <u>embedded thunderstorm</u>.

Note: Generally it's best to avoid the `<u>` tag; underlining should be reserved for hyperlinks.

Superscript <sup>	Avogadro's number is approximately equal to 6.022 × 10²³	Avogadro's number is approximately equal to 6.022×10^{23}
Subscript <sub>	log_ex	$\log_e x$
Font Size <font size=...>	I want a <font size=+2>huge </font> house, a <font size=+1>big</font> dog, and a <font size=-1> small</font> waist.	I want a huge house, a big dog, and a small waist.
Font Color <font color=...>	An airplane's navigation lights are <font color=green>green</font> on the right wing and <font color= "#ff0000">red</font> on the left.	An airplane's navigation lights are green on the right wing and red on the left.

Note: A table of colors and their hexadecimal equivalents is available from http://falco.elte.hu/COMP/HTML/colors.html

Font Face <font face=...>	The <font face="arial narrow, arial, helvetica">NASA Aviation Safety Program</font> is the only source of innovation.	The NASA Aviation Safety Program is the only source of innovation.
Typewriter Text <tt>	The terminal forecast called for winds <tt>02015G25KT</tt>, which means from the northeast at 15 knots, gusting to 25 knots.	The terminal forecast called for winds 02015G25KT, which means from the northeast at 15 knots, gusting to 25 knots.

Pre-formatted Text `<pre>`	Winds aloft for Buffalo, Boston, and Nantucket, at 3000, 6000, and 9000':
	`<pre>`
	`` 3000 6000 9000
	BUF 0517 0215+01 3306-01
	BOS 2218 2325+08 2321+03
	ACK 2118 2012+08 1917+03```
	`</pre>`
		Winds aloft for Buffalo, Boston, and Nantucket, at 3000, 6000, and 9000':
		
		`` 3000 6000 9000
		BUF 0517 0215+01 3306-01
		BOS 2218 2325+08 2321+03
		ACK 2118 2012+08 1917+03```

Blockquote `<block-quote>`	Aviation safety quote: `<blockquote>` All life is the management of risk, not its elimination. ` ` -- Walter Wriston, former Chairman of Citibank `</blockquote>`	Aviation safety quote: All life is the management of risk, not its elimination. —Walter Wriston, former Chairman of Citibank

It's generally considered more tasteful to use logical markup instead of physical markup. It has become especially important now that there is such a wide variety of devices on which to browse Web sites, for example, mobile phones and handheld devices. A phone might ignore `<font size>` tags, but it will probably try to make headlines (`<h1>`) stand out.

Hyperlinks

Hyperlinks, often just called *links*, allow the user to jump to a new page or a new location within the same page. Hyperlinks are generally represented by blue, underlined text. Although it is possible to change how hyperlinks appear to the user, we recommended against it; users expect a consistent user interface for Web pages.

An *absolute link* is a hyperlink that specifies the full URL of the destination. Example:

```
<a href="http://aviationweather.gov/">aviationweather.gov</a>
```

Relative links are hyperlinks to documents in relation to the location of the current document. You do not need to specify the server name in the URL. Example:

```
<a href="glossary">Glossary</a>
```

embedded in a file in the directory `/seia/` will take a user to the `glossary` file in the same directory.

You can make a Web page open up in a new browser window by specifying a target window:

```
<a href="glossary" target="glossary_window">Glossary</a>
```

If there is no browser window named `glossary_window`, a new window will pop up. However, you should use this feature sparingly because the appearance of new windows can be confusing to users. Furthermore, a number of users have pop-up ad blockers installed; these ad blockers will also prevent legitimate windows from popping up.

You can also link to specific locations within a document so that your user doesn't have to scroll down to find a particular item on the page. To accomplish this, first you have to mark the location in the document to which you need to link. For example,

```
<a name="DNS">DNS</a>
```

Then you can link to that location within the file with:

```
see the <a href="glossary#DNS">glossary entry for DNS</a>
```

Note that if you want to link to another location within the same file you can omit the file name, for example, `<a href="#DNS">DNS</a>`.

You will often see a question mark followed by form variables at the end of a URL; this is called the *query string*. For example,

```
<a href="http://groups.google.com/groups?hl=fr&group=rec.aviation
.student">rec.aviation.student newsgroup</a>
```

The variables in this query string are `hl` (headline language?) and `group`. Most Web programming APIs provide convenient facilities for reading the values of query string variables.

Breaks

All whitespace is treated equally in HTML, meaning that spaces, tabs, and linebreaks are all rendered as single spaces. To force a newline to occur, you need to use a tag.

Here are some common breaks:

Tag	Code Example	Typical Rendering

Paragraph `<p>`	`<p>`
	`"I'll be seeing you,"`
	`he said.`
	`</p>`
		"I'll be seeing you," he said.

	`<p>`
	`Then he walked away.`
	`</p>`
		Then he walked away.

Line Break ` `	`Carson's Plumbing ` `123 Main St. ` `Seattle, WA 98101`	Carson's Plumbing 123 Main St. Seattle, WA 98101

Horizontal Rule `<hr>`	`And they lived happily`
	`ever after.`
	`<hr>`
	`The End`
		And they lived happily ever after.
		———————————
		The End

Notice that `<br>` and `<hr>` have no closing tags. Additionally, the `</p>` tag is optional; the browser assumes that, when it encounters a new `<p>` tag, the old paragraph has ended.

Lists

The most common types of lists are ordered lists, in which the browser places a number before each list item, and unordered lists, which appear as a series of bulleted items. You can also create definition lists, useful for online dictionaries or glossaries.

Tag	Code Example	Typical Rendering

Ordered List `<ol>`	Alaska summer survival gear:
	`<ol>`
	`<li>`rations for each occupant
	`<li>`one axe or hatchet
	`<li>`one first aid kit
	`</ol>`
		Alaska summer survival gear:
		1. rations for each occupant
		2. one axe or hatchet
		3. one first aid kit

	Common training airplanes:
	`<ol type=A>`
	`<li>`Cessna 172
	`<li>`Diamond DA20
	`<li>`Piper Tomahawk
	`</ol>`
		Common training airplanes:
		A. Cessna 172
		B. Diamond DA20
		C. Piper Tomahawk

	Class B VFR Weather Minimums:
	`<ol type=i>`
	`<li>`3 statute miles visibility
	`<li>`clear of clouds
	`</ol>`
		Class B VFR Weather Minimums:
		i. 3 statute miles visibility
		ii. clear of clouds

Unordered List `<ul>`	Checklist for Mexican Flying:
	`<ul>`
	`<li>`proof of airplane ownership
	`<li>`proof of liability insurance
	`<li>`pilot's license and medical
	`<li>`seldom asked-for documents:
	  `<ul>`
	  `<li>`radio station license
	  `<li>`radio operator's license
	  `</ul>`
	`<li>`border-crossing flight plan
	`</ul>`
		Checklist for Mexican Flying:
		• proof of airplane ownership
		• proof of liability insurance
		• pilot's license and medical
		• seldom asked-for documents:
		  ○ radio station license
		  ○ radio operator's license
		• border-crossing flight plan

| Definition List `<dl>` | `<dl>` `<dt>IFR` `<dd>Instrument Flight Rules` `<dt>VFR` `<dd>Visual Flight Rules` `<dt>VOR` `<dd>Very High Frequency Omni Ranging radio navigation beacon` `</dl>` | IFR Instrument Flight Rules VFR Visual Flight Rules VOR Very High Frequency Omni Ranging radio navigation beacon |

Images

Images are stored as separate files, not part of the HTML page. An image can be included in a page as follows:

```
<img src="http://www.eveandersson.com/alex.jpg">
```

This tag instructs the user's browser to make a new request, possibly to a different server than the one from which the HTML document was obtained, for the image.

There are many optional attributes for images. The most important are the `width` and `height` attributes; by telling the browser the size of the image, it can render the entire Web page, leaving space for the image, before it has downloaded the image file itself.

Attribute	Code Example	Typical Rendering
Dimensions width/ height	`<img width=100 height=100 src="http:// www.eveandersson.com/ alex.jpg">`	

Border
border

```
<img width=100 height=100
border=2
src="http://
www.eveandersson.com/
alex.jpg">
```

Alignment
align

```
<img align=right
width=100 height=100
src="http://
www.eveandersson.com/
alex.jpg">
Canine-American
```

Canine-American

Alignment
align

```
<img align=left
width=100 height=100
src="http://
www.eveandersson.com/
alex.jpg">
Canine-American
```

 Canine-American

Horizontal
Space (on
both sides)
hspace

```
<img hspace=10
align=left width=100
height=100
src="http://
www.eveandersson.com/
alex.jpg">
Canine-American
```

 Canine-American

Vertical
Space (top
and bottom)
vspace

```
<img vspace=10
width=100 height=100
src="http://
www.eveandersson.com/
alex.jpg">
```

Tables

Here are the tags used when creating HTML tables:

`<table>, </table>`	start and end a table
`<tr>, </tr>`	table row
`<td>, </td>`	table cell
`<th>, </th>`	table heading; like a table cell except that the text is bold and centered

Many of these tags can have attributes, for example, to specify alignment, borders, cell spacing and padding, and background colors. Examples:

Code Example

```
<table border=2
  cellspacing=5
  cellpadding=5>
<tr>
 <th>Year</th>
 <th>Revenue</th>
 <th>Expenditures</th>
 <th>Profits</th>
</tr>
<tr>
 <td>1999</td>
 <td>$58,295</td>
 <td>$73,688</td>
 <td>$(15,393)</td>
</tr>
<tr>
 <td>2000</td>
 <td>$902,995</td>
 <td>$145,400</td>
 <td>$757,595</td>
</tr>
</table>
```

Typical Rendering

Year	Revenue	Expenditures	Profits
1999	$58,295	$73,688	$(15,393)
2000	$902,995	$145,400	$757,595

Year	Revenue	Expenditures	Profits
1999	$58,295	$73,688	$(15,393)
2000	$902,995	$145,400	$757,595

```
<!-- reduce the
cellspacing and
right-align the
text in the cells -->
<table border=2
  cellspacing=2
  cellpadding=5>
<tr>
 <th>Year</th>
 <th>Revenue</th>
 <th>Expenditures</th>
 <th>Profits</th>
</tr>
<tr>
 <td>1999</td>
 <td align=right>
   $58,295</td>
 <td align=right>
   $73,688</td>
 <td align=right>
   $(15,393)</td>
</tr>
<tr>
 <td>2000</td>
 <td align=right>
   $902,995</td>
 <td align=right>
   $145,400</td>
 <td align=right>
   $757,595</td>
</tr>
</table>
```

Year	Revenue	Expenditures	Profits
1999	$58,295	$73,688	$(15,393)
2000	$902,995	$145,400	$757,595

```
<!-- remove the
border -->
<table border=0
   cellspacing=2
   cellpadding=5>
<tr>
 <th>Year</th>
 <th>Revenue</th>
 <th>Expenditures</th>
 <th>Profits</th>
</tr>
<tr>
 <td>1999</td>
 <td>$58,295</td>
 <td>$73,688</td>
 <td>$(15,393)</td>
</tr>
<tr>
 <td>2000</td>
 <td>$902,995</td>
 <td>$145,400</td>
 <td>$757,595</td>
</tr>
</table>
```

Year	Revenue	Expenditures	Profits
1999	$58,295	$73,688	$(15,393)
2000	$902,995	$145,400	$757,595

```
<!-- shade every
other row -->
<table border=0
   cellspacing=2
   cellpadding=5>
<tr bgcolor="#cecece">
 <th>Year</th>
 <th>Revenue</th>
 <th>Expenditures</th>
 <th>Profits</th>
</tr>
```

```
<tr bgcolor=white>
 <td>1999</td>
 <td>$58,295</td>
 <td>$73,688</td>
 <td>$(15,393)</td>
</tr>
<tr bgcolor="#cecece">
 <td>2000</td>
 <td>$902,995</td>
 <td>$145,400</td>
 <td>$757,595</td>
</tr>
</table>
```

Forms

To collect data from users, use the form tag:

```
<form method=POST action=/register/new>
```

The action is the URL to which the form is submitted, which may correspond to a computer program in the server file system, for example, a Java Server Page, a PHP or Perl script, and so forth.

The form's method can be either GET or POST. The only difference is that, with method=GET, the variables that the user submits are presented in the query string of the following page's URL. This is useful if you want the user to be able to bookmark the resulting page. However, if the user is expected to enter long strings of data, method=POST is more appropriate because some old browsers only handle query strings containing fewer than 256 characters (newer browsers can handle a few thousand). Note further that if you use the GET method, the form variable values will appear in the server access log and could create a security or privacy risk.

Code Example

```
<form method=POST action=/survey/demographic>
<input type=hidden name=user_id value=2205>
Age: <input type=text size=2><br>
Sex: <input type=radio name=sex value=m>male
     <input type=radio name=sex value=f>female<br>
What are you interested in (check all that apply)?
<input type=checkbox name=interest value="aerobatics">Aerobatics
<input type=checkbox name=interest value="helicopters">Helicopters
<input type=checkbox name=interest value="IFR">IFR
<input type=checkbox name=interest value="seaplanes">Seaplanes
<br>
Where do you live?
        <select name=continent_live>
        <option value=north_america>North America
        <option value=south_america>South America
        <option value=africa>Africa
        <option value=europe>Europe
        <option value=asia>Asia
        <option value=australia>Australia
        </select>
        <br>
Which continents have you visited?<br>
        <select multiple size=3 name=continent_visited>
        <option value=north_america>North America
        <option value=south_america>South America
        <option value=africa>Africa
        <option value=europe>Europe
        <option value=asia>Asia
        <option value=australia>Australia
        </select>
        <br>
Describe your favorite airplane trip:<br>
<textarea name=favorite_trip_story rows=5 cols=50></textarea>
<p>
<input type=submit value="Continue">
</form>
```

Typical Rendering

Special Characters

A wide variety of non-alphanumeric characters can be specified in HTML. Here is a small sampling:

Entity	Code Example	Typical Rendering
n, tilde ñ	piñata	piñata
e, acute accent é	café	café
inverted question mark ¿	¿Qué pasa?	¿Qué pasa?

non-breaking space	a b	a b
greater-than >	4 > 3	4 > 3
less-than <	5 < 6	5 < 6
copyright ©	© 2004	© 2004
pound sterling £	£50	£50

A more complete special character reference can be found at http://webmonkey .wired.com/webmonkey/reference/special_characters/.

HTML Document Structure

Up to this point, we have looked at individual tags within an HTML document. But what is the overall structure of an HTML document?

HTML documents are broken into two main sections: the *head* and the *body*. The head contains information pertaining to the entire document (most importantly, the document's title). The body contains the content of the page that appears within the browser window. Here is a basic HTML document:

```
<html>
<head>
    <title>This is the Title</title>
</head>
<body>
    ... This is the content of the page. ...
</body>
</html>
```

News pages often include instructions that the browser refetch the page. Here's a tag, located in the head, from news.google.com:

```
<meta HTTP-EQUIV="refresh" CONTENT="900">
```

If you load this page into a browser and step back from the computer, you should notice it updating itself every 900 seconds (15 minutes).

Also within the head, you can specify keywords and a description of the page. These tags were originally intended to help search engines index pages, but now they are often ignored due to abuse such as page authors using incorrect keywords to get more hits.

```
<META NAME="description" CONTENT="An owner's review of the Diamond Star DA40">
<META NAME="keywords" CONTENT="Diamond Star DA40 review Cirrus SR20 SR22">
```

You can modify properties of the Web page by using <body> tag attributes. For example:

```
<body bgcolor=white text=black link=blue vlink=purple alink=red>
```

However, you should use this sparingly; users are accustomed to the standard text colors and may become frustrated if they can't tell what's a link and what isn't.

Cascading Style Sheets

Ever since the development of the Web, there has been a tension between people who focus on content and those who are more interested in presentation. The content people want to get relevant information on every page, possibly marking up a phrase with the H3 tag to say "this is a headline." The presentation folks say things like "move this two pixels to the right," "stick this in 18-point Helvetica Bold and make it red," and "stick this in 14-point Times Italic." They use tricks such as blank images for spacing and tags such as font and color.

Here are some of the problems with filling up site content and scripts with tags like font and color:

- Older browsers will ignore them; the latest and greatest tags tend to have been introduced with the latest and greatest browsers; <h3> and <em>, however, are understood by browsers going back to the early 1990s.

- Newer browsers will ignore them; mobile phones, palmtops, and hiptops often have very basic browsers that understand only the basic tags.

- When your service hires a new graphic designer, the programmers will have to edit 10,000 HTML documents and thousands of scripts.

A site-wide cascading style sheet addresses all of these issues. Here's part of the cascading style sheet for the online version of this book (http://philip.greenspun .com/seia/style-sheet.css):

```
body {margin-left: 10% ; margin-right: 10%}

P { margin-top: 0.3em; text-indent : 2em }

P.stb { margin-top: 12pt }
P.mtb { margin-top: 24pt; text-indent : 0in}
P.ltb { margin-top: 36pt; text-indent : 0in}

p.marginnote { background: #E0E0E0;
               text-indent: 0in ; padding-left: 5%; padding-right: 5%;
               padding-top: 3pt; font-size: 75%}
p.bodynote { background-color: #E0E0E0 }
...
```

Each line of the style sheet gives formatting instructions for one HTML element and/or a subclass of an HTML element. The body tag is augmented so that all of the pages will have extra left and right whitespace margins. The next directive, for the P tag, tells browsers not to separate paragraphs with a full blank line, but rather to indent the first line of a new paragraph by "2em" and add only a smidgen of blank vertical space ("margin-top: 0.3em"). Now paragraphs will be mushed together like those in a printed book or magazine. Books and magazines do sometimes use whitespace, however, mostly to show thematic breaks in the text. We therefore define three classes of thematic breaks and tell browsers how to render them. The first, "stb" (for "small thematic break") will insert 12 points of white space. A paragraph of class "stb" will inherit the 2em first-line indent of the regular P element. For medium and large thematic breaks, more whitespace is specified, as well as an override for the first-line indent.

How does one use a style sheet? Park it somewhere on the server in a file with the extension ".css." This extension will tell the Web server program to MIME-type it "text/css." Inside each document that uses the cascading style sheet, put the following link element inside the document head:

```
<LINK REL=STYLESHEET HREF="/seia/style-sheet.css" TYPE="text/css">
```

The first time the user's browser sees a page that references this style sheet, it will come back and request "http://philip.greenspun.com/seia/style-sheet.css" before rendering any of the page. Note that this will slow down page viewing a bit, although if all of our pages refer to the same site-wide style sheet, users' browsers should be smart enough to cache it. If you read ten chapters from this book online, for example, the browser should request the common style sheet only once.

Okay, now the browser knows where to get the style sheet and that a small thematic break should be rendered with an extra bit of whitespace. How do we tell the browser that a particular paragraph is "of class stb"? Instead of "<P>", we use

```
<P CLASS="stb">
```

An excellent CSS reference can be found at http://www.w3schools.com/css/default.asp.

Frames

Frames consist of independent windows within a single Web page. Usually each window can be scrolled separately. Often, when you click a link, only one frame is updated with a new URL; the rest of the page content stays the same.

Frames sounded like a good idea at the time (mid-1990s), but have proven to be painful for both users and developers for the following reasons:

- *Frames waste screen space*   Often frames have their own scrollbars, which take up valuable space within the browser window. Furthermore, if you are only interested in one frame and you scroll down within that frame, the other frames remain in place, leaving less space for the content you want.

- *Frames make it difficult to bookmark pages*   When the user follows links that only update one frame, the URL of the page does not change. Suppose Joe User visits a travel site, follows five links within frames to get to a page about a tour of Mexico's Copper Canyon, and then bookmarks that page; the bookmark will point to the front page of the travel site, not the Copper Canyon page.

- *Frames make it difficult to share pages*   Suppose Joe User wants to see if his friend is interested in going on the Copper Canyon tour. While looking at the tour advertisement, he cuts and pastes the URL from the browser's Address field into an email message. Joe's friend clicks on the URL and gets the travel site home page, not the interior page about the Copper Canyon tour.

- *Frames make it difficult to report errors*   Consider a frame-using site with 200 scripts. A user isn't happy with the way a page works. You ask her "What's the URL of the broken script?" She looks in her browser's Address field and gives you the URL of the site's front page.

- *Frames make scrolling more difficult*   Experienced users know that you don't have to use a mouse to scroll through a Web page; you can use the space bar or arrow keys. However, if the page uses frames, the user must first click on the frame in which they wish to scroll.

- *Frames break the Reload button*   In our hypothetical travel site, if Joe User pushes Reload when looking at the Copper Canyon page, the browser will often show the travel site home page, because the URL has not been updated.

- *Frames break the Back button*   In some browsers, frames break the Back button; if a user visits a frame-based site and clicks 100 times on interior links, a click on the Back button may take the user back 101 steps rather than 1.

- *Search engines send users to subpages*   Suppose your site uses two frames: one for navigation and one for content. Since each frame is defined by a separate HTML document at a separate URL, a public search engine such as Google is most likely to send the user to the HTML document containing content only. That user will never see the navigation frame and therefore won't be able to find the other parts of your site.

HTML Considered Harmful?

Vanilla HTML imposes limits on how you can display and collect information. Users can't drag and drop objects. There are no sliders, no paintbrushes, no real-time direct manipulation of screen objects. You can get around these limitations with a Java applet, Flash, or code targeted at another browser plugin, but it might not be a good idea.

Part of the genius of HTML and the Web is that all sites using HTML markup and forms work the same. A user who has learned to use amazon.com can apply his or her experience to using Google. Users visit a Web site because they are looking for unique content and services, not a unique interface.

Administration pages may constitute an exception to the "custom interface is bad" rule. Suppose you hire and train customer service agents who will be using the administration pages on a daily basis. If a Macintosh/Windows-like drag-and-drop interface saves them a lot of time (and you money), it is perfectly reasonable to write custom code that will run in their browsers. You may have to spend fifteen minutes training each agent, an unacceptably long time for a casual user, but the long-run productivity dividends make it worthwhile.

The Future

In the practical world, HTML is king. In the conference rooms of standards committees, however, it has been superseded by Extensible Hypertext Markup Language (XHTML). Should you wish to keep up with events in this area, visit http://www.w3.org/MarkUp/.

More

- visit your favorite Web page and use the browser command "View Source"
- HTML tag reference: http://www.w3schools.com/html/html_reference.asp (Web) and *HTML & XHTML: The Definitive Guide* by Chuck Musciano and Bill Kennedy (O'Reilly, 2002) (print)
- Colors and their hexadecimal equivalents: http://falco.elte.hu/COMP/HTML/colors.html
- Special characters: http://hotwired.lycos.com/webmonkey/reference/special _characters/
- Cascading Style Sheets: http://www.w3schools.com/css/default.asp

B Engagement Management

This section was primarily authored by Cesar Brea.

Most of this book is about building a great experience for the users. In parallel, however, it is important to ensure that you're creating a great experience for your client and his or her sponsors during your team's engagement with this client. These are the folks who will pay the bills and sing your praises.

Whether or not your praises get sung depends primarily on whether the application that you build delivers the benefits your client expects. Thus it is important at all times to keep in mind an answer to the question "What does my client expect?" One comforting factor is that you have a lot of control over the client's expectations. You are preparing the planning documents, you are writing the schedule, and you are bringing agendas to meetings with clients.

This chapter presents an engagement management worksheet, a lightweight tool for managing your relationship with the client.

Definitions:

- *Organization*—the company or non-profit corporation for whom you are building the application; if you're working for an enormous enterprise, for example, a university or Fortune 500, it is probably best to put down a particular department or division as the organization

- *Sponsor*—the person whose budget is paying for this, or who is accountable for business results the application supports; in some cases, if you are working directly for the top manager at a small organization, the sponsor will be the board of directors

- *Client*—the manager, typically a subordinate of the sponsor, who is your day-to-day contact

The worksheet has five sections:

- About the Organization
- About the Application
- About the Project
- Sign-Offs
- Assets Developed

We recommend you go through this formally with your team at least once a week. You can also use it to structure introductory and update meetings with your client, though the worksheet is primarily for your team.

About the Organization

To contribute to discussions about scope and which features are critical, you need to understand what the client's organization is trying to accomplish as a whole. It helps to know a bit about not just the organization's purpose, but about its size, resources, and trends in its fortunes.

It also helps to understand your client personally, and to understand his/her place and influence in the organization. How much can be forced through? What must be proven before the application will get support from higher management?

Organization Name	
Organization Purpose (does what? for whom?)	
Organization Size (# people? annual budget?)	
Organizational Performance (revenue/ profit/budget trend, actual vs. plan)	

Sponsor's Name, Title, and Organizational Role/Level (person whose budget is paying for this, or who is accountable for business results the application supports)	
Client's Name, Title, and Organizational Role/Level (person responsible for what gets delivered)	
Business Goals Served by Application (doing exactly what "better, more, faster, cheaper," quantifiably how much?)	
Client Clout (leader, has say, follower?)	
Client Tenure In Job (new, mid-term, leaving)	
Client Technical Knowledge (none, some, lots)	

About the Application

You want to document at a high level what the client wants, what you think the client should want (if different), and if there are differences, what the plan for persuading the client to follow your lead is. Some of these items are confusing and they are explained below.

Topic	What the Client Wants	What We Think	Persuasion Plan*
Capabilities for Site-Wide Administrator	First, Next, Nice		
Capabilities for Registered Community Member	First, Next, Nice		
Capabilities for Unregistered Casual Visitor	First, Next, Nice		
Capabilities for User Class N	First, Next, Nice		
Design Preferences			
Performance Requirements	Page loading times		
Technical Infrastructure Constraints			
Application Maintenance Plans/ Resources			
Budget Through First Year			
Deadlines	Soft launch, full rollout, first business benefit		

Capabilities for site-wide administrator   For this as for other user class items, list those features that are needed first (must-have to launch the service in any form), next (what you'd do if you had a little bit of extra time and effort available), and nice-to-have. One example for the site-wide administrator user class is the following:

```
First = publish / manage content
Next = spam members with news/offers
Nice = track activity at individual registered user level
```

Design preferences   If your organization has an existing Web site or sites you can probably infer their design style. If they suggest Flash, frames, a lot of JavaScript, you've got a potential problem and might want to point out that Google, Amazon, eBay, and the other successful Internet applications stick to a plain, fast-loading, easily understood design.

Performance requirements/expectations   Start by suggesting your own standards of loading times in seconds for the index page and more complex pages on the site. Let the client react to these suggestions. If everyone agrees on sub-second page loading times, that will make it a lot easier to kick out the worst user interface ideas, such as Flash introductions.

Technical infrastructure constraints   A small or medium-sized organization will generally have only expertise and staff appropriate for maintaining one kind of server. If you're not building the project on top of that server, you're implicitly asking the organization to spend $100,000 per year to bring in additional maintenance staff and/or push the new service out to a contract hosting organization. It is best to be clear up front about what will need to happen when it comes time to move the system into production.

Application maintenance plans/resources   Who's going to look after what you deliver? How experienced is this person?

Budget   What is the total budget for hardware, software, integration, launch (including populating with content), training, and maintenance?

Deadlines   You'll probably use other tools to keep a detailed schedule. Use this worksheet to keep track of some high-level scheduling goals that both you and the client are working towards. Avoid the temptation of stereotypical technical people to think in terms of their own requirements and tasks. Your client and sponsor don't care about SQL. They care about the date on which full business benefit (FBB) is realized for this application, that is, when is the system adding to profitability or otherwise contributing to organizational goals.

Working back from that date and recognizing that one or two version launches will probably be necessary to achieve FBB, establish a public launch date. Working back from the public launch date, establish a soft launch or full user test date. Working back from that date, establish a "feature-complete build" date on which the programmers are only testing and fixing bugs rather than adding new features.

Persuasion plan   For each item in this section, if differences of opinion arise during initial meetings, document a persuasion plan. Here are some elements of the plan that should be sketched in this worksheet:

- battle worth fighting?
- objective: total victory? acceptable compromise?
- agreement driven by facts/logic? emotion/relationship?
- who else should be involved? (e.g., course staff or experienced alumni engineers)

About the Project

You'll have more detailed project management documents than this section of the worksheet. Consider this a high-level summary of how things are going. Try to have as many face-to-face meetings as possible, supplemented by telephone conferences and email, always anchoring the discussion with documents and written schedules. At a minimum, try to do a face-to-face meeting every three weeks and a phone call every week. This section of the worksheet should be updated every two weeks and will serve to flag any major problems.

It's tempting to blow this off, but projects need to be managed face-to-face (at least occasionally) and in writing. These disciplines force you and your client to be honest and realistic with each other. You don't have to overdo it with endless meetings and thick reports. A meeting at the beginning, middle, and end will do just fine, supplemented by weekly phone calls. And the table below will be plenty to flag major problems. Review it at least once every two weeks.

Date of most recent face-to-face meeting with Client	
Date of most recent telephone meeting with Client	
Date of most recent face-to-face meeting with Sponsor	
Date of most recent telephone meeting with Sponsor	
Engagement letter (see below) signed by Client and Sponsor?	
Current specs signed by Client and Sponsor?	
Weekly update meeting minutes signed by Client? (includes changes requested/agreed/under discussion)	
Estimated delivery date vs. committed delivery date	
Estimated budget vs. committed budget	
Client mood (unhappy to happy)	
Team mood	
Mood of the average user who has tried the application	

A good engagement letter covers at least the following subjects:

- overall description of client situation and need
- summary of application to be built
- deadlines
- budgets
- mutual obligations
- other terms

Sign-Offs

Try to schedule comprehensive project reviews every three weeks or so, ideally face-to-face. Notes and decisions from those reviews should be signed by both sides (team or team leader and client). Requiring a signature has a way of forcing issues to closure.

Assets Developed

In building a profitable business or a professional reputation it is important to learn from and build on experience. Here are some of the things that you can take away from a project:

- experience with the problem domain and knowledge of how to solve a similar problem in the future
- lessons about dealing with this particular organization
- lessons about working with this particular team
- general lessons about teamwork and working with organizations of a particular size
- data models, stored procedures, and maybe even some page scripts for re-use on the next Internet applications that you build
- a good reference from the Client
- magazine or newspaper articles describing the application
- a "white paper" describing your team's achievement to a technical audience
- some sort of written summary describing your team's achievement to a business audience

At the midpoint of the project, write down what you're hoping to take away from the experience. At the end, write down what you actually did take away.

C Grading Standards

These are the grading standards used by the authors in 6.171 at MIT. If you're a student in 6.171, please keep these in mind throughout the semester. If you're an instructor at another school, you might find these a useful model.

Our overall goal in 6.171 is producing professionally competent software engineers. If by the end of the semester, you have the skills of a professional programmer you will get an A for the class.

A professional programmer ought to be able to pick worthwhile problems to attack. Engineering is the art of building cost-effective solutions to problems that society regards as significant. A person who blindly does what he or she is told, without independently figuring out the context and significance of the problem, is not doing engineering. A professional programmer needs to be able to sit at a meeting with decision-makers, prepared with substantial domain knowledge, and make significant contributions to the discussion. In evaluating your performance in 6.171, we look at (i) how well you've steered your client into solving the most important problems for users first, (ii) what you've said during in-class discussions of potential projects, and (iii) whether you've made useful suggestions to other teams in the realm of service design.

A professional programmer needs to be skilled at realizing clean-sheet-of-paper designs: (i) taking vague organizational aspirations and turning them into concrete specifications, (ii) selecting appropriate tools for a substrate, (iii) building and testing a prototype, (iv) using that prototype to obtain feedback from users and the sponsoring organization, (v) implementing and launching Release 1.0, (vi) refining the specs for Release 2.0 based on experience with 1.0. In evaluating your performance in 6.171, we look at whether you managed to launch your service to real users and how successful your project was at meeting technical and organizational goals. The mid-term exam is also aimed at figuring out whether you can look at a desired user experience and perform the most critical aspects of system design such as data modeling.

Notice that a critical element of the realization process, *selecting appropriate tools*, requires that a programmer maintain a network of professional colleagues. It is extremely risky to pick software tools based on vendor claims, 99 percent of which have proven to be, uh, optimistic. A programmer who can draw on a group of friends and get unbiased information as to which tools are reliable is much more effective than a programmer working in isolation, reading press releases and advertising. You'll get extra credit in 6.171 if you can say "I really liked feature X from Team Y's project so I asked them how they did it and adapted their ideas and code for our project."

A professional programmer needs to have a dedication to the quality of the end-user experience. A coder, ripe for outsourcing to the Third World, can unthinkingly implement whatever system design that results from management and graphic designer whims. An engineer, however, makes sure that what he or she is doing makes effective use of the end-user's time, partially by reference to established principles of user interface design and partially by conducting prototype tests with a handful of potential users. In evaluating your performance in 6.171, we look at whether you made effective use of user testing, ideally beyond the minimum required in the exercises.

A professional programmer is skilled in communicating. This means writing documentation that will enable another programmer to take over a project. Communicating also means writing white papers that explain the significance of a problem, how it was attacked, and what the results were. A programmer also ought to be good at making short oral presentations that communicate the main points of a project to a technical or non-technical audience. Finally, a programmer should know how to make good use of face-to-face interactions with users and customers. In evaluating your performance in 6.171, we ask "Can we understand all of this structure and source code purely by reading what is in the /doc directory?" We also look at (i) whether you gave clear and compelling presentations in class, (ii) whether your client felt that he or she was kept apprised of project status, and (iii) the quality of your final overview document.

A professional programmer is not afraid of a challenge. An MIT graduate certainly should never be afraid of a challenge. You get extra points in 6.171 for tackling a hard problem and solving it in an elegant or clever way.

Speaking of challenges ... most software projects are too difficult for one person to tackle alone. Consequently, a professional programmer is good at working within a team, managing risks, establishing milestones, and meeting deadlines. In evaluating your performance in 6.171, we'll look at whether you helped your projectmates function as a team and whether you discharged the responsibilities for the role(s) that you assumed within the team.

For a software engineer to have a successful career, he or she must have a portfolio of projects that actually launched and customers who were satisfied and say "I would really like to work with this engineer again." We look at whether you did the last painful 5 percent of work that is necessary to push your project out into the hands of real users and how your client feels about the overall experience of working with you.

Glossary

Abstract URL   An abstract URL is one without a file extension, e.g., `http://foobar.com/contact-info` rather than `http://foobar.com/contact-info.html` or `http://foobar.com/contact-info.aspx`. If you publish only abstract URLs, you have the freedom to change your implementation technology without breaking users' bookmarks and links from other sites.

Acceptance Test   A test performed by an end-user or system owner to verify that the delivered software functions correctly and meets requirements.

ACID Test   A test proposed by IBM in the 1960s for transaction database management systems: Atomicity, Consistency, Isolation, Durability. An ACID-compliant database such as Oracle or SQL Server can guarantee that two updates will be done together (atomicity), that rules for integrity can be established and enforced (consistency), that concurrent users won't see each others' half-finished work (isolation), that information won't be lost even if a hard disk dies (durability). See the "Basics" chapter and *SQL for Web Nerds* at http://philip.greenspun.com/sql/ for more.

Application Server   See "Middleware."

AOLserver   Released in early 1995 as "NaviServer," AOLserver remains one of the most powerful Web server programs on the market and it is free and open-source. It is a multi-threaded server that provides a lot of support for connecting to relational database management systems. AOLserver is documented at www.aolserver.com.

Apache   Vies with Microsoft Internet Information Server for the title of "world's most popular Web server." Apache was never very technically advanced, but it was the best of the free and open-source Web servers for a time and grew to dominance. More: http://philip.greenspun.com/panda/server.

API   Application Programming Interface. An abstraction barrier between custom/ extension code and a core, usually commercial, program. The goal of an API is to let you write programs that won't break when you upgrade the underlying system. The authors of the core program are saying, "Here are a bunch of hooks into our code. We guarantee and document that they will work a certain way. We reserve the right to change the core program, but we will endeavor to preserve the behavior of the API call. If we can't, then we'll tell you in the release notes that we broke an old API call."

ASP   Active Server Pages, introduced by Microsoft in the mid-1990s. This is the standard programming system for Internet applications hosted on Windows servers. It is bundled with Internet Information Server (IIS) when you buy Windows. The fundamental idea is that you write HTML pages with little embedded bits of Visual Basic, C# or other languages, that are interpreted by the server.

Audit Trail   A record of past activity. For instance, a log of all past values held by columns in a database row. Or a sequence of all cash register transactions over the last three months. Or a print-out of all customer service interactions related to a given order, regardless of whether communication takes place by telephone, email, or live chat with a representative.

Blog   An online journal, published frequently (often daily). Readers can post comments on each journal entry. Some blogs gain a wide readership, such as this one: http://blogs.law.harvard.edu/philg/. The term *blog* is a shortening of *weblog*.

Bozo Filter   An individual user request that the server filter out contributions from some particular other community member.

Cable Modem   A cable modem is an Internet connection provided by a cable TV operator, typically with at least 1.5 Mbits per second of download bandwidth (50–100 times faster than modems that work over analog telephone lines).

Cache   Computer systems typically incorporate capacious storage devices that are slow (e.g., disk drives) and smaller storage devices that are fast (e.g., memory chips, which are 100,000 times faster than disk). File systems and database management systems keep recently used information from the slow devices in a *cache* in the fast device.

CGI   Common Gateway Interface. This is a standard that lets programmers write Web scripts without depending on details of the Web server program being used. Thus, for example, an Internet service implemented in CGI could be moved from a site running AOLserver to a site running Apache. CGI scripts, which run as separately launched operating system processes, are typically very slow compared to scripts than run inside a Web server program.

Client/Server   In the 1960s, computers were so expensive that each company could have only one. "The computer" ran one program at a time, typically reading instructions and data from punch cards. This was *batch processing*. In the 1970s, that computer was able to run several programs simultaneously, responding to users at interactive terminals. This was *timesharing* (it would be nice if modesty prevented one of the authors from noting that this was developed by his lab at MIT circa 1960). In the 1980s, companies could afford lots of computers. The big computers were designated *servers* and would wait for requests to come in from a network of *client* computers. The client computer might sit on a user's desktop and produce an informative graph of the information retrieved from the server. The overall architecture was referred to as *client/server*. Because of the high cost of designing, developing, and maintaining the programs that run on the client machines, Corporate America is rapidly discarding this architecture in favor of *Intranet*: Client machines run a simple Web browser and servers do more of the work required to present the information.

Code Freeze   The point at which all coding stops, usually to allow software testing without the introduction of new bugs.

Collaborative Filtering   If you can persuade a group of people to rate movies on a 1–10 scale, for example, it becomes possible to identify people whose tastes are similar. Given a new movie that only a few people have seen and rated, a *collaborative filter* can identify others in the community who might like it. Some e-commerce sites provide this service, noting for example that "customers who bought the product you're looking at right now also tended to buy these other three things." Collaborative filtering is easy to program, but ultimately is a poor substitute for human reviewers and editors.

Community Site   A community site exists to support the interaction of an online community of users. These users typically come together because of a shared interest and are most vibrant when there is an educational dimension, i.e., when the more experienced users are helping the novices improve their skills.

Compression   When storing information in digital form, it is often possible to reduce the amount of space required by exploiting regular patterns in the data. For example, documents written in English frequently contain "the." A compression system might notice this fact and represent the complete word "the" (24 bits) with a shorter code. A picture containing your friend's face plus a lot of blue sky could be compressed if the upper region were described as "a lot of blue sky." All popular Web image, video, and sound formats incorporate compression.

Content Repository   Instead of having one SQL table for every different kind of content on a site, e.g., `articles`, `comments`, `news`, `questions`, `answers`, it is possible to define a single *content repository* table that is flexible enough to store all of these in one place. This approach to data modeling makes it simpler to perform queries such as "show me all the new stuff since yesterday" or "show me all the content contributed by User 37." With a content repository, it is also easier to program and enforce consistent site-wide policies regarding approval, editing, and administration of content.

Cookie   The Cookie protocol allows a Web application to conveniently maintain a "session" with a particular user. The Web server sends the client a "magic cookie" (piece of information) that the client is required to return on subsequent requests. The original specification is at http://home.netscape.com/newsref/std/cookie_spec.html.

Data Model   A data model is the structure in which a computer program stores persistent information. In a relational database, data models are built from tables. Within a table, information is stored in homogeneous columns, e.g., a column named `registration_date` would contain information only of type `date`. A data model is interesting because it shows what kinds of information a computer application can process. For example, if there is no place in the data model for the program to store the IP address from which content was posted, the publisher will never be able to automatically delete all content that came from the IP address of a spammer.

DNS The Domain Name System translates human-readable hostnames, e.g., `www.google.com`, into machine-readable and network-routable IP addresses, e.g., `216.239.57.100`. DNS is a distributed application in that there is no single computer that holds translations for all possible hostnames. A domain registrar, e.g., www.register.com, records that the domain servers for the google.com domain are at particular IP addresses. A user's local *name server* will query the name servers for google.com to find the translation for the hostname `www.google.com`. Note that there is nothing magic about "www"; it is merely a conventional name for a computer that runs a Web server. The procedure for translating a hostname such as `froogle.google.com` is the same as that applied for `www`. *Round robin DNS* was an early load-balancing technique in which multiple computers at different IP addresses were configured to serve an application; browsers asking the DNS servers to translate the site's hostname would get different answers depending on when they asked, thus spreading out the users among the multiple computers hosting the application.

DTD Document Type Definition. The specification of an XML document's schema, including its elements, attributes, and data structure. DTDs are used for validating that an XML document is well-formed. You can also share a DTD with your collaborators in order to agree upon the structure of XML documents that will be exchanged.

Dynamic Site A dynamic site is one that is able to collect information from User A, serve it back to Users B and C immediately, and hide it from User D because the server knows that User D isn't interested in this kind of content. Dynamic sites are typically built on top of relational database management systems because these programs make it easy to organize content submitted by hundreds of concurrent users. An example of a simple dynamic site would be a classified ad system.

Emacs World's most powerful text editor, written by Richard Stallman (RMS) in 1976 for the Incompatible Timesharing System (ITS) on the PDP-10s at MIT. Emacs has been subsequently ported to virtually every kind of computer hardware and operating system between 1976 and the present (including the Macintosh, Windows 95/NT, and every flavor of Unix). Good programmers tend to spend their entire working lives in Emacs, which is capable of functioning as a mail reader, USENET news reader, Web browser, shell, calendar, calculator, and Lisp evaluator. Emacs is infinitely customizable because users can write their own commands in Lisp. You can find out more about Emacs at ftp://publications.ai.mit.edu/ai-publications/pdf/AIM-519A.pdf (Stallman's 1979 MIT AI Lab report), at www.gnu.org (where you can download the source code for free), or by reading *Learning Emacs* (Debra Cameron et al. [O'Reilly, 1996]). If you want to program Emacs, then you'll want *Writing Gnu Emacs Extensions* (Bob Glickstein [O'Reilly, 1997]).

Filter   The best Web server APIs allow the programmer to say "run this little piece of code before [or after] serving files that match a particular URL pattern." Filters that run after a file is served are useful if you want to add extra logging to an application. Filters that run before a file is served or a script is run are useful for implementing a security policy in a consistent fashion, rather than relying on the authors of individual scripts to insert an authentication check.

Firewall   A computer that sits between a company's internal network of computers and the public Internet. The firewall's job is to make sure that internal users can get out to enjoy the benefits of the Internet while external crackers are unable to make connections to machines behind the firewall.

Flat-file   A flat-file database keeps information organized in a structured manner, typically in one big file. A desktop spreadsheet application is an example of a flat-file database management system. These are useful for Web publishers preparing content because a large body of information can be assembled and then distributed in a consistent format. Flat-file databases typically lack support for processing transactions (inserts and updates) from concurrent users. Thus, collaboration or e-commerce Web sites generally rely on a relational database management system as a back-end.

GIF   Graphical Interchange Format. Developed in 1987 by CompuServe, this is a way of storing compressed images with up to 256 colors. It became popular on the Web because it was the only format that could be displayed in-line by the first multi-platform Web browser (NCSA Mosaic). The JPEG image file format results in much better looking images with much smaller-sized files.

HTML   Hyper Text Markup Language. Developed by Tim Berners-Lee, this specifies a format for the most popular kind of document distributed over the Web (via HTTP). Documented sketchily in this book, documented badly at http://www.w3.org, and documented well in *HTML: The Definitive Guide* (Chuck Musciano and Bill Kennedy [O'Reilly, 2002]).

HTTP   Hyper Text Transfer Protocol. Developed by Tim Berners-Lee, this specifies how a Web browser asks for a document from a Web server. Question such as "How does a server tell the browser that a document has moved?" or "How does a browser ask the time that a document was last modified?" may be answered by reference to this protocol, which is documented badly at http://www.w3.org and documented well in various books such as *HTTP: The Definitive Guide* (David Gourley and Brian Totty [O'Reilly, 2002]).

IIS   Internet Information Server. A threaded Web server program that is included by Microsoft when you purchase the Windows operating system.

Java   Java is first a programming language, developed by Sun Microsystems around 1992, intended for use on the tiny computers inside cell phones and similar devices. Java is second an interpreter, the Java virtual machine, formerly compiled into popular Web browsers (back when Netscape Navigator was popular and before Sun sued

Microsoft). Java is third a security system that purports to guarantee that a program downloaded from an untrusted source on the Internet can run safely inside the interpreter. Java is the only realistic way for a Web publisher to take advantage of the computing power available on a user's desktop. Java is generally a cumbersome language for server-side software development. For more background on the language, see the "Java" chapter from *Database Backed Web Sites* at http://philip.greenspun.com/wtr/dead-trees/53008.htm.

JPEG   Joint Photographic Experts Group. A bunch of people who sat down and designed a standard for image compression, conveniently titled "IS 10918-1 (ITU-T T.81)." This standard works particularly well for 24-bit color photographs. C-Cube Microsystems came up with the JFIF standard for encoding color images in a file. Such a file is what people commonly refer to as "a JPEG" and typically ends in ".jpg" or ".jpeg." The main problem with JFIF files is that they record only 8 bits per color, a vastly smaller range of intensities than is present in the natural world and significantly smaller than the 12- and 14-bits-per-color signals that come out of the best digital scanners and cameras. This defect and more are remedied in the JPEG 2000 standard. See www.jpeg.org for more about the standard.

LDAP   Lightweight Directory Access Protocol. A typical LDAP server is a simple network-accessible database where an organization stores information about its authorized users and what privileges each user has. Thus, rather than create a new employee account on 50 different computers, the new employee is entered into LDAP and granted rights to those 50 systems. If the employee leaves, revoking all privileges is as simple as removing one entry in the LDAP directory. LDAP is a bit confusing because original implementations were presented as alternatives to the Web and the relational database management system. Nowadays many LDAP servers are implemented using standard RDBMSs underneath, and they talk to the rest of the world via XML documents served over HTTP.

Linux   A free version of the Unix operating system, primarily composed of tools developed over a 15-year period by Richard Stallman and Project GNU. However, the final spectacular push was provided by Linus Torvalds who wrote a kernel (completed in 1994), organized a bunch of programmers Internet-wide, and managed releases.

Lisp   Lisp is the most powerful and also easiest-to-use programming language ever developed. Invented by John McCarthy at MIT in the late 1950s, Lisp is today used by the most sophisticated programmers pushing the limits of computers in mathematical physics, computer-aided engineering, and computer-aided genetics. Lisp is also used by thousands of people who don't think of themselves as programmers at all, e.g., people who want to define shortcuts in AutoCAD or the Emacs text editor. The best introduction to Lisp is also the best introduction to computer science: *Structure and Interpretation of Computer Programs* (Harold Abelson and Gerald Sussman [MIT Press, 1996]).

Log Analyzer   A program that reads a Web server's access log file (one line per request served) and produces a comprehensible report with summary statistics, e.g., "You served

234,812 requests yesterday to 2,039 different computers; the most popular file was /samoyed-faces.html."

Magnet Content   Material authored by a publisher in hopes of establishing an online community. In the long run, a majority of the content in a successful community site will be user authored.

Middleware   A vague term that, when used in the context of Internet applications, means "software sold to people who don't know how to program by people who don't know how to program." In theory, middleware sits between your relational database management system and your application program and makes the whole system run more reliably, just like adding a bunch of extra moving parts to your car would make it more reliable.

MIME   Multi-Purpose Internet Mail Extensions. Developed in 1991 by Nathan Borenstein of Bellcore so that people could include images and other non-plain-text documents in email messages. MIME is a critical standard for the World Wide Web because an HTTP server answering a request always includes the MIME type of the document served. For example, if a browser requests "foobar.jpg," the server will return a MIME type of "image/jpeg." The Web browser will decide, based on this type, whether or not to attempt to render the document. A JPEG image can be rendered by all modern Web browsers. If, for example, a Web browser sees a MIME type of "application/x-pilot" (for the .prc files that PalmPilots employ), the browser will invite the user to save the document to disk or select an appropriate application to launch for this kind of document.

Multi-modal   A multi-modal user interface allows you to interact with a piece of software in a variety of means simultaneously. For example, you may be able to communicate using a keyboard or stylus, or with your voice, or even with hand or face gestures. These are all "modes" of communication. The advent of GPRS makes simultaneous voice/keypad interaction possible on cellular telephones.

Operating System (OS)   A big, complicated computer program that lets multiple, simultaneously executing, big, complicated computer programs coexist peacefully on one physical computer. The operating system is also responsible for hiding the details of the computer hardware from the application programmers, e.g., letting a programmer say "I want to write ABC into a file named XYZ" without the programmer having to know how many disk drives the computer has or what company manufactured those drives. Examples of operating systems are Unix and Windows XP. Examples of things that try to be operating systems but mostly fail to fulfill the "coexist peacefully" condition are Windows 98 and the Macintosh OS.

Oracle   Oracle is the most popular relational database management system (RDBMS). It was developed by Larry Ellison's Oracle Corporation in the late 1970s.

Perl   Perl is a scripting language developed by Larry Wall in 1986 to make his Unix sysadmin job a little easier. It unifies a bunch of capabilities from disparate older Unix tools. Like Unix, Perl is perhaps best described as "ugly but fast and useful." Perl is free, has particularly powerful string processing operators, and quickly developed a large following and, therefore, a large library for CGI scripting. For more info, see www.perl .com or www.perl.org.

Historical note: Lisp programmers forced to look at Perl code would usually say "if there were any justice in this world, the guys who wrote this would go to jail." In a rare case of Lisp programmers getting their wish, in 1995 Intel Corporation persuaded local authorities to send Randal Schwartz, author of *Learning Perl* (O'Reilly, 2001), to the Big House for 90 days (plus 5 years of probation, 480 hours of community service, and $68,000 of "restitution" to Intel). Sadly, however, it seems that Schwartz's official crime was not corrupting young minds with Perl syntax and semantics. Most Unix sysadmins periodically run a program called "crack" that tries to guess user passwords. When crack is successful, the sysadmins send out email saying "your password has been cracked; please change it to something harder to guess." Obviously they do not need the passwords since they have root access to all the boxes and can read any of the data contained on them. At a university, you get paid about $50,000/year for doing this. In Oregon if you do this for a multi-billion-dollar company that has recently donated $100,000 to the local law enforcement authorities, you've committed a crime. See http://www .lightlink.com/spacenka/fors/ for more on *State of Oregon v. Randal Schwartz*.

Persistence   The continued existence of data. A *persistence mechanism* is something that provides long-term data storage, even when the application that created the data is no longer running. Examples include RDBMSs, XML documents, and flat-file databases.

RDBMS   Relational Database Management System. A computer program that lets you store, index, and retrieve tables of data. The simplest way to look at an RDBMS is as a spreadsheet that multiple users can update. The most important thing that an RDBMS does is provide transactions.

Request Processor   Portion of a Web server program that decides how to handle an incoming request. A well-designed request processor enables a publisher to expose only abstract URLs, e.g., "glossary" rather than "glossary.html." The job of the request processor is to dig around in the file system and find a document to deliver or a script to execute.

RMS   Richard M. Stallman. In 1976, he developed Emacs, the world's best and most widely used text editor. He went on to develop gcc, the most widely used compiler for the C programming language and won a $240,000 MacArthur fellowship in 1990. Stallman is the founder of the free software movement (see www.fsf.org), and Project GNU, which gave rise to Linux.

Robot   In the technologically optimistic portion of the 20th century, robots were intelligent anthropomorphic machines that understood human speech, interpreted visual scenes, and manipulated objects in the real world. In the technologically realistic 21st century, robots are absurdly primitive programs that do things like "Go look up this book title at three different online bookstores and see who has the lowest price; fail completely if any one of the online bookstores has added a comma to their HTML page." Also known as *intelligent agents* (an intellectually vacuous term, but useful for getting tenure if you're a university professor). Some simple, but very useful examples of robots are the spiders or Web crawlers that fill the content database at public search engine sites such as AltaVista.

Scalable   A marketing term used to sell defective software to executives at big companies. Internet applications are fundamentally concerned with processing updates from thousands of concurrent users. This is what database management systems were built for. Smart engineers build Web applications so that if the database is up and running, the Web site will be up and running. Period. Adding more users to the site will inevitably require adding capacity to the database management system, no matter what other software is employed. The thoughtful engineer will realize that a provably *scalable* site is one that relies on no other software besides the database management system and the thinnest of software layers on top, such as Apache, AOLserver, or Microsoft IIS.

Semantic Tag   The most popular Web markup language is HTML, which provides for formatting tags, e.g., "this is a headline" or "this should be rendered in italics." This is useful for humans reading Web pages. What would be more useful for computer programs trying to read Web pages is a *semantic tag*, e.g., "the following numbers represent the price of the product in dollars," or "the following characters represent the date this document was initially authored." More: http://www.w3.org/RDF/.

SOAP   Simple Object Access Protocol. A way for a Web server to call a procedure on another, physically separate Web server, and get back a machine-readable result in a standardized XML format. Useful for building a Web page that combines dynamic information pulled from multiple foreign sites. Also useful for building a single Web form that can perform multiple actions at foreign sites on behalf of a user. See http://msdn.microsoft.com/soap/ and http://www.w3.org/TR/SOAP/.

SGML   Standard Generalized Markup Language, standardized in 1980. A language for marking up documents so that they could be parsed by computer programs. Each community of people that wishes to author and parse documents must agree on a Document Type Definition (DTD), which is itself a machine-parsable description of what tags a marked-up document must or may have. HTML is an example of an SGML DTD. XML is a simplified descendant of SGML.

Soft Launch   Placing a server on the public Internet, but only telling a handful of people about it gives the developers a chance to see how real users interact with the system, fix bugs, and see how the servers handle a gradually increasing load. A *soft launch* like this is much safer than a Big Bang-style launch in which the server is made public just as a massive advertising campaign airs.

Spider   A spider or *Web crawler* is a program that exhaustively surfs all the links from a page and returns them to another program for processing. For example, all of the Internet search engine sites rely on spider robots to discover new Web sites and add them to their index. Another typical use of a spider is by a publisher against his or her own site. The spider program makes sure that all of the links function correctly and reports dead links.

SQL   Structured Query Language. Developed by IBM in the mid-1970s as a way to get information into and out of relational database management systems. A fundamental difference between SQL and standard programming languages is that SQL is declarative. You specify what kind of data you want from the database; the RDBMS is responsible for figuring out how to retrieve it. A full tutorial on SQL is available at http:// philip.greenspun.com/sql/.

Static Site   A static Web site comprises content that does not change depending on the identity of the user, the time of day, or what other users might have contributed recently. A static Web site is typically built using static documents in HTML format with graphics in GIF format and images in JPEG format. Collectively, these are referred to as *static files*. Contrast with a dynamic site, in which content can be automatically collected from users, personalized for the viewer, or changed as a function of the time of day.

TCP/IP   Transmission Control Protocol and Internet Protocol. These are the standards that govern transmission of data among computer systems. They are the foundation of the Internet. IP is a way of saying "send these next 1000 bits from Computer A to Computer B." TCP is a way of saying "send this stream of data reliably between Computer A and Computer B" (it is built on top of IP). TCP/IP is a beautiful engineering achievement, documented beautifully in *TCP/IP Illustrated, Volume 1* (W. Richard Stevens [Addison-Wesley, 1994]).

Transaction   A set of operations for which it is important that all succeed or all fail. On an e-commerce site, when a customer confirms a purchase, you'd like to send an order to the shipping department and simultaneously bill the customer's credit card. If the credit card can't be billed, you want to make sure that the order doesn't get shipped. If the shipping database can't accept the order, you want to make sure that the credit card doesn't get billed. RDBMSs such as Oracle provide significant support for implementing transactions.

UDDI   Universal Description, Discovery, and Integration. Like a worldwide Yellow Pages, this is an XML-based registry where companies can list the Web services they provide. More: uddi.org.

Unix   An operating system developed by Ken Thompson and Dennis Ritchie at Bell Laboratories in 1969, vaguely inspired by the advanced MULTICS system built by MIT. Unix really took off after 1979, when Bill Joy at University of California, Berkeley released a version for Digital's VAX minicomputer. Unix fragmented into a bewildering variety of mutually incompatible versions, thus enabling Microsoft Windows to take over most of the server market. The only surviving variants of Unix are Sun's Solaris and Linux.

URL   Uniform Resource Locator, also Uniform Resource Identifier (URI). A way of specifying the location of something on the Internet, e.g., "http://philip.greenspun.com/seia/glossary" is the URL for this glossary. The part before the colon specifies the protocol (HTTP). Legal alternatives include encrypted protocols such as HTTPS and legacy protocols such as FTP, news, gopher, etc. The part after the "//" is the server hostname ("philip.greenspun.com"). The part after the next "/" is the name of the file on the remote server. Also see "Abstract URL." More: http://www.w3.org/Addressing/.

USENET   A threaded discussion system that today connects millions of users from around the Internet into newsgroups such as rec.photo.equipment.35mm. The original system was built in the late 1970s and ran on one of the wide-area computer networks later subsumed into the Internet.

Version Control System   A system for keeping track of multiple versions of a file, usually source code. Version control systems are most useful when many developers are working together on a project, to help prevent one developer from overwriting another developer's changes, and to make it easy to revert to a previous version of a file. An excellent open-source version control system is CVS, Concurrent Versions System: www.cvshome.org.

VoiceXML   A markup language used for the development of voice applications. Using only a traditional Web infrastructure, you can create applications that are accessible over the telephone. With VoiceXML, you can specify call flow, speech recognition, and text-to-speech. See the "Voice" chapter for more.

W3C   The World Wide Web Consortium. The W3C is a vendor-neutral industry consortium that promotes standards for the World Wide Web. Popular W3C standards include HTML, HTTP, URL, XML, SOAP, VoiceXML, and many more: www.w3.org.

WAP   Wireless Application Protocol. A set of standard communication protocols for wireless devices. See the "Mobile" chapter for more.

Web Service   These days, the term *Web service* typically refers to a modular application that can be invoked through the Internet. The consumers of Web services are other computer applications that communicate, usually over HTTP, using XML standards including SOAP, WSDL, and UDDI. Sometimes *Web service* will still be used in the older sense of the word, as a user-facing application like amazon.com or photo.net.

Weblog   See "Blog."

Windows NT/2000/XP   A real operating system that can run the same programs with more or less the same user interface as the popular Windows 95/98 system. Windows NT was developed from scratch by a programming team at Microsoft that was mostly untainted by the people who brought misery to the world in the form of Windows 3.1/95. The latest versions of Windows work surprisingly well.

WML   Wireless Markup Language. An out-of-date markup language for the development of mobile browser applications. Replaced by XHTML-MP.

Workflow   The management of steps in a business process. A workflow specifies what tasks need to be done, in what order (sometimes linearly, sometimes in parallel), and who has permission to perform each task. Most tasks are performed by humans, but they can also be automated processes.

WSDL   Web Services Description Language. A way for a Web server to answer, in a machine-readable form, the question "what services do you provide?" with said services ultimately to be provided by SOAP. See http://www.w3.org/TR/wsdl.

WYSIWYG   What You See Is What You Get. A WYSIWYG word processor, for example, lets a user view an on-screen document as it will appear on the printed page, e.g., with text in italics appearing on-screen in italics. This approach to software was pioneered by Xerox Palo Alto Research Center in the 1970s and widely copied since then, notably by the Apple Macintosh. WYSIWYG is extremely effective for structurally simple documents that are printed once and never worked on again. WYSIWYG is extremely ineffective for the production of complex documents and documents that must be maintained and kept up-to-date over many years. Thus Quark Xpress and Adobe Framemaker facilitated a tremendous boom in desktop publishing, while Microsoft FrontPage and similar WYSIWYG tools for Web page construction have probably hindered development of interesting Web applications.

XHTML   The next generation of HTML, compliant with XML standards. Although it is very similar to the current HTML, it follows a stricter set of rules, thus allowing for better automatic code validation. This structure also makes it possible to embed other XML-based languages such as MathML (for equations) and SMIL (for multimedia) inside of XHTML pages. More: www.wdvl.com/Authoring/Languages/XML/XHTML/.

XHTML-MP   XHTML Mobile Profile. A strict subset of XHTML, used as a markup language for wireless application development. See the "Mobile" chapter for more.

XML   Extensible Markup Language, a simplified version of SGML with enhanced features for defining hyperlinks. As with SGML, it solves the trivial problem of defining a syntax for exchanging structured information, but doesn't do any of the hard work of getting users to agree on semantic structure.

To the Instructor

Thank you for considering this textbook. This section is intended to help you use it effectively for students at the following levels:

- juniors and seniors in Computer Science taking a one-term cram course in Internet application design (the MIT way)
- juniors and seniors in Computer Science taking a one-year "capstone" course in software engineering
- seniors in Computer Science doing a capstone independent study project or bachelor's thesis
- sophomores in Computer Science or non-majors spending a semester learning about building modern information systems

With respect to these goals, we will treat the following issues: (1) what to do during lectures, (2) how to find clients for your students, (3) what to put on exams, (4) how to find and use alumni mentors, and (5) evaluation and grading.

Before plunging into these issues, let's take a step back and reflect on the rationale for teaching this material at all.

A Step Back

Why is software engineering part of the undergraduate computer science curriculum? There are enough mathematical and theoretical aspects of computer science to occupy students through a bachelor's degree. Yet most schools have always included at least some hands-on programming. Why? Perhaps there is a belief that someone with an engineering degree ought to be able to engineer the sorts of systems that society demands. In the 1980s, users wanted desktop applications. Universities adapted by teaching students how to build a computer program that interacted with a single user at a time, processing input from the mouse and keyboard and displaying results graphically. Starting in the early 1990s, however, demand shifted toward server-based Internet applications. With 1,000 users potentially attempting the same action at the same instant, the technical challenge shifts to managing concurrency and transactions. Given stateless protocols such as HTTP, software engineers must learn to develop stateful user experiences. Given the ubiquitous network and evolving standards for remote procedure calls, students can learn practical ways of implementing distributed computing.

Once we've taught students how to build Internet applications, it is gratifying to observe their enormous potential. A computer science graduate in 1980 was, by his or her efforts alone, able to reach only a handful of users. Thanks to the ubiquitous Internet, a computer science student today is able to write a program that hundreds of thousands of people will use before that student ever graduates. One of our student teams, for example, built a photo-sharing service launched to the users of photo.net. Through November 2005, the software built by the students is holding more than one million photographs on behalf of roughly 87,000 users.

What Deep Principles Do They Need to Learn?

To contribute to the information systems of the next twenty years, in addition to teaching the material in the core computer science curriculum, we have to teach students:

- object-oriented design where each object is a Web service (distributed computing, demonstrating the old adage that "The exciting thing in computer science is always whatever we tried twenty years ago that didn't work.")
- about concurrency and transactions
- how to build a stateful user experience on top of stateless protocols
- about the relational database management system
- that they're only as good as their last user test

Universities have long taught theoretical methods for dealing with concurrency and transactions. The Internet raises new challenges in these areas. A dozen users may simultaneously ask for the same airline seat. Twenty responses to a discussion forum question may come in simultaneously. The radio or hard-wired connection to a user may be interrupted halfway through an attempt to register at a site. Starting in 1994 there has been a convergence of solutions to these problems, with the fundamental element of the solution being the relational database management system (RDBMS). At a school like MIT, where the RDBMS has not been taught, this textbook gives an opportunity to introduce SQL and data modeling with tables. At a school with an existing database course, this textbook can be used to get students excited about using the RDBMS as a black box before they embark on a more formal course where the underpinnings are explained.

Scientists measure their results against nature. Engineers measure their results against human needs. Programmers ... don't measure their results. As a final overarching deep principle, we need to teach students to measure their results against the end-user experience. Anyone can build an Internet application. The applications that are successful and have impact are those whose data model and page flow permit the users to accomplish their tasks with a minimum of time and confusion.

What Skills Do They Need to Learn?

In a world where it seems that every villager in India has learned Java, we want our graduates to be more than mere coders. A graduate who can do nothing more than sit in a corner and code Java classes from specs is doing a job that is certain to be sent to a low-wage country eventually.

We'd like our students to be able to take vague and ambitious specifications and turn them into a system design that can be built and launched within a few months, with the features most important to users and easy to develop built first, and the difficult bells and whistles deferred to a second version. We'd like our students to know how to test prototypes with end-users and refine their application design once or twice within even a three-month project. We'd like our students to be able to think on their feet and speak up with constructive criticism at design reviews.

These desires translate into some aspects of how we use this textbook at MIT: real clients so that students are exposed to the vagueness and confusion of real-world problems; user testing built into the homework problems; "lecture" time primarily devoted to student-student interaction, with the instructors moderating the discussion.

Survey Courses Considered Helpful?

Suppose that one were convinced that the foregoing are the correct topics to teach a computer science undergraduate. Should we teach them one at a time, in-depth? Or should we start with a survey course that teaches all the concepts simultaneously in the context of building actual applications (this book)?

Students in a traditional computer science curriculum will

- spend a term learning the syntax of a language
- spend a term learning how to implement lists, stacks, hash tables
- spend a term learning that sorting is $O(n \log n)$
- spend a term learning how to interpret a high-level language
- spend a term learning how to build a time-sharing operating system
- spend a term learning about the underpinnings of several different kinds of database management systems
- spend a term learning about AI algorithms

Students in MIT course 6.001 (Structure and Interpretation of Computer Programs, based on the Abelson/Sussman textbook of the same name) learn all of the above in one semester, albeit not very thoroughly. By the end of the semester, they're either really excited about the challenges in computer science or ... they've wised up and switched to biology.

Survey courses have been similarly successful on the electrical engineering side of our department. In the good old days, MIT offered 6.01, a linear networks course. Students learned RLC networks in detail. But they forgot why they'd wanted to major in electrical engineering. Today the first hardware course is 6.002, where students play with op-amps before learning about the transistor!

One of the most celebrated courses at MIT is the Aeronautics and Astronautics department's Unified Engineering. Here is the first semester's description from the course catalog:

Presents the principles and methods of engineering, as well as their interrelationships and applications, through lectures, recitations, design problems, and labs. Disciplines introduced include: statics, materials and structures, dynamics, fluid dynamics, thermodynamics, materials, propulsion, signal and system analysis, and circuits. Topics: mechanics of solids and fluids; statics and dynamics for bodies systems and networks; conservation of mass and momentum; properties of solids and fluids; temperature, conservation of energy;

stability and response of static and dynamic systems. Applications include particle and rigid body dynamics; stress and deformations in truss members; airfoils and nozzles in high-speed flow; passive and active circuits. Laboratory exposure to empirical methods in engineering; illustration of principles and practice. Design of typical aircraft or spacecraft elements.

Note that this is all presented in one semester, albeit with double the standard credit hours. For almost every topic in the course description, MIT has one or more full-semester courses exclusively devoted to that topic.

Experiences like these led us to develop *Software Engineering for Internet Applications* and the corresponding survey course in building computer systems for collaboration.

Using This Book for a Thesis Project

Most computer science programs require bachelor's candidates to engage in an open-ended development project, either as a "capstone" project or a thesis. Oftentimes the freedom inherent in this requirement serves as a quantity of rope sufficient for a student to hang him or herself. The student might choose to build anything from a graphics system to a compiler. A faculty member supervising the project might have to do a fair amount of work merely to determine what standards are appropriate in the student's chosen area. For example, if it is a compiler project, is it reasonable to expect the student to develop a complete Ada compiler in Lisp in one year? The core of an ML type-inferencer? A simple optimizing modification to gcc?

If you agree with the student to work within the framework of *Software Engineering for Internet Applications*, the project has enough structure that risk is minimized, yet enough flexibility that the student's creativity can flower. For example, using this book means that the student will be using a relational database management system. All of the code that you have to review will be in SQL. Yet the student is free to experiment with the operating system and HTML glue environment of his or her choice. The student will be building an Internet application that has user registration, content management, a discussion forum, and full-text search, and a combination of the book and the public Internet provide a good context for evaluating the student's achievement in these areas. Yet almost any client will put before the student idiosyncratic challenges that should give the student an opportunity to build something unusual.

We consider Mozart to have been creative although he did not develop new musical forms, relying instead on the structure laid down by Haydn. A student will accomplish more if he or she can spend the first months of a project working rather than figuring out what field in which to work, roughly what the scope of the project should be, what tools to choose from an unlimited palette, and so forth.

The One-Term Cram Course

When teaching this material in one semester, it is important that students set up their environments before the first class meeting. A student might have to reinstall operating systems and relational database management systems, contact technical support, or abandon an initial choice of tools.

The One-Year Thorough Course

There are several possible reasons for spreading this material over a full year:

- students who don't appreciate or can't handle a gung-ho pace
- students working individually rather than in teams (more coding per student)
- opportunity to go deeper into some of the underlying concepts and systems
- opportunity to launch services to real users mid-way through the course

If we had an extra semester, we would devote more attention to the inner workings of the relational database management system, demystifying the SQL parser and the various methods for handling concurrency. We would have the students look more carefully at the HTTP standard, possibly building their own simple Web server. We would cover some of the more exotic Web Consortium work, such as semantic Web and RDF and multi-modal interfaces. We would devote more time to performance measurement and engineering. We would push the teams and clients to launch their sites to real users as quickly as possible so that the students could learn from user activity and user feedback.

It would be nice to include a section on high-level formal specification of page flow and data model. Unfortunately, as of 2005, there are no tools available for this that compile into standard executable languages such as SQL and

Java. A quick glance at Unified Modeling Language (UML) might make one think that this is a useful nod in the direction of formal specification of Internet applications. However, UML cannot be compiled into a working system nor can it be verified against a system built in executable languages such as SQL and Java. Even if students mastered the 150 primitives of UML, the only thing that they would learn is that people in the IT industry can get paid high salaries, despite never having learned to write clear English prose. Object Role Modeling (ORM), however, is a high-level formal specification language that looks promising for automatic code generation in the coming years.

A Course for Sophomores

Less mature engineers are going to have more difficulty choosing an appropriate set of tools, more difficulty with tool installation and administration, and are going to be less resourceful in seeking assistance when appropriate. Thus if you are using this textbook with sophomores, it is probably a good idea to reduce flexibility and increase the physical rootedness of the students and the amount of hands-on assistance available.

Juniors and seniors might have had summer jobs working with Oracle and PHP on Debian Linux or with Microsoft .NET and SQL Server. They will probably be most productive if they can continue using their familiar tools. Furthermore, having a variety of tools in use during the semester provides all the students with an opportunity to learn a little bit about other development styles. The main risk to having students choose their tools is that some get sucked in by software vendor hype and elect to use, for example, three-tiered architectures and application servers. At MIT the students have three weeks before the start of the semester in which to install their chosen tools. All of the MIT students who decided to go the application server route were unable to get their systems up and running in time to do the "Basics" problem set and hence were forced to drop the class.

For sophomores, it is less likely that students will have extensive development experience with a particular set of tools and the risk of a student choosing an inappropriate set of tools is increased. It may be best to standardize on one set of tools so that everyone in the class is using the same systems.

Universities spend hundreds of millions of dollars on dormitories so that students can drink beer together, but are seemingly reluctant to spend a dime on shared workspaces for students. This is a shame because for learning most technical material it is much more effective for students to work together and live separately. A student working in a common laboratory with teaching assistants and fellow students nearby won't get stuck on something simple, such as "how do I launch SQL*Plus?" If you can possibly arrange a room with a bunch of desks and PCs and make that the center of your class, this will be an enormous help to less experienced students.

What to Do during Lectures

We try to keep our mouths shut during class meeting times (two 80-minute sessions per week). Students in 6.171 are learning to present their work to other engineers and to offer on-the-fly constructive criticism in response to an engineering presentation by others. If we're talking, they're not learning these skills. At various times in the semester, notably at the beginning of the course, the students won't have anything to present. We might fill a meeting time with a 25-minute lecture on RDBMS fundamentals, followed by a collaborative project in which students break up into teams to solve a data modeling problem.

At a minimum, the meeting room must have one Web browser connected to a video projector. Ideally the room will also have extra Web browsers and keyboards distributed around the room, one for every 3–6 students, and blackboards or whiteboards for collaborative work by small teams.

Here is a sample schedule, the goal of which is to drive the student projects to public launch as quickly as possible:

- *Three weeks before the first meeting* Students informed that they are accepted into the class, thus giving them time to prepare their computing environments. Inform students that they ought to make sure their environment works by building at least one Web page that returns data queried from the RDBMS. They may simply wish to do "Basics" problems 1 through 6.

- *Week 1, Meeting 1* Schedule, grading standards, and other bureaucracy relegated to handouts and a URL reference; we establish a precedent that class time is devoted to engineering. After a 5-minute "welcome to the course" in which we explain what we want them to learn, we give a 15-minute lecture on why online learning communities are important and what are the required elements for a sustainable online community. To get the students accustomed to the idea that they are going to be speaking up in class, we pick a few examples of online communities from the public Internet and ask students to criticize the features and user interface. We follow this with a 20-minute introduction of the RDBMS. Remind students that they must turn in the "Basics" problems in one week or be dropped from the class.

- *Week 1, Meeting 2*   In grappling with the "Basics" problem set, the students have now had a chance to work with SQL. We give a 20-minute lecture on serialization and concurrency control in the RDBMS, pointing out the practical differences between optimistic and pessimistic locking. The rest of the class time is devoted to pitches by prospective clients. The clients introduce themselves and explain what they want to accomplish with their Internet application. Each client should get about 5 minutes. For those projects where the client is unable to present in person, an instructor gives the pitch on behalf of the client.

- *Week 2, Meeting 1*   Students turn in the "Basics" problems. Today is the day that you assign teams to clients, and hence today is the day that you decide who is staying in the class. Drop anyone who did not turn in the problem set. They are not capable of building database-backed Web pages and hence are very unlikely to catch up. Most of the class time is devoted to code review on the "Basics" problems. You have secretly been surfing around before class looking at source code from various students. You're looking to get a discussion going on at least the following issues: (a) lack of commenting or identified authorship, (b) error handling in the comparative shopping problem, (c) different approaches to generating unique keys in the face of concurrency, (d) escaping single-quote characters in the search pages, (e) user interface design for the quote personalization system (tables versus bulleted lists, "kill" buttons versus checkboxes and a submit button), (f) different ways of parsing XML. Spend the last 5–10 minutes of class with some hints on working with the client. Students often have the most trouble contacting their client. They'll say "I sent him email a week ago, but he hasn't responded." Remind them to pick up the phone twice per day until they get a phone or in-person meeting with their client.

   (Giving students one week to do the "Basics" problem set seemed harsh to us, and hence we decided one term to give them two weeks to do it. Rather than spreading the work out, the result was that most students did nothing until two or three days before the due date and ended up staying up all night.)

- *Week 2, Meeting 2* Students break up into groups and work on a data modeling problem, e.g., "design an airline reservation system." The specification is open-ended, but you supply English-language queries that they'll have to translate into SQL against their tables and columns. A group can be one project team or two project teams working together. Ideally the classroom will have many separate blackboards. The instructors walk around answering questions and coaching the groups. After 30–40 minutes, you ask two or three of the best groups to present their work. After each presentation you moderate a discussion of the merits of the data model and how much work the RDBMS will have to do in answering the queries. You close the meeting time by introducing the B-tree index and explaining how to add indices to a data model to improve query performance.

- *Week 3, Meeting 1* Students turn in their work on "User Registration and Management" exercises. Class time is devoted to presentation and discussion of different teams' approaches to the "User Registration" chapter problems. At least a couple of teams will have been successful in meeting with their clients and drafting solutions to the "Planning" chapter. Devote 5–10 minutes of class time to discussing the work of the farthest-along teams in this area as a way of inspiring the rest of the class.

- *Week 3, Meeting 2* Students turn in their work on "Planning" and Exercises 1 through 3 in "Content Management" (up to but not including the skeletal implementation). Class time is devoted to presentation and discussion of teams' approaches to content management data models. Consider breaking up into teams to take a single-table data model and put it into Third Normal Form.

- *Week 4, Meeting 1* Devoted to look-and-feel criticism of public Internet applications and the more advanced teams' projects.

- *Week 4, Meeting 2* Students complete all exercises in "Content Management," including client sign-off. Class time devoted to team presentations of work so far and plans for immediate future.

- *Week 5, Meeting 1* Students complete all exercises in "Software Modularity." Class time devoted to team presentations of their design decisions and documentation.

- *Week 5, Meeting 2* Students complete exercises in the "Discussion" chapter up to, but not including the usability test.

- *Week 6, Meeting 1* Students complete all exercises in the "Discussion" chapter except execution of the refinement plan. Class time devoted to discussion of usability test results and whether the numbers could have been predicted from the page flow and HTML designs.

- *Week 6, Meeting 2* Students present their refined discussion forum systems. Class time devoted to presentation of the refined systems. Close with an exhortation that students spend the weekend starting the "Mobile" and "VoiceXML" problems in parallel so that if they are stuck with the tools they'll have an early warning.

- *Week 7, Meeting 1* Students complete all exercises in the "Mobile" chapter. Class time devoted to presentations and discussion of the wireless interfaces to the applications.

- *Week 7, Meeting 2* Students complete all exercises in the "VoiceXML" chapter. Class devoted to presentations and discussion. It would be very helpful to have an amplified telephone system so that the entire class can hear interactions between a team's system and a user.

- *Week 8, Meeting 1* Students complete all exercises in the "Scaling Gracefully" chapter. Take-home mid-term exam handed out (an individual rather than a team project). Class discussion of scaling exercises, ideally starting with each answer being presented by a separate team.

- *Week 8, Meeting 2* Exercises 1 and 2 from "Search" due. Discussion of team designs for full-text search.

- *Week 9, Meeting 1* Mid-term exam due. All exercises from the "Search" chapter due. Class time devoted to discussion of exam questions, answers, and implications.

- *Week 9, Meeting 2* "Planning Redux" exercises due. Note that the instructors must interview the clients as part of this chapter. Team presentations of their work and plans for public launch.

What to Put on Exams

You might think that exams are unnecessary in a project-oriented course such as this one. We give exams for the following reasons:

- we want to make sure that a student isn't being carried by his or her teammates

- we want to make sure that students are reading and re-reading the principles outlined in this textbook
- we want to make sure that students understand data modeling and concurrency
- we want to see if a student is capable of writing good analyses of Internet applications and compelling justifications of his or her design work
- by giving take-home exams rather than in-class quizzes we are able to create an experience that will add to the students' skills

A good style of question involves asking the students to try out a particular public Internet service and then build a data model that would support what they've just seen. The students should then load their data model and try to solve some SQL puzzles against them.

Another good question asks the students to visit a public Internet application, try it out, and write a critique of the user experience. In our exam we include the following admonition: "Your critique should be clear concerning what is wrong with the current system. Your critique should be explicit about what to change, such that a junior programmer could implement your improvements without depending on his or her own taste and judgment."

You might also want to ask the students to propose and justify a hardware and software architecture to handle a specific service and user load.

Note that all of these questions are sufficiently open-ended to lead to interesting classroom discussion. Note further that these exams must be graded by someone experienced with software engineering and data modeling.

Finding Clients

A real-world client has much to offer your students. A real-world client will phrase problems in vague and general terms. A real-world client will bring content and users to flesh out what would otherwise be a purely academic exercise. A real-world client can provide students with performance feedback. A real-world client forces students to confront the challenge of demonstrating their achievement to a non-technical audience.

What can your students offer real-world clients? In some cases, a student team will build a launchable, documented, maintainable, high-performance system that the client can run for years. This happy result, however, is not necessary in order for a client to get value from participating in a course based on this textbook. Oftentimes working with a student team will enable a client to make decisions and formulate precise specifications. Most people are unable to make good decisions about information systems without seeing a prototype. We don't promise clients that their student team will solve their problem, but we do promise clients that the experience will clarify their goals and, whatever else, will be over in 3.5 months.

Working groups within your own university can be a good source of clients. Groups that need to work with off-campus people, such as alumni, parents, or colleagues at other institutions, are especially logical candidates for online community support. Non-profit organizations can also be good sources of projects because they are usually much more patient than for-profit corporations and can afford to (a) wait for your semester to start, and (b) start over if necessary at the end of your semester in the event that the student team does not produce a launchable system. For-profit organizations can provide well-organized and highly motivated clients. Both cash-starved startups and small neglected departments within larger companies may be attracted to working with a student team. With any potential client, however, try to make sure that they have enough resources to gather content and users.

A bit of diversity among the client projects is nice, but at their cores all of the client projects should be online communities. At the very least, a project needs to have a discussion forum where User A can ask a question that User B will answer. Much of the value in this course comes from student teams comparing their differing approaches to the similar challenges of user registration, content management, and discussion support. If a client wants a 100-percent voice interface, their team won't be able to learn from other teams very effectively nor will other teams building primarily Web browser sites be able to learn from the voice-browser-only team. If a client says "I want an online store," just respond "no." If a client says "I want an online store where the customers talk to each other," respond with "Okay, but the students aren't going to build the checkout pages until the end of the term, and you'll have to offer them summer jobs if you want e-commerce admin pages."

Here are some criteria for selecting among clients:

- spirit of the project; does it look like an online learning community in which the users share a common purpose and the more experienced will teach the less experienced?

- availability of magnet content and users; is the client dreaming or does he or she have compelling unique content that will draw users or some other way of bringing users to the application?

- availability of the client; the university calendar is unforgiving and the client needs to be able to respond within 24 hours to a request for a critique

- long-term resources; it is great if students can go into a job interview and say "point your Web browser at http://www.foobar.org to see what I built," but this won't happen unless the client has the long-term wherewithal to host and maintain an Internet application

Alumni Mentors

In 1950 tuition at Ivy League schools was about $500 and the average new car cost nearly $2,000 (4 times tuition). In 2003 tuition is approaching $30,000 per year and a beautiful Honda Accord can be had for $15,000 (1/2 of tuition). Thanks to improvements in design and manufacturing engineering, the relative price of an automobile has fallen by a factor of 8 while its quality has improved dramatically. Why has the cost of a university education soared relative to automobiles and other manufactured goods? Consider the classroom circa 1950: 25 students, 1 teacher, 1 blackboard, 25 chairs. Compare to the classroom experience circa 2005: 25 students, 1 teacher, 1 blackboard, 25 chairs. Even if universities were to exercise restraint in the hiring of administrative staff, the cost of tuition is doomed to outstrip inflation because education is the only industry in America where there are no productivity improvements.

This problem is not too severe for teaching Physics 101. The school pays one instructor and fills a room with 300 tuition-paying students. But teaching software engineering effectively requires that students be given an apprenticeship. No school will want to pay the army of instructors that would represent an optimum-sized teaching staff for a software engineering project course like this one. Even if a school had an infinite amount of money, professors and graduate students are probably the wrong people for the job. How much experience does the average academic computer scientist have in comparing a collection of software source code to a statement of user requirements and suggesting improvements?

We can solve the staffing and expertise problems in one stroke by bringing in alumni volunteers. A typical school has 10 or 20 times as many alumni as current students. If students are broken up into teams of 3 and each volunteer can assist two teams, we only need to convince approximately 1 percent of our alumni to volunteer each semester. As working software engineers, our graduates will likely do a much better job of assisting students than a fresh graduate student would and perhaps even a better job in some areas than a seasoned professor.

A course based on *Software Engineering for Internet Applications* is uniquely amenable to alumni mentoring because all of the students' work is accessible from any Web browser anywhere on the Internet. Between the plans and the /doc directory and the mandated "View Source" links at the bottom of every student-authored page, an alumnus 3,000 miles away ought to be able to contribute almost as effectively as someone who is willing to come down to campus two nights per week.

Evaluation and Grading

The daily cost of attending a top university these days is about the same as the daily rate to stay at the Four Seasons hotel in Boston, living on room-service lobster and champagne. It is no wonder, then, that the student feels entitled to have a pleasant experience. Suppose that you tell a student that his work is substandard. He may be angry with you for adversely affecting his self-esteem. He may complain to a dean, who will send you email and invite you to a meeting. You've upheld the standards of the institution, but what favor have you done yourself? Remember that the A students will probably go on to graduate school, get Ph.Ds., and settle into $35,000/year post-docs. The mediocre students are the ones who are likely to rise to high positions in Corporate America, and these are the ones from whom you'll be asking for funding, donations of computer systems, and so on. Why alienate paying customers and future executives merely because they aren't willing to put effort into software engineering?

In teaching with *Software Engineering for Internet Applications*, you have a natural opportunity to separate evaluation from teaching. The quality of the user experience and the solution engineered by a team is best evaluated by their client and the end-users. If the client responds to the questionnaire in Exercise 3 of the "Planning Redux" chapter by saying "Our team has solved all of our problems and we love working with them," what does your opinion matter?

Similarly if a usability study shows that test users are able to accomplish tasks quickly and reliably, what does your opinion of the page flow matter? During most of this course we try to act as coaches to help our students achieve high performance as perceived by their clients and end-users. We use every opportunity to arrange for students to get real-world feedback rather than letter grades from us.

The principal area where we must retain the role of evaluator is in looking at a team's documentation. The main question here is "How easy would it be for a new team of programmers, with access only to what is in the /doc directory on a team's server, to take over the project?"

Sample Contract (between the Student Team and Client)

This is an agreement made _____ (today's date) between _____ ("Client") and the Student Team whose members are listed below.

Ownership of computer programs developed during the software engineering course in which the Student Team is enrolled remains with the individual students who developed that software. However, in exchange for the Client's advice, supervision, and participation in the class, the undersigned members of the Student Team grant the Client a perpetual royalty-free license to use that software.

The intent of this agreement is that the students are free to reuse the software that they've developed in future projects, in which, for example, user registration and a discussion forum are required. The Client has the right, without payment of any fees, to continue operating an Internet or intranet service based on the software developed by the Student Team and may hire any programmers whom it wishes to make modifications and extensions to the code.

The Client acknowledges that this software is delivered with no warranty. The Student Team is licensing this software to the Client under the terms of the GNU General Public License ("GPL"), the full text of which is available from http://www.gnu.org/licenses/gpl.txt. The effect of this license is that the Client cannot demand that Student Team fix bugs beyond the last day of the class. Nor can the Client hold members of the Student Team responsible for any economic losses that result from the operation of software delivered by the Student Team.

All copyrighted site content provided by the Client remains the property of the Client or the content author(s).

Signed by the Client

Print name: _____

for Organization: _____

by (signature): _____

Signed by the Student Team

Print name: _____

Signature: _____   Date: _____

Print name: _____

Signature: _____   Date: _____

Print name: _____

Signature: _____   Date: _____

Print name: _____

Signature: _____   Date: _____

Print name: _____

Signature: _____   Date: _____

About the Authors

Eve Andersson

Eve is Senior Vice President and Chair of the Bachelor of Science in Computer Science at Neumont University in Salt Lake City, Utah. She has engineered dozens of enterprise Web applications and a handful of voice applications. Her open-source software for building online communities and e-commerce sites has been adopted by thousands of Internet application operators worldwide. Eve is a co-author of Stephen Breitenbach et al., *Early Adopter VoiceXML* (Wrox Press, 2001).

Eve holds a B.S. from Caltech in Engineering and Applied Science, and an M.S. from U.C. Berkeley in Mechanical Engineering (1998). She was Visiting Professor of Computer Science at Galileo University in Guatemala in 2002, where she led the development of the university's learning management system. She can recite the first few hundred digits of pi from memory, although she confesses that she knows fewer than 100 digits of e. More: eveandersson.com.

Philip Greenspun

Philip has been in and around the Massachusetts Institute of Technology since 1979. In addition to teaching Software Engineering for Internet Applications, the course in which this text is used, he has helped teach many of the core electrical engineering classes, including circuits, signals and systems, and probability theory. Greenspun holds a commercial pilot's certificate with instrument, multi-engine, seaplane, and helicopter ratings and has flown small aircraft across most of the North American continent and portions of three other continents.

In the mid-1990s, Greenspun founded the Scalable Systems for Online Communities research group at MIT and spun it out into a profitable $20 million (revenue) open-source enterprise software company. Greenspun has participated in the design and engineering of more than 200 collaborative applications of the Internet. More: philip.greenspun.com.

Andrew Grumet

Andrew holds a Ph.D. in Electrical Engineering and Computer Science from MIT. He has been building database-backed Internet applications since 1999, leading development teams that built systems for Hewlett-Packard Company, the World Bank, and MIT Sloan School of Management. He is the author of a standard open-source toolkit for building mobile applications, and the applications that he developed are in daily use by more than 100,000 people.

As of May 2003, Andrew is the technical architect for iLearn, a collaborative effort of the Sloan School and Microsoft to build innovative educational software using the .NET Development Framework. More: grumet.net.

Cesar Brea

Cesar contributed primarily to the reference chapter on engagement management. After undergraduate life at Harvard, Cesar received an MBA from Dartmouth's Tuck School. He has been a banker, management consultant at Bain, head of marketing for a $30 million software business, head of sales and marketing at Razorfish until its acquisition by SBI, and is now CEO of Contact Network Corporation, a Boston-based enterprise software firm.

Cesar serves on the Executive Board of the .LRN Consortium (dotlrn.org), and is a frequent writer and speaker on enterprise software strategy and high-technology marketing.

Index